Europe and the Superpowers

Europe
1971

ATLANTIC

OCEAN

NORWAY

Oslo

NORTH
SEA

SCOTLAND

Glasgow

Edinburgh

N.
IRELAND

DENMARK

Copenhagen

UNITED
KINGDOM

EIRE

Dublin
*Irish
Sea*

Liverpool

Kiel
Lubeck
Hamburg EAST

Birmingham

ENGLAND

Amsterdam NETH.

London

*The
Hague* GERMAN

Berlin

Ghent *Antwerp*

Hanover

Potsdam

English Channel

Essen

GERMANY

Brussels

Dresden

Brest

BELG.

Bonn

Le Havre

FEDERAL

Reims

LUX.

Frankfort

Prague

Paris

LORRAINE

Nantes

Strasbourg

Nurnberg

Loire R.

Seine R.

Rhine R.

REP.

Danube R.

ALSACE
Basel

Munich

Salzburg

BAY OF
BISCAY

FRANCE

Berne
SWITZ.

AUSTRIA

Bordeaux

Lyons

Milan

Venice

Bilbao

Garonne R.

Rhone R.

Genoa

Po R.

Bologna

ADRIATIC

Oporto

Ebro R.

Toulouse

ANDORRA

Florence

PORTUGAL

Duero R.

SPAIN

Madrid

Marseilles

MONACO

Barcelona

CORSICA

ITALY

Lisbon

Tagus R.

Rome

*Guadiana
R.*

Valencia

Majorca *Minorca*

Naples

BALEARIC IS.

TYRRHENIAN
SEA

Strait of Gibraltar

Malaga

Granada

Tangier *Ceuta*

Gibraltar

SARDINIA

SICILY

MEDITERRANEAN

Rabat

Algiers

Tunis

MALTA

MOROCCO

ALGERIA

TUNISIA

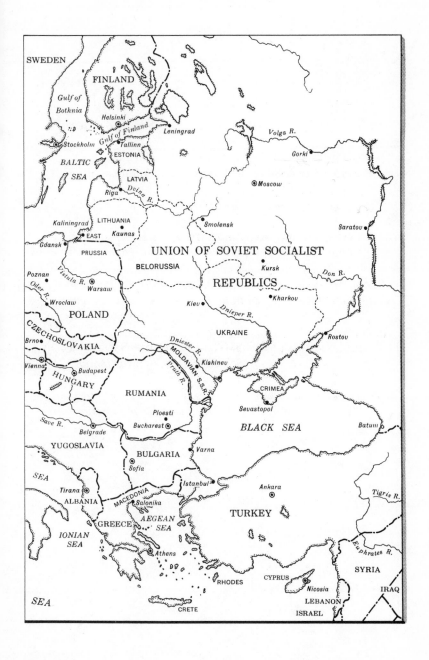

By the Same Author

THE NATO INTERNATIONAL STAFF/SECRETARIAT, 1952–57: A Study in International Administration

GOVERNMENT AND POWER IN WEST AFRICA

INTERNATIONAL ADMINISTRATION: Its Evolution and Contemporary Applications *(editor and contributor)*

PROBLEMS IN INTERNATIONAL RELATIONS *(co-editor and contributor to the 3rd edition, with Andrew Gyorgy and Hubert Gibbs)*

MULTINATIONAL COOPERATION: Economic, Social and Scientific Development *(editor)*

POLITICAL LEADERSHIP IN POSTWAR WESTERN EUROPE: Studies in Multinational Diplomacy *(in preparation)*

Europe and the Superpowers

Perceptions of European International Politics

editor and contributor

ROBERT S. JORDAN

*Professor of Political Science and
Chairman of the Department
State University of New York
at Binghamton*

1976

Allyn and Bacon, Inc.
Boston

Library of Congress Catalog Card Number:
70-132781

Printed in the United States of America.

to the memory of

Edgar S. Furniss, Jr., Late Director
Social Science Program
The Mershon Center for Education
in National Security
The Ohio State University

and

Charles O. Lerche, Jr., Late Dean
School of International Service
The American University

CONTENTS

Map   ii

Foreword   *Andrew W. Scott*   xi

Introduction   *Robert S. Jordan*   1

Prologue — An Analysis of Contemporary European
International Politics   *Pierre Hassner* / Robert S. Jordan   13

Part I   The Political Involvement of the Superpowers in Europe   23

1   The Political Involvement of the United States in Europe
Robert S. Jordan   27

2   The Political Involvement of the Soviet Union in Europe
Robert Ranger   47

Part II   The Central Problem of Central Europe   71

3   Europe East of the Elbe   *Pierre Hassner*   74

4   Europe West of the Elbe   *Pierre Hassner*   101

viii

*Part III The Growth of Nationalistic
Particularism in Central and Eastern Europe
(Including the Balkans)*   *131*

5   The Contemporary West German National Outlook
    Waldemar Besson   134

6   Nationalistic Interests in the Balkans and Eastern
    Mediterranean   *Viktor Meier*   149

*Part IV   Can Europe Be United? Variations
on the Continental Pattern*   *167*

7   The Dilemma of Great Britain   *Ian Taylor*   170

8   The Special Conditions of the Baltic Subregion
    Nils Andren   193

Epilogue — Economic and Political Integration: From
Schuman Plan to the European Communities
    Harold K. Jacobson / Robert S. Jordan   231

Chronology of Major European Developments   254

Suggestions for Further Reading   290

Index   295

ix

ABOUT THE CONTRIBUTORS

NILS ANDREN has been Professor of Political Science at the University of Copenhagen, and a Visiting Professor at the Brookings Institution in Washington, D.C. He is now working for the Swedish Defense Research Institute, and also is an External Research Associate at the Institute of International Studies, University of South Carolina. He received his doctorate from the University of Uppsala, and has written extensively about the governments of the Nordic subregion, including *Modern Swedish Government, Government and Politics of the Nordic Countries,* and *Power-Balance and Non-Alignment.*

WALDEMAR BESSON is Professor of Political Science at the University of Konstanz. He has traveled widely and lectured in the United States, as well as having done research at Harvard University. He took his doctorate in Germany.

PIERRE HASSNER lectures at the Fondation Nationale des Sciences Politiques in Paris, and at the Bologna Center of the School of Advanced International Studies, Johns Hopkins University. He has written widely on European politics, including, for the Institute for Strategic Studies, two Adelphi Papers entitled *Change and Security in Europe.*

HAROLD JACOBSON is Professor of Political Science at the University of Michigan. He has been a Visiting Professor at the Graduate Institute of International Studies in Geneva, Switzerland, and consultant to various research organizations. He has written or edited several books, including *America's Foreign Policy,* and *Foreign Policy in the Sixties.*

VIKTOR MEIER for several years has been the correspondent in Washington, D.C. for leading West German newspapers. He has also been a correspondent in Central Europe, and has written and lectured on contemporary international politics. He took his doctorate in Germany.

ROBERT RANGER is a member of the Department of Political Studies, Queen's University, Canada. He has taught, and took his doctorate, at the London School of Economics and Political Science, and has been a Research Associate at the Institute of War and Peace Studies, Columbia University. He wrote a widely acclaimed article on "NATO's Reaction to Czechoslovakia," in *The World Today,* January 1969.

IAN TAYLOR is a graduate of the University of Keele and has been doing research on post-1934 French foreign policy toward Eastern Europe. In research, he has contributed to a study of East-West relations in Europe written under the auspices of the Norwegian Peace Research Institute.

FOREWORD

This study of the European states and the Superpowers appears at a fortunate moment. The analysis in this volume will help the reader understand some of the many changes now taking place in the international system, and particularly the European international system. Since 1947 the cold war has provided the framework for European policy and for relations between the Superpowers. Now the intensity of the cold war is waning and relationships that have been frozen for years have begun to thaw and long-fixed patterns of behavior have become changeable. Every European state and every state closely associated with Europe must adjust to changing circumstances. Attitudes and policy stances developed in response to the cold war must be reviewed and, in many cases, modified.

The states of Western Europe no longer find their post-World War II political relationship with the United States satisfactory and have been trying to define a new and more attractive one. They must also try to find a way to handle the economic challenge of the United States and to see whether there are important political implications of improving relations with the states of Eastern Europe. Is time running out for the integration movement? Does the future lie with a broader "Europe"?

The Western European states have common problems and, in addition, each has its special problems. The German Federal Republic, for example, has long pursued the goal of German reunification by means of implacable hostility to the German Democratic Republic and by refusing to grant official recognition to its existence. This policy bore little fruit and in 1965 the "grand coalition" of Christian Democrats and Social Democrats began to explore the idea of an "opening to the East." This tactic has continued under the Brandt government. The government of the Federal Republic is saying, in effect, that perhaps progress can be made on certain problems in an atmosphere of increasing friendliness which could not be made in one of unrelieved hostility. The division of Germany is part of the larger division of Europe and in a time of détente and easing of East-West tensions it would not be easy for either German government to maintain a stance of complete hostility toward the other. This suggests that the German Democratic Republic may also be forced to adjust its policy before long. Perhaps the political aspects of German reunification can be left in suspension for a time while the people of the two Germanies learn to interact again in non-political ways.

The Soviet Union is also being forced to adapt to changing realities both with respect to the non-Communist states and Communist states. It is having to recognize that it has some interests in common with the United States and a number of conflicting interests with "socialist" China. It is having to adjust to the fact that the Eastern European bloc is not a complete success and that the level of disaffection in Eastern Europe remains high. It has been forced to recognize that trade and increasing interaction with Western Europe is very attractive to the Eastern European states. For many years the Soviet Union sought to discourage the Eastern European states from reaching out to the West but now it appears to be learning to live with that desire. The Soviet Union appears to be ready to discard the bogeyman of German resurgence with which it long tried to frighten Eastern bloc states, and to welcome improved relations between the two German states and between the Federal Republic and the states of Eastern Europe.

The present volume is addressed to Americans; that is just as well for we too have a great deal of adjusting to do. While the attention of the United States has been primarily focused on Vietnam, changes have been taking place in Europe. The Western European states have learned to be less reliant upon the United States and have begun to interact increasingly with the European states to the East. A Europe oriented increasingly toward the East would not offer the same policy opportunities to the United States as one oriented toward the West. For example, the concept of a developing Atlantic Community may not be consistent with an eastward-looking Europe and it is perhaps significant that the rhetoric about an Atlantic Community is heard less often these days. Perhaps that concept must be regarded as a product of the cold war; it might be one of the early casualties following from an easing of East-West tensions.

The United States must adjust to the fact that when the United States talks about NATO its European partners have ceased to listen very attentively. The credibility of the Soviet threat has waned very greatly and, in addition, there is a widespread belief in Europe that the real defense of the continent against a possible

Soviet attack does not lie in NATO forces located in Europe but in the nuclear deterrent capability of the United States. If that is the case, Europeans ask, why should they strain their resources to supply a few thousand more troops for NATO? While the will to maintain it has been weakening among our allies, American thinking has remained closely tied to NATO. It is time to realize that NATO was a response to a particular set of circumstances and that as those circumstances change new responses are appropriate. The United States cannot realistically hope to keep the alliance in a vigorous and healthy state while simultaneously pursuing a policy of détente with the Soviet Union, and if it must choose between them there can be little doubt what its choice must be.

If the United States, as a practical matter, no longer regards the Soviet Union as exclusively a continuing and immediate military threat, it must acknowledge this fact and carefully examine its manifold policy implications. It must acknowledge more openly that the relations between major states are seldom all of a kind but consist, rather, of a mix of competing and common interests. If Americans have been preoccupied with interest conflicts with the Soviet Union during the past two decades, they must now become aware of the interests that the two Superpowers may share. If conflicting interests are to be expressed by means of appropriate foreign policies so, too, must shared interests. Almost all of these issues are explored in this thoughtful volume.

In spite of the Fulbright program and the myriad excursions to Europe of American students and faculty members since 1945, there is all too little intellectual exchange between American students of international politics and their opposite numbers in Europe. To a degree this reflects the parochialism of American publishing and reading habits. This is all the more reason to welcome a thoughtful and lucid discussion by European writers at this juncture.

ANDREW M. SCOTT
Professor of Political Science
University of North Carolina
Chapel Hill, North Carolina

For more than a generation, Europe, and France in the heart of Europe, has been a passive observer of history rather than a participant. For a continent so rich in men and resources, this situation is becoming increasingly intolerable. With a leadership class intellectually obsessed with an American pattern it copies clumsily with a 15-year lag, and with a working class equally obsessed by a Soviet pattern whose disastrous rigidity has been obvious in Eastern Europe for several years, the nations of Western Europe have looked like—and still look like—psychologically conquered territories.

—*J. J. Servan-Schreiber*

INTRODUCTION
The Outlooks of Europeans toward the Dominance of the Superpowers

A leading political analyst once observed:

Americans tend to think of recent history in terms of the expansionism of Russia and China. They have seen their own role as one of containing those two foreign and alien countries. Yet in the eyes of the rest of the world the picture has seemed somewhat otherwise. As seen by others, the most striking feature of history since the end of World War II has been the expansion of American power and influence. In the name of containing others, the United States has in fact expanded its own power faster and farther than the others.[1]

[1] Joseph C. Harsch, "Nixon Turns Foreign Policy Page," *Christian Science Monitor*, 2–4 August 1969.

1

One of those misperceptions between the Americans and the Europeans, in this post-World War II period, has been the fact of a massive American intervention in Europe, in the name of containing expansionist Russia. To the Americans, this has appeared to be a selective, constructive, and essentially permissive intervention, based upon various notions of "partnership," leading by the latter 1950's to "interdependence." From the European view, this trans-Atlantic relationship has been seen as a quasi-permanent American entry into European power politics.

At the beginning of this contemporary period, the alignment of America with Europe, and especially that part west of the Elbe, was highly desired by Europeans and Americans alike. The paramountcy of the United States in Western Europe became a politico-military-economic counter to the paramountcy of the Soviet Union in Eastern Europe, with Germany being divided between them. How else, so all parties in the West reasoned, could Western Europe fend off the Russians' temptation to extend their influence and control even farther westward than they were already? The notion of a "Superpower" has as much to do with this shared dominance of Europe, which previously had been itself the center of world politics, as with the acquisition of first the atomic and then the thermonuclear capabilities by these two super-states. In other words, control of European politics passed from the European states themselves to the two great peripheral—but nonetheless, politically-speaking, European—Superpowers.

It is important, therefore, that students of post-war international politics take into account the feelings and reactions of the Europeans to this situation as it has unfolded. The calculations of American and Soviet intentions have been written about at length and in great depth, and this literature is readily available to students. The reactions of the Europeans, and their interpretations of the intentions of the Superpowers, as regards the European aspects of the global struggle of the United States and the Soviet Union, are not as readily available. It is the purpose of this book to remedy in a small way this deficiency. For this reason, the chapters have been structured to reveal the outlooks of the European toward the dominance of the Superpowers. Most of the chapters have been written by Europeans especially for this book, and their writings reflect essentially European impressions about the Superpowers, rather than reflecting explanations of American or Soviet outlooks.

Part I, "The Political Involvement of the Superpowers in Europe," provides a necessary overview of the convolutions of American and Russian policies as they concern Europe. The position taken by the authors of these chapters is not one of defense or explanation, but rather one of description and analysis, allowing the reader to draw his own conclusions. American students must attempt to remove themselves from their own (and quite natural) national political frames of reference if they are to understand their country's behavior in Europe as well as the behavior in Europe of their country's primary adversary.

Part II, "The Central Problem of Central Europe," examines the political outlooks of Europe from the two dimensions set by the Superpowers at the end of World War II—eastward and westward from the Elbe. In the past decade, both the East and West have tended to view the growth of a mélange of inter-subregional relationships (sometimes called "bridge-building") with mixed feelings of anxiety and approbation. As the Europeans on both sides of the Elbe are quick to point out, the Superpowers made the first moves to "fish in each other's troubled waters" politically and economically before their client (or satellite) states in their respective subregions started to do the same. Therefore, Europeans have asked, why do the Superpowers expect to get away with "do as I say and not what I do" policies? Furthermore, since the advent of the "Grand Coalition" in the German Federal Republic, followed by the coming to power of the Social Democrats, the shift in West German policy toward Eastern Europe and toward the German Democratic Republic has noticeably been away from an attitude of isolation and hostility, to an attitude of attempting to establish relationships and to open channels of communication that could bring about a measure of political reconciliation. Thus, the scene from Central Europe is one of movement and fluctuation, with the Superpowers attempting to retain the military and political rigidities of a divided Europe while at the same time not being willing or able to control in every case the trans-European connections being formed, so to speak, under their noses.

Part III, "The Growth of Nationalistic Particularism in Central and Eastern Europe," follows from the changes taking place in Central Europe. In the case of Germany, its bifurcation, coming less than a century after its unification and after three European wars involving a unified Germany, is a key aspect of the political future of Europe and the role of the Superpowers in Europe. It has been said—and I believe rightly—that from the historian's perspective, the North Atlantic Treaty Organization (NATO) will have served almost as much as a means to control a potentially resurgent Germany in the West as to have dealt with the menace of the Soviet Union from the East.

The Balkan and East Mediterranean subregion presents an equally complex, although different, picture. Greece, Turkey, Bulgaria, Yugoslavia, and Albania have had various long-term, historic interrelationships, which have not died out in the face of the Superpowers' dominance.

Part IV, "Can Europe Be United? Variations on the Continental Pattern," focuses more on the duality of the European-extra-European traditions and relationships of Great Britain and of the Baltic States. All are primarily trading states with mixed feelings about being drawn too closely into the affairs of the continent. While the problems of Germany are essentially European problems, the problems of Great Britain can be seen as only partially European. We all know that the British have, historically, pursued a policy of selective engagement on the continent; they have viewed European politics within the framework of their global needs, aspirations, and rivalries. In some ways, the Britain of the nineteenth century resembles the America of the mid-twentieth century. But the Britain of the mid-twentieth century, as former Secretary of State Dean Acheson put it, is a nation in search of a role. Its role vis-à-vis Europe must, of necessity, be a special topic in this book because the broad question of the definition of a united Europe cannot be achieved without taking into account the special situation of Britain.

In the Baltic subregion there is not nearly the same rigidity in relationships between East and West that has existed in Central Europe. The Baltic subregion inclines neither completely in the eastern direction, nor completely in the western direction. Finland, remaining neutral in a pro-Soviet stance, is balanced by Sweden, remaining neutral in a pro-West stance. Denmark and Norway, while being in the North Atlantic Alliance and hence anti-Soviet as far as Central Europe is concerned, also are anti-German and pro-Scandinavian. These various tendencies, which can be seen as possessing both centripetal and centrifugal characteristics, are examined in this Part.

Finally, it would be appropriate, it seems to me, to take up the question of "What is Europe?", and then to suggest the various directions which such a Europe might take in the future.

WHAT IS EUROPE?

I am struck with an observation made not long ago that Europe is not an entity, but merely an expression. As M. Berl, a distinguished French historian, said:

> [Europe] . . . . is no easier to localize in time than in space . . . . People have argued that the Roman Empire was a first sketch of Europe, but it excluded Frankfurt, Copenhagen and Amsterdam. Spengler holds that Europe appears with the Holy Roman Empire of the German nation, but this excluded all Spain, all the Balkans, and the whole of Eastern Europe. The birth of Europe is no better known to us than its boundaries.[2]

One could add that America is an extension of Europe, a transplantation of much that characterized the Europe evolving in the eighteenth and nineteenth centuries. In other words, it is difficult and even misleading to regard Europe only in geographic terms. Its cultural and political influences have spread beyond the peninsula of the Eurasian continent; and even within this peninsula, the variety of cultures which grew up, flourished, dominated, and then declined are fascinating to contemplate but difficult to define.

Another difficulty is the temptation to discuss Europe within the context of a particular period in time. The Europe of the seventeenth century, quite obviously, is not that of the eighteenth century; pre-industrial Europe cannot be regarded in the same way as an industrialized Europe. The political unification of some states antedated their cultural consolidation; whereas in other parts of Europe cultural consolidation tended to accompany, if not precede, the political unification of the state. One thing is clear—over the centuries, the Slavic influences and traditions of Eastern Europe have been closely identified with the Russian national state, as have more recently, the Anglo-Saxon influences and traditions of Western Europe been identified with the American national state. In a sense, this contrasting differentiation can be seen as having a lot to do with

[2] As quoted in Max Beloff, *Europe and the Europeans* (London: Chatto and Windus, 1957), p. xiv.

the outlooks of each of the Superpowers toward the other, and of the subordinate states within the East and the West of Europe toward the Superpowers.

One can with some accuracy speak of Europe as being "from the Atlantic to the Urals." Russia has to a large extent been a part of Europe since the days of Peter the Great. By the nineteenth century, European politics had become the struggle for power carried on by Russia, Prussia, Austria-Hungary, and France, with Great Britain playing an offshore role, and the crumbling Ottoman Empire being seen as "the sick man of Europe." World War I destroyed this European political configuration, often described as "the balance of power." As A. J. P. Taylor put it:

> The seventy years between 1848 and 1918 were the last age of the European Balance of Power, a Balance reinforced by political and economic developments which had been expected to destroy it. The first twenty-three years were a period of turmoil, when the old order seemed to be crumbling. It ended with "the lesser revision"; the new national states of Germany and Italy were fitted into the system of the Balance of Power; and Europe combined vast change with international peace for more than a generation. Then the Balance grew top-heavy and was challenged anew. But the First World war had none of the traditional outcomes. The Balance was not restored; a single Great Power did not dominate the Continent; there was not even universal revolution. The intervention of the United States overthrew all rational calculations. Henceforward, what had been the centre of the world became merely "the European question."[3]

One of the most confusing aspects of the attempt to settle the peace after World War I was the policy adopted to settle the political future of the peoples of central and southern Europe. President Woodrow Wilson insisted that the principle of national self-determination, expressed through elections or plebescites of the ethnic "minorities," should be the means of legitimizing the new states and their rulers, and of defining the territorial dimensions of these successor states to the Austro-Hungarian and Ottoman Empires. One of the responsibilities that the League of Nations was asked to fulfill was to preserve the "political independence and territorial integrity" of these states. We know, of course, that the attempts to

[3] A. J. P. Taylor, *The Struggle for Mastery in Europe 1848–1918* (Oxford: The Clarendon Press, 1954), pp. xxxv–xxxvi.

chart the map of Europe along ethnic and territorial lines produced new tensions and sources of conflict which resulted in another European conflagration. The outcome of the second all-European (and world-wide) war ratified indisputably American preeminence in the West and Russian preeminence in the East. Winston Churchill had anticipated the division during the war, in a famous exchange with Premier Stalin:

> The moment was apt for business, so I said, "Let us settle about our affairs in the Balkans. Your armies are in Rumania and Bulgaria. We have interests, missions, and agents there. Don't let us get at cross-purposes in small ways. So far as Britain and Russia are concerned, how would it do for you to have ninety per cent predominance in Rumania, for us to have ninety per cent of the say in Greece, and go fifty-fifty about Yugoslavia?" While this was being translated I wrote out on a half-sheet of paper:
>
> | | |
> |---|---|
> | Rumania | |
> | Russia | 90% |
> | The others | 10% |
> | Greece | |
> | Great Britain | 90% |
> | (in accord with U.S.A.) | |
> | Russia | 10% |
> | Yugoslavia | 50-50% |
> | Hungary | 50-50% |
> | Bulgaria | |
> | Russia | 75% |
> | The others | 25%[4] |

To some extent, then, as the foregoing discussion indicates, the question "What is Europe?" can be answerable only in reference to the situation that obtains at a particular time. "Europe" to the Americans after World War II was coterminous with the Europe that had been created after World War I, the creation of which Soviet intransigence had frustrated. But, as pointed out earlier, "Europe" to the Europeans after World War II meant a Europe which included the physical presence of the United States. There has been little dissent among America's NATO allies about the desirability of having the United States politically and militarily in Europe; the differences in NATO have been over the form that the American presence should take and the role of its allies in the Alliance.

[4] Winston S. Churchill, *Triumph and Tragedy* (Boston: Houghton Mifflin Company, 1953), pp. 227–228.

It is interesting that as the cold war heightened in the late 1940's and early 1950's, the territorial aspect of the Soviet-American rivalry in Europe became almost an end in itself. Neither the Soviet Union nor the United States could permit any transferral of territory in Europe from one "camp" to the other, and even today NATO is often cited as being a success because no territory guaranteed by the Treaty has changed hands. This preoccupation with the territorial aspect of the Superpowers' rivalry in Europe has been cited by some scholars as begging the question. It enhanced the tendency of both sides to retain policies toward each other and toward the states of Europe over which they exerted a dominating influence long beyond that point where perhaps their respective national vital interests were being served. It is only in the late 1960's that the territorial aspect of the cold war has given way to more flexible, and perhaps more traditional, Great Power maneuvering. The primary ingredient of the pre-World War I European balance of power was shifting coalitions; it is very likely that in the 1970's the coalitions formed around the two Superpowers will become more shifting than in the 1950's and 1960's.

We should also take note of the ideological aspect of the Soviet-American confrontation in Europe. The territorial aspect appeared to be intertwined with the ideological aspect during the 1950's, when the American military doctrine of massive retaliation guaranteed that any attempt of the Soviet Union to penetrate Europe westward from the Elbe would not go unpunished.[5] Ideologically, most historians of the post-World War II period trace the American commitment to a global but European-centered ideological rivalry with the Soviet Union to the declaration of the Truman Doctrine in 1947. The Doctrine, which was introduced to meet the immediate crisis of the threat of a Communist guerrilla takeover in Greece in March of that year, actually expanded the American commitment so that the United States appeared dedicated to opposing Communist aggression and subversion wherever it might occur. Professor Hans Morgenthau commented early in 1951: "As a guide to political action, it [the Truman Doctrine] is the victim . . .

[5] Professor Hans Morgenthau, however, in his book *A New Foreign Policy for the United States* (New York: Frederick A. Praeger, 1969), claims that the Dulles period of "brinkmanship" was in fact the time of the beginning of the Soviet-American tendencies toward détente.

of two congenital political weaknesses: the inability to distinguish between what is desirable and what is possible, and the inability to distinguish between what is desirable and what is essential."[6] To the so-called revisionist school of contemporary historians, this weakness of the Truman Doctrine ensured Soviet-American hostility.

A final analytical dimension, which takes us directly into the present, is the appearance of nationalistic, or particularistic, influences on national foreign policies. The term "polycentrism" has been used to describe how the states of Europe east of the Elbe have in their respective ways been reasserting their nationalistic tendencies (albeit still Communistic) in the face of persisting Russian attempts to maintain and consolidate an "international system" in the area. In Europe west of the Elbe nationalistic tendencies are appearing that are reminiscent of pre-World War II national political forms of behavior. At the same time Western Europe has been moving toward new forms of unity. Even if Europe west of the Elbe cannot be bound together by a common Church, or by a common notion of political legitimacy, it can, possibly, find common ties through economic integration and a greater melding of national services, agricultural and industrial resources, and parliamentary traditions. (This is surveyed in the Epilogue.) Perhaps the two halves of the Europe that have emerged will become so attracted toward each other (assuming an acceptable resolution of the problem of the two Germanies) that an even wider form of European unity might evolve. Whether all of this will eventuate and how, is one of the great issues facing the contemporary world. Perhaps, then, Europe can once again play a role in world affairs commensurate both with its own rich past, and with its vast potential.

ACKNOWLEDGEMENTS

In closing, I must pay tribute to the encouragement given me from the beginning of this project by my colleague in the School of Public and International Affairs and the Department of Political Science while I was at The George Washington University, Professor Andrew Gyorgy. I am grateful to Professor Andrew Scott for

[6] Hans J. Morgenthau, *In Defense of the National Interest* (New York: Alfred A. Knopf, 1951), p. 117—as quoted in *ibid.*, p. 10.

his advice on those aspects of the manuscript dealing with Western Europe, and for consenting to write a Foreword. Philip Windsor and Robert Hunter, both of the London School of Economics and Political Science and the Institute for Strategic Studies, were instrumental in the planning of several chapters. It would be a dereliction not to mention the invaluable research assistance of Thomas Geoffrey Bolle, and the assistance of Miss Kathleen Peterson, Mrs. Margo von Kaenel, and Stuart Greenberg, as well as the encouragement and help of my wife in preparing the manuscript for publication. Lastly, I would like to acknowledge the common membership—and mutual interest—which I share with my colleagues on the Committee on Atlantic Studies, several of whom contributed to this book.

Robert S. Jordan

If East is East and
West is West, where
will Europe come to rest?

—*Pierre Hassner*

NOTE TO THE PROLOGUE

Probably because of the immense power which the United States can and does wield in the world, but also because of the fact that the people of the United States have not, until recently, experienced over an impressionable length of time the national frustrations which come from encountering some degree of impotence in international politics, Americans often assumed an interpretation of international affairs that was close to being mechanistic in character. "If we only put so many dollars into such-and-such"; "If we can only get X and Y together, we can make them see the right way"; "If a little input of force is made now at this point, then a larger input of force won't be needed later at that point." Or, put in more abstract terms, we have often heard the phrase "organizing the peace."

If the world at one time could effectively be viewed in this way by Americans, such is not the case today. The varieties of traditions, political motivations, and conceptions of interest make any kind of mechanistic approach to understanding and manipulating the international politics of Europe (or anywhere else) misleading, if not dangerous. This Prologue gives us a brief analysis of the ways in which Europe can be viewed by Europeans in terms of contemporary international politics. It is a fitting way to begin the systematic analytical and informational tour de force which this book is intended to provide the student. He should, it is hoped, come

away from reading about Europe and the Superpowers with a
heightened appreciation—one might say respect—for Europe and
for Europeans, and this may help us as Americans to avoid the
temptation to view the international politics of Europe—of which
the United States is so much a part—in a mechanistic fashion.

**PIERRE HASSNER and
ROBERT S. JORDAN**

PROLOGUE
An Analysis of
Contemporary European
International Politics

This Prologue starts on a note of poetic doubt rather than of political science, because perhaps the main observation to be made about our subject bears upon the difficulty of defining it.

When we speak of Europe, we usually specify its division along geographic lines. Something of this geographic division is present when we refer to the "East-West struggle," but is it the same East and the same West to everyone? Perhaps not. They are, in this book, "seen through foreign eyes." Furthermore, central to our subject is the notion of the Superpowers and their struggle: their competition or their collaboration, their collision or their collusion. Are these Superpowers part of Europe? Is the East-West relationship *their* relationship, whose consequences are simply felt by various sub-regions of Europe (just as by various regions of the world) in different ways? Or is the split a European split, opposing two different kinds of Europe, a western and an eastern one? And is the Superpower relationship today both influenced and limited by this division of Europe which has developed its own structure and its own dynamics?

TWO BASIC OPPOSITIONS IN EUROPE

We have, then, the two basic oppositions—the horizontal East-West opposition, and the vertical, or Superpower versus Small

13

or Middle Power opposition. We also have, in between, the question first of Europe, of its definition and status in relation to these two oppositions and hence of the political reality or meaning of Europe as a whole (with or without both Superpowers or one of them). Then we have the question of Western Europe and of Eastern Europe (with or without their specific multinational organizations), and of Central Europe which in one way comprises them both. In another way, having been suppressed by their division, it tends to re-emerge whenever Europe's division tends to decrease. Later in this book, we will speak of "The Central Problem of Central Europe" when speaking of Eastern and Western Europe. But the very facts that the boundary that divides them is the Elbe and that we will also in this book speak of the problem of Germany shows how much the national problem of a specific divided state, Germany, is both essential to any definition of Europe and of its parts, and is controlled today by the opposition between East and West.

How can one, indeed, speak of Europe in a coherent way when the three Powers which play the most decisive role for its orientation and its fate—Germany, the Soviet Union, and the United States—have these two features in common: first, they raise, by their peculiar size and power—actual or potential—difficult problems of balance for the other European states; second, the other European states are precisely those whose ultimate identity or presence are most ambiguous either because, like Germany, they are made of one nation but at least two states or because, like the Soviet Union and the United States, they are both in Europe and out of Europe. The Superpowers are unavoidably in the picture, their global outlook and power making them more dominant, though less inescapably present and committed, than the purely continental states.

FIVE LEVELS OF INTERNATIONAL POLITICS

One can say, then, that Europe is involved on five levels of international politics: the various European states; the various European subregions; the continent of Europe; the two continental Superpowers; the East-West opposition. Of these five, two (the

European continent and the East-West opposition) have a more abstract and speculative character; they represent the two perspectives (one, perhaps, belonging more to the past and one to the future) which give direction or meaning to the relations between the actual entities which constitute the other three. It is among these— the states, the subregions, and the Superpowers, together with the organizations which either tie the first two to the third or differentiate them from it—that the real game is played.

Yet, here again, we shall find it impossible to study the vertical aspect—the relationship of a given subregion with its respective states and its respective Superpower—without crossing the Iron Curtain to examine the effects of the horizontal relations—between the two Berlins, the two Germanies, the two Europes, the two Superpowers, and hence between the incipient reunification of Europe and the resilient opposition between East and West.

What makes the study of European politics fascinating is that none of these relationships can be isolated from the others, yet none can simply be considered as their mere consequence or reflection. What happens in one half of Europe is influenced by what happens in the other half, yet is not identical with it. There are striking parallels and obvious differences that can be due to interaction or to separate evolutions, and the influence itself can go in the direction of imitation or of contrast. Similarly, it is hard to determine whether the relation of each half of Europe with its respective Superpower is more influenced by the relationships between the Superpowers themselves, or whether the latter is more a function of their respective relations with their allies or satellites. Indeed, the Superpowers can have a relatively symmetrical attitude toward each other, yet maintain fundamentally different positions and hence elicit fundamentally different reactions, within their respective spheres.

The difficulty is both compounded and alleviated by the fact that these relationships and indeed those relationships between relationships, are strikingly different according to domains, problems, or issues. Perhaps the main characteristic of international politics in our time, and particularly in the especially intricate continent of Europe, is the discrepancy in the size of political units, in the scope of loyalties, and in the direction and intensity of alignments, links, and conflicts, whether one speaks of agriculture or of defense, of cultural ties or of foreign policy alignments, of the aspirations of citizens, or of the authority of rulers. For example, agricultural interests put Western Europe into opposition with the United States, yet defense interests still tend to draw them together. As another example, cultural affinities and popular aspirations draw Czechoslovakia closer to Western Europe, yet ideological alignment and military power bring it back under Soviet rule.

According to states, issues, and periods, the Superpowers are often at the same time welcomed as protectors and cursed as oppressors. Their economic or their cultural presence are both sought and feared in one case, or dismissed as an irrelevant by-product of their power in another. This explains that perhaps the most central fact about the continent today is that both its division and the presence of the Superpowers, and hence organizations like NATO which are based on both of these realities, are at the same time obsolete and irreplaceable. The presence of the Superpowers seems less and less natural and desired, yet the hopes of diminishing the Soviet presence in Eastern Europe or of finding a substitute for the American presence in Western Europe have also decreased. The two Superpowers have failed in whatever hopes they may have entertained of bringing a permanent or institutional character to their presences by building a monolithic Soviet bloc or an integrated Atlantic community. Yet their troops are still along the Elbe and the reasons why they are there—to balance each other and to prevent the emergence of undesirable policies in the two Germanies—are as valid as ever.

There have been two extreme descriptions of their role in the division of the continent. The "cold war" role saw a permanent ideological opposition between two worlds or, politically speaking, two civilizations, each headed and represented by a Superpower. The "Gaullist" or neo-traditionalist role, in contrast, saw the division as the passing consequence of the military occupation of Europe by two external Powers who would try to impose their unnatural presence until they could be persuaded to allow the continent to find its natural balance by withdrawing their troops. In fact, each view has proved just wrong enough to be challenged by the course of events, yet right enough not to be replaced by its opposite. Hence, the only way of describing the ambiguous and contradictory nature of the Superpowers' relations to Europe and to each other in Europe is to distinguish between the different levels of international reality and the different ways in which they are affected by the winds of change. These levels appear valid for the whole of the continent, but the very different ways in which common elements or trends are reflected by specific regional realities and balances will help us to understand the differences between Western and Eastern Europe as much as their similarities.

THREE BASIC ASPECTS OF
CONTEMPORARY INTERNATIONAL POLITICS

We suggest a distinction among three basic aspects, which are probably useful to any analysis of contemporary international politics, but particularly to the understanding of the politics of Europe. These three levels are: the international security system, the states, and the societies; or, put another way: the security structure, the diplomatic constellations, and the "transnational" technological, economic, social, cultural, and psychological forces or trends. The first, primarily military, aspect shows the continuing importance of bipolarity and of the Superpowers. The second, primarily diplomatic, aspect shows the emergence of certain possibilities for multipolar or polycentric aspirations, decisions, and moves. The third aspect shows that there is more to international politics than either the Superpower confrontation or the inter-state game; that the passage of events and the shifts in influence whose source cannot be identified with any definite center of power may erode the most solid structure and obstruct the most skillful calculations.

From the first aspect, that of the military-territorial balance, nothing much has changed since 1945. All talk about the end of the post-war world notwithstanding, the European system is still characterized, from the point of view of security, by the direct presence of the two Superpowers and the division of Europe, of Germany, and of Berlin along a line resulting from the military situation of 1945. Their troops create a military balance of sorts on the ground and, more important, an immediate link between the confrontation on the continent and the global, strategic balance. The more one allows, mentally, the two-bloc division to disappear, the more the skeleton takes the shape of a divided Germany occupied by the Soviet Union and the United States. Three concentric circles appear on the map of Europe, with the two Superpowers and Germany providing the basic structure, and the other European states—east and west of the Elbe—constituting a more hazy and mobile intermediate zone.

But it is precisely in this zone, and hence related to the second polycentric aspect, that things have seemed for a time to be happening. The more the territorial division and the military balance have been observed as stable, or the more the confrontation of the two Superpowers has seemed to evolve into an ambiguous relationship of mutual acceptance and "cooperative bipolarity," the more the second aspect has begun to emerge: that of competing national interests and diplomatic flexibility. Once the two leading Powers no longer seemed to regard or to brand each other as an immediate and total threat, their allies and satellites had lost at least one basic reason for accepting an unconditional and automatic alignment. Hence the exploratory groping and maneuvering toward new combinations both within and outside the existing blocs that has been symbolized by French and Rumanian diplomacy.

Finally, the third aspect, more constant and less visible but ultimately less easy to control or to stop, is the subterranean stream through which societies' attitudes and beliefs are transformed. Sometimes, as in 1968, it suddenly bursts into the open, revealing a gap between institutions and expectations, or between generations in the same state, or between states of the same bloc.

The double danger of error has always been either in ignoring this multiplicity of aspects or in neglecting their interaction. The whole European problem lies in the question of their interaction—is the slow evolution of the third aspect going to erode or even to explode the barrier of the first? Are the moves and countermoves of states likely to accelerate or to complicate the process? Or are states going to use and influence the third aspect by channeling it in various possible directions? Or could it be that states have only a superficial effect—like stones thrown into the water—on what would remain the essential dialogue between social forces and military force?

While the three aspects have always coexisted to some extent, and while the present phase, in 1971, seems particularly striking in this respect, each of them did tend in the past to play the main role during a given post-war historical period. During the period of the cold war proper, between 1947 and 1962, the territorial division of Europe and the military occupation of its eastern half by the Soviet Union were definitely the decisive realities. In the East, the diversity of national situations was felt, but it was a diversity of reactions to Soviet actions, to Stalin's empire-building and to Khrushchev's attempt to give it new life on a new basis by making it at the same time more relaxed and more expansive. In the West, beyond the preoccupation of defense against the Communist East, the economic recovery of Western Europe and the attempt at building European unity through multilateral organizations, certainly showed a new vitality on the old continent and gave rise to the distant hope of challenging the bipolar situation. But the Western European construction was based on the assumptions of the existence of the division of Germany and of the continent, of the Soviet danger and, above all, of the protection, encouragement, and often initiative of the United States, which often was the prime mover in those very enterprises whose success would one day tend to reduce its role.

In this sense at least, the years 1962–1963 were indeed a watershed. While it is probably incorrect to speak of an end to the cold war, what they certainly did mark was the end of any dramatic "grand design" of the Superpowers. Within three months, Khrushchev's grand design was effectively killed by President Kennedy over Cuba; and Kennedy's grand design was killed just as effectively by General de Gaulle over Britain's admission to the Common Market.

THE GLOBAL PLANE AND THE EUROPEAN PLANE

From then on, the scene shifted to two main planes, which cut across both the alliances. On the global plane, the groping of the two Superpowers for a bilateral detente, entente, and cooperation (from Test Ban to Non-Proliferation Treaty) was, both in its motivations and its difficulties, more strategic and extra-European than political and European. It was bound to produce political reactions in Europe. On this second, European, plane the initiative began to pass to the individual Medium or Small Powers and especially

France in the West and Rumania in the East. In retrospect, the American efforts in favor of the multilateral nuclear force (MLF) in 1964, and the Soviet efforts to use COMECON in 1964–1965 and the Warsaw Pact in 1965–1966 as ways of restoring unity and control appear as unsuccessful efforts to turn back the tide. (See the Chronology for further events of this period.)

By the latter date, the situation was becoming even more serious, with more important characters getting into the act. With the Christian Democratic-Social Democratic Grand Coalition in West Germany, German diplomacy began, however cautiously, to explore possibilities with the East instead of relying exclusively on American protection and European integration. On the other hand, the Soviet Union started to revive its 1954–1955 proposal for a European security conference leading to a European security system as an alternative to the two alliances. Both switches were tentative and cautious; they did not give away anything essential from the bipolar structure. However, while the French and Rumanian initiatives were innocuous enough as long as they stayed French and Rumanian, they indirectly began to challenge the system when their impact was felt on the two Germanies. The establishment of diplomatic ties between the Federal Republic and Rumania, and the intense and effective East German reaction, represented a landmark which foreshadowed some of the aspects of the Czechoslovak crisis of 1968. Interestingly enough, less than a year after the Czechoslovak invasion, the Soviet Union seemed to be returning to the more mobile and ambiguous European diplomacy foreshadowed in 1965–1966, and this time to include, as did Poland, West Germany among the recipients of its overtures. The reactions in Bonn were not significantly cooler than before Czechoslovakia. Indeed, since events in Czechoslovakia have shown that ultimately the decisive influence on Eastern European affairs is still held by the Soviet Union, the possibility of a dialogue with the Russians was bound to elicit not only even more scepticism but also more interest than before. Even more predictably, East Germany has reacted with as much displeasure (if with more discretion) to Russia's and Poland's new attitudes or new tones toward the Federal Republic than it did to Rumania's two years before.

We may witness, then, a certain revival on the European scene of the diplomatic agitation which had seemed to have been stopped by Soviet rigidity in 1968. But precisely because this time the Soviet Union is at the center of the stage, because it makes no bones about its refusal to relax its grip on Eastern Europe, because its European diplomacy clearly has to be seen in the context of its triangular relations with China and the United States, and because to the extent that it looks toward Western Europe, it looks to the economic and, potentially, military power of West Germany rather than to the diplomatic and potentially illusory power of France, the real meaning of 1968 retains all its validity. And this meaning lies in the relative cutting-down to size of the second, diplomatic, aspect, or of polycentric nationalism, both through the spectacular emergence of the third aspect and through the no less spectacular reassertion of the first (see above).

Both France's and Rumania's freedom of action have been severely narrowed, directly or indirectly, by unforeseen events which started by domestic evolutions or explosions in France and in Czechoslovakia, and led to economic consequences in France and to military consequences in Eastern Europe. On the one hand, both the French and Czechoslovak "springs" of 1968 showed the fundamental importance, even for international politics, of domestic tensions and transformations. On the other hand, both the French and Czechoslovak "summers" of 1968 showed the conservative and reactive power of the established structures, provided that their leaders are ready to use force. In the very moments, days, weeks, or months where it displayed its ideological or spiritual weakness, the established structure—domestic or international—showed it could reassert itself as long as it had not decided to abdicate. At the same time, while its victory may not be Pyrrhic since we cannot see where a real challenge to its power may come from, things can no longer be as they were. The legitimacy and self-assurance of the "establishment" have been shattered, and it has been led to adopt some of the policies of the defeated rebels without being able to reconcile or to appease them.

Not too much should be made, of course, of this analogy between domestic crises in the West and in the East, or between both and the crisis in the European international system. One of the intended results of this Prologue is to show the very different ways in which the dialectics of rebellion and conservatism, of change and stability, operate in these different contexts and the very different results they are likely to produce. Whatever may be the different patterns, or levels of political reality—the realities of power balances, social structures, and institutions—and the intangibles of aspirations, expectations and frustrations, they are the basic features that can serve as a guiding thread to an analysis of the relations between the two Europes and the Superpowers as much as to an analysis of the respective states themselves.

PART I

The Political Involvement of the Superpowers in Europe

Europe, if she wants to live, will have to accept common arrangements for defense and internal prosperity, but she does not have to surrender her other diversified institutions and manners, which constitute her historical heritage, still precious in an age of mass civilization.

—*Hajo Holborn*

INTRODUCTION

Quite obviously, in this post-World War II period, we must look at Europe in ways which are fundamentally different from any earlier period of European history. The major differences are: the massive interventions of the United States and the Soviet Union into the politics of Europe; the acquisition of first, atomic and then, nuclear weaponry, and the expressed willingness of the two Superpowers to use them against each other, and perhaps against Europe; the shrinking of the colonial possessions of Europe or, to put it another way, the "re-Europeanization" of the states of Western Europe; and the dual tendencies of the states of Europe, militarily divided at the Elbe, to draw into respective Eastern and Western groupings, while at the same time reaching out across the division into new or re-established relationships directly with each other.

Whatever happens in regard to any of these contemporary aspects of European politics, the United States and the Soviet Union will be participants, shaping events as best they can to their own advantage and hopefully to the disadvantage of the other. Many people confuse a "spirit of detente" with some notion of reconciliation between former enemies. Conflict and cooperation go on simultaneously between and among states. But it is only since American and Russian mutual involvements have become more diffuse, with the diffusion accelerating after the public onset of Sino-Soviet hostilities in 1959, that the cooperative aspects of Soviet-American relations have come into clearer perspective.

For example, during the period when the United States held a monopoly of the atomic bomb, and the capability to deliver it on the Soviet Union, this undisputed military advantage was not exploited to its fullest potential. The reason, as expressed by Secretary of State James Byrnes was:

> . . . we must not imagine wishfully that overnight there can arise full grown a world government wise and strong enough to protect all of us, and tolerant and democratic enough to command our willing loyalty. If we are to preserve the continuity of civilized life, we must work with the materials at hand, improving and adding to existing institutions until they can meet the stern test of our time . . . the creation and development of safeguards to protect us all from unspeakable destruction is . . . the responsibility of all governments. Without the united effort and unremitting co-operation of all the nations of the world, there will be no enduring and effective protection against the atomic bomb.[1]

It is thus not inaccurate to characterize Soviet-American relationships vis-à-vis Europe as reflective of both cooperation and conflict, but not necessarily of reconciliation. The "parallelism" of common interests need not, and perhaps should not, bring with it total friendship, just as even during the coldest period of the cold war, the United States and the Soviet Union did not regard each other as total enemies. It is too easy to let the rhetoric of foreign policy lead students into conclusions about the range and nature of inter-state relationships which are either oversimplified or too self-serving for his own particular state. We need only note how in the short period of five years the United States accomplished a major reversal of alliances which made the pronouncements of the period 1943–45 seem oddly dissonant to the pronouncements of 1949–51. And the repudiation by the United States of the behavior of its chief cold war allies during the first Suez Crisis of 1956 was accompanied by a degree of de facto cooperation with America's chief public enemy which cannot be explained except by recognizing that international political enmities need not be total, just as international political friendships need not be total. Another example would be the long-contemplated Soviet-American Strategic Arms Limitation Talks (SALT), if they were to bear fruit. Changes in governments, or in attitudes of governments, can and do move more quickly than do the shifts of those fundamental and enduring conditions guiding the coexistence of states. Often, like flickering

[1] James F. Byrnes, *Speaking Frankly* (London: William Heineman Ltd., 1947), p. 266.

colors against a continuous backdrop, the changes in governmental attitudes can momentarily obscure the continuities of international political interests and behavior.

The discussions which follow in Chapters 1 and 2 are designed to give us an overview of the convolutions of American and Russian policies toward Europe, set against their respective outlooks toward each other, which will illustrate even further the points made above.

ROBERT S. JORDAN

1   The Political Involvement of The United States in Europe

The United States entered into world politics as a major power at the turn of this century, as has often been pointed out in the literature on American diplomacy. But also it should be noted that the American domestic national experience up to that time had ill-prepared the United States to accept the fact of its Great Power involvement. For example, although the victory of Germany over France in 1870–1871 presaged a fundamental realignment of the Powers in Europe, the consequences for the United States of this realignment were not perceived until World War I. It is worth noting, as an aside, that America's one major diplomatic venture prior to World War I into the international politics of Asia and the Pacific—the bringing-about by President Theodore Roosevelt of the Treaty of Portsmouth between Japan and Russia to settle the Russo-Japanese War of 1904–1905—produced lasting ill-feelings toward the United States on the part of a victorious Japan, the first non-European state to defeat a European state in war in modern times.

THE UNITED STATES AND THE EUROPEAN POLITICAL SYSTEM

With the entry of the United States as a co-belligerent in Europe in 1917, the stage was set for a definition of America's European interests which could result in new and more dynamic foreign policies. Yet even with the widespread popularity of President Woodrow Wilson's liberal democratic political principles, and his formula for a "just peace" as promulgated in the famous Four-

teen Points, responsibility for the failure to settle the peace of World
War I must be shared by the United States. As Professor Hajo
Holborn put it: ". . . the depth of the revolutionary changes that
World War I had caused in the social structure and attitude of na-
tions was hidden from the view of the peacemakers."[1]

The League of Nations was in practice, with the absence of the
United States, a revival of the coalition of European Great Powers,
but with the complication of being identified with the punitive
aspects of the Treaty of Versailles. Regrettably, a new world political system, based on the rule of law, did not emerge from the set-
tlements of World War I. Instead, grievances and nationalistic
aspirations tended to overwhelm the peacekeeping machinery of the
League. As a participant in European affairs during the interwar
period of 1919–1939, the United States was as much at fault in
permitting this situation to occur as were the European states
themselves. The way that the United States finally mobilized its
political will to cope with the changes in Europe which led to World
War II was by aligning itself against the totalitarianism of the
Fascist dictatorships, while at the same time nurturing a deep-
seated measure of hostility and suspicion toward the totalitarianism of the Communist dictatorship of the Soviet Union. Thus,
Europe was viewed during the interwar period as being in what
E. H. Carr has called "the twenty years crisis." It simply was not
possible for the states of Europe to resume the balance of power
form of international politics which was destroyed by World War I,
and another system of carrying on their conflicts and rivalries,
through the League, proved unworkable in the face of various
nationalistic pressures.

The Wilsonian dream of a Europe composed of liberal democracies ascribing to the principles of national self-determination and
political independence, ironically led to international confusion as
well as to international reconciliation. After World War II, American persistence in continuing to base its policy toward Europe on
the Wilsonian model also failed to produce a reconciliation. The
two major victors, the United States and the Soviet Union, soon
fell into wrangling about how the map of Eastern Europe should be

---

[1] Hajo Holborn, *The Political Collapse of Europe* (New York: Alfred A. Knopf, 1951), p. 109.

drawn. For example, the United States objected to what it considered were Soviet violations of an agreement reached at Yalta that the United States, the United Kingdom, and the Soviet Union "will jointly assist the peoples liberated from the Axis to form interim governmental authorities broadly representative of all democratic elements in the population and pledged to the earliest possible establishment, through free elections of governments responsive to the will of the people."[2]

The frustration of these operative principles, as evidenced by the 1948 Czechoslovak takeover through a pro-Soviet Communist coup, produced a resurgence in the United States of severe anti-Soviet feelings, in part because of conflicting national interests, but equally because of resentment of the nature of the totalitarian dictatorship of the Soviet Union. It was thought that the continuation of the "natural" political evolution of Europe—i.e., a Europe composed of liberal democracies with their political independence and territorial integrity guaranteed by the Superpowers—was being systematically frustrated by the Soviet Union, just as it had been nearly obliterated by the German and Italian dictatorships in the interwar period. Hence, in 1947, the Truman Doctrine was conceived to oppose Communist-led aggression, whether overt or covert. It was assumed at this time that once these anti-democratic intentions could be effectively frustrated, in the Eastern Mediterranean and in Western Europe, but also hopefully in Eastern Europe, it would be possible to construct a European political system that would restore the stability to world politics lost since 1914.

Such, however, was not to be the case, either in Europe or elsewhere. The de facto dismemberment of Germany, the inability to do much about restoring the lands lost to the Poles from Russian encroachments and lands lost to the Germans from Polish encroachments, the exclusion of liberal democratic political parties in the governments of the territories that came under the military and then political domination of the Soviet Union, and the inability of the wartime allies to agree on the implementation of the various agreements to settle the peace of Europe, and especially concerning Germany, led to the onset of the cold war, which pitted the Superpowers against each other in Europe.

---

[2] As quoted in Byrnes, *op. cit.,* p. 49.

CONSEQUENCES OF THE FAILURE
TO SETTLE THE PEACE IN EUROPE

In the light of the failure of the Superpowers to get along, each Power moved, in the latter 1940's, to consolidate its respective position in Eastern and Western Europe. With American encouragement, Great Britain and France joined with the Benelux states and Italy to form the Brussels Treaty Organization in 1948. Then, in 1949, the United States and Canada joined them to form the North Atlantic Treaty Organization (NATO), which also included Portugal, Norway, Denmark, and Iceland. (In 1951 Greece and Turkey joined, and the German Federal Republic was permitted to enter in 1955.) NATO at this time was primarily an anti-Russian coalition, designed to ensure to the weak states of Western Europe that the United States intended to protect them as well as itself against the hostile and aggressive intentions of the Soviet Union. By the early 1950's, through NATO, American military power was restored in Europe to confront the Soviet Union.

Along with this military manifestation of the Truman Doctrine, the early 1950's witnessed the conversion of the successful Marshall Plan economic aid program into a program of Atlantic and Western European rearmament. The Americans' sense of urgency for rearmament arose not only from the outbreak of the Korean War in June, 1950, but also from their realization that the breaking of the American atomic and then nuclear monopoly by the Soviet Union made it essential that a Soviet-American war in Europe should not "go nuclear." To avoid this eventuality, even while continuing to prepare for a nuclear war and to assert a willingness to use nuclear weapons if a war with Russia were to break out, the United States actively promoted the building-up of non-nuclear, or conventional, forces in Western Europe. This led to a crisis in NATO because in order to facilitate rapid Western European rearmament, the United States proposed to its NATO allies in the fall of 1950 that steps should be taken to rearm Western Germany.

The reaction in Western Europe, and especially in France, was one of alarm. Was the immediacy of the Russian military threat as great as that? There was some doubt in Western Europe, although apparently little doubt in Washington. The result, however, was a proposal to create a Western European-oriented security system. This European Defense Community (EDC) would be a parallel with the newly-formed European Coal and Steel Community (ECSC). The ECSC Treaty had been signed by the Benelux states, Italy, France, and West Germany in 1950 to pool their iron and steel industries, thus implementing the notion that a recurrence of Franco-German warfare, already having brought on three European wars, could best be prevented by the integration of the two states' primary war-making industrial capabilities. (See the Epilogue for a more detailed discussion of these events and their consequences.) In reality, this gave France a control over West Germany which the EDC proposals further advanced, in that they would have given France control over an integrated Western European armed force which would have included West Germany.

Debate over the EDC dragged on for nearly four years, with the Americans becoming impatient over the delay in getting West German rearmament underway, and the French becoming more uncertain about whether they wanted West German rearmament in any form. Finally the delay was terminated in 1954 with the setting-aside of the EDC proposals and the incorporation of West Germany directly into NATO, thus reaffirming the Atlantic military connection. France still retained some control over West German rearmament by virtue of the rearrangement at this same time of the Brussels Treaty Organization into the Western European Union (WEU) so that France, along with Britain, Italy, and the Benelux states, could exercise supervision over the ban on West Germany to manufacture (but not necessarily to acquire) so-called "ABC" weapons (atomic, bacteriological, and chemical).

During this same period, the United States introduced in Western Europe nuclear weapons designated tactical or "battlefield" to distinguish them from the strategic nuclear deterrent forces of the American Strategic Air Command and the British Bomber Command, which were not a part of NATO but linked to NATO for targeting and warfare contingencies. The Europeans, already aware of the mutually deterring effect of the Soviet-American retaliatory nuclear strike capabilities, never undertook their own non-nuclear, or conventional, rearmament as enthusiastically as the Americans desired.

EXTRA-EUROPEAN PRESSURES ON
AMERICAN-WESTERN EUROPEAN RELATIONS

The tensions that NATO and West German rearmament had produced were just being ameliorated when the United States found itself once again publicly at odds with its Western allies. This time it was over differing outlooks toward decolonization. Essentially, the first Suez crisis can be regarded as a consequence of the divergence between American global opposition to the spread of Communist influences and French and British concern about surrendering their dominance in non-European areas. The cancelling of American aid for the Aswan High Dam as a punishment to Egypt for buying Communist-supplied arms (previously denied to them by the United States) forced Egypt in President Nasser's judgment to nationalize the Suez Canal, thereby acquiring the Canal's revenues to help in financing the Dam. Egypt's cotton crop had already been mortgaged to pay for the arms. The result of the Franco-British reaction to the Egyptian takeover of the Canal was military intervention, ostensibly to impose a cease-fire between the Israelis and Egyptians and to protect the Suez Canal itself.

The United States unequivocally opposed the actions of Britain and France; these states' major NATO ally worked in a de facto manner in the United Nations with the declared enemy of NATO, the Soviet Union, to bring about a cease-fire and withdrawal. It was a humiliating experience to the British and the French, as evidenced by the Eden government in London and the Mollet government in Paris giving way shortly thereafter to the leadership of men whose reputations were not publicly identified as closely with this episode. The bad feeling that had arisen between Washington and London and Paris caused some serious reflection in NATO. President Eisenhower's general attitude of lecturing to his French and British counterparts had not helped matters, given the fact that the United States also in the post-war period had reserved to itself the discretion to use its armed forces in the first instance to protect what it regarded as its vital interests. The following statement by President Eisenhower could only have annoyed America's chief European allies:

We cannot—in the world, any more than in our own nation—subscribe to one law for the weak, another law for the strong; . . . There can be only one law—or there will be no peace. . . . We value—deeply and lastingly—the bonds with those great nations [Britain and France], those great friends, with whom we now so plainly disagree. And I, for one, am confident that those bonds will do more than survive. They can—my friends, they must—grow to new and greater strength. But this we know above all: there are some firm principles that cannot bend—they can only break. And we shall not break ours.[3]

From this situation, as mentioned, there emerged an "agonizing reappraisal" within the North Atlantic Alliance about the need for greater political consultation, which resulted in a document called the Report of the Committee of Three on Non-Military Co-operation.[4] The major point made in the report, to which all the allies in the coalition agreed, was:

NATO has not been destroyed, or even weakened by the threats or attacks of its enemies. It has faltered at times through the lethargy or complacency of its members; through dissension or division between them; by putting narrow national considerations above the collective interest. It could be destroyed by these forces, if they were allowed to subsist. To combat these tendencies, NATO must be used by its members far more than it has been used, for sincere and genuine consultation and co-operation on questions of common concern. For this purpose, resolution is more important than resolutions; will than words. It is easy to profess devotion to the principle of political—or economic—consultation in NATO. It is difficult and has in fact been shown to be impossible, if the proper conviction is lacking, to convert the profession into practice. Consultation within an alliance means more than exchange of information, though that is necessary. It means more than letting the NATO Council know about national decisions that have already been taken; or trying to enlist support for those decisions. It means the discussion of problems collectively, in the early stages of policy formation, and before national posi-

[3] As quoted in Dwight D. Eisenhower, *Waging Peace, 1956–1961* (Garden City, New York: Doubleday and Company, 1965), p. 83.

[4] For a summary of the background of this Report, see Robert S. Jordan, *The NATO International Staff / Secretariat, 1952–1957: A Study in International Administration* (London and New York: Oxford University Press, 1967).

tions become fixed. At best, this will result in collective decisions on matters of common interest affecting the Alliance. At the least, it will ensure that no action is taken by one member without a knowledge of the views of the others.[5]

The United States and its Western European allies had to heal the political breach which Suez had opened among them. The tensions within Western Europe and the Atlantic area, stemming from the divergence of American global anti-Communist reactions and European decolonial reactions, were major factors in a calculation of American interests in Europe in the mid-1950's.

AMERICAN ATTITUDES TOWARD
WESTERN EUROPEAN INTEGRATION

By the latter half of the 1950's the United States had become preoccupied with the Middle East (the Jordan and Lebanon crises) and the Far East (the Formosan and Pescadores Islands crises). The states of Western Europe, feeling secure within the Atlantic Alliance and preoccupied with increasing their living standards, began to explore among themselves the potential of more formal economic collaboration. The result, as is well known, was the Treaty of Rome, signed in 1957. The Treaty laid out a pattern for the gradual creation of a European Economic Community (EEC), the first step of which was to create a Common Market among the six signator states—France, Italy, West Germany, and Benelux.

The United States supported this move, since it reflected the growing possibility that France and Germany could indeed "bury the hatchet" through economic functionalism. None of the participants, however, and certainly not Great Britain, anticipated the extent and the rapidity of the economic growth in Common Market trade which would result. By 1960 the volume of trade had increased sharply. Britain, having initially declined to enter the Market, now was having second thoughts. Britain's three major earlier reservations (in addition to not wanting to be a part of what was thought would be a marginally successful venture) were considerations of the effect of the Market on British Commonwealth

[5] *Ibid.*, p. 76.

ties, on British agriculture, and on the so-called "special relation-ship" of Britain with the United States which in defense affairs had permitted Britain to become the third nuclear Power in the world.

Prime Minister Harold Macmillan, however, sensing that Britain should take more seriously the trans-Channel challenge that the Market might present, moved to form a more loosely conceived grouping of states, known as the European Free Trade Association (EFTA). This grouping, consisting of Britain, Sweden, Portugal, Norway, Denmark, Austria, and Switzerland (with Finland having an Agreement of Association) was seen as a bargaining counter for these states as they moved, under British leadership, to investigate the possibilities of "entering into Europe." Thus by the early 1960's, not only was Europe divided into eastern and western parts, but also the western part was divided into the "inner Six" and the "outer Seven." This latter fractionalization was not entirely welcome to the United States, which looked for a larger community of European states even while not objecting to a retention and strengthening of Atlantic ties among the states individually and also collectively through NATO and through a broadened Organization for Econom-ic Cooperation and Development (OECD—formerly the Organi-zation of European Economic Cooperation, an outgrowth of the Marshall Plan).

DIFFERENCES IN ATTITUDE TOWARD MILITARY STRATEGY

The growth of European economic prosperity was not matched, however, in American eyes, with a sufficient growth of Western European willingness to assume more of the common de-fense "burden." As mentioned earlier, a primary reason for this was that the states in Europe of the Atlantic Alliance were con-vinced that the real deterrent to a Soviet threat lay in the nuclear dimension, over which they had very little control, and with the exception of Britain even less capability to create for themselves. It was only after the Soviet Union had demonstrated in 1957, through Sputnik, that the Russians could directly attack the conti-nental United States with nuclear weapons that the crisis of confidence about the American guarantee to Western Europe came out into the open.

Although beginning as early as 1956, when France began laying plans for its own nuclear force after the Suez debacle, the advent of General de Gaulle to power in 1958 brought on what eventuated in an open split between France and the United States on the question of the reliability of the American nuclear "umbrella" and the role of Britain in American nuclear affairs. The events which made it possible for France to actually move in foreclosing British entry into the Common Market were directly tied to Britain's "special relationship" with the United States in strategic nuclear weaponry. The United States had offered to Britain in 1960 the Skybolt ballistic missile, which would have given the British a delivery system for its nuclear warheads to replace the "V" series of manned bombers, which were becoming obsolete. Then, in 1962, upon very short notice, the American Secretary of Defense, Robert McNamara, informed Britain that the United States would no longer continue the development of Skybolt, but that the British could do so if they would assume the costs.

This episode occurred just at the time that Prime Minister Macmillan was meeting with President de Gaulle about the question of British membership in the Common Market. Macmillan, quite rightly, asked immediately to meet with President Kennedy since Britain obviously could not assume the development costs of Skybolt, and in the eyes of the British public the Macmillan government had suffered a stinging national humiliation at the hands of the Americans, similar to the earlier Suez crisis.

The two leaders met at Nassau in December, 1962, out of which came the "Declaration of Interdependence," which was designed to emphasize the compatibility of the two national partners in a common defense mission. Unfortunately for Britain, the Nassau meeting and the Declaration conveyed to President de Gaulle that Britain was so excessively dependent in defense matters on the United States as to be an unreliable European partner. So, with this episode fresh before all the member states of the Common Market, de Gaulle announced his opposition to Britain's entering the Market. He did so with the satisfaction that the immediate opportunity lay in the confusion of Britain's nuclear relationship to the United States, which had all along been a source of French irritation and resentment.[6]

French rejection of the British application was followed by moves to disengage France from the confines of the NATO military organizational structure. These arrangements had emphasized common integrated military commands together with a network of Alliance logistical arrangements, but the nuclear deterrent forces of the United States had not been made a part of these organizational arrangements.

The ill-fated Multilateral Nuclear Force (MLF) and Atlantic Nuclear Force (ANF) proposals of the early 1960's, suggesting a greater sharing of the nuclear dimension, proved more divisive than otherwise. Even the British were not enthusiastic about the principle of "mixed-manning" of NATO warships equipped with nuclear weapons, but still possessing an American check on their use. General Lauris Norstad while NATO Supreme Commander had advocated a NATO European nuclear force, yet even his own government was not sympathetic with him on this matter. The occasional revival of the possibility of an Anglo-French nuclear force might have been another means of strengthening NATO militarily, but neither state has vigorously pressed the matter. Finally, the reluctance of West Germany and Italy, and the outright refusal of France to sign the Nuclear Non-Proliferation Treaty points up the difference in outlook over these matters between the United States and Western Europe.

As long as America could unequivocally guarantee the security of Western Europe through unilateral nuclear deterrence, the Alliance was fulfilling its basic anti-Soviet purpose. Almost from the time of the signing of the Treaty in 1949, however, the question of the credibility of the United States military guarantee to Europe

[6] For example, in 1958 de Gaulle had proposed to the United States and Britain that a preferential relationship be established among these three Powers in NATO, not only to plan the affairs of NATO and Western Europe, but also to consult together on world-wide problems of mutual concern. According to de Gaulle, he had been rebuffed by President Eisenhower. According to Eisenhower, he had informed de Gaulle that such an arrangement would have created two classes of members in NATO, which would have been inconsistent with the intentions of the Treaty.

was not entirely foreclosed, for it was also at this time that the Soviet Union had demonstrated its capability to build atomic weapons, thus depriving the United States of its monopoly. As mentioned earlier, after Sputnik, America's allies could publicly ask: was it *really* in the interests of the United States to accept the destruction of, say, New York for retaliating directly against the Soviet Union if Russian troops were to move westward into NATO territory? By 1966, de Gaulle summarized his doubts thus:

> There has been a change in the nature of the threats to the Western world, and particularly to Europe, which had led to the conclusion of the Treaty. They are no longer as imminent or as menacing as they were formerly. Moreover, the European countries have restored their economies and have therefore recovered means for action. In particular, France is equipping herself with atomic weapons, the very nature of which precludes her integration. Thirdly, the substitution of the balance of nuclear power between the Soviet Union and the United States for the United States' monopoly in this field has transformed the general conditions of Western defence. Finally, it is a fact that Europe is no longer the centre of international crisis. This centre is now elsewhere, particularly in Asia, where the countries of the Atlantic alliance as a group are obviously not involved.[7]

France, thus, by the mid-1960's appeared to be frustrating American interests in Europe in two significant ways. First, Britain was being denied access to the growing and prospering Common Market. In the eyes of France and perhaps less vocally in the eyes also of other Common Market states, the British were doing little to rearrange their affairs with the Commonwealth (especially in agriculture), or their special ties with the United States, both of which would be necessary to become a serious candidate for entry into the Market. Second, as regards NATO, the prime vehicle through which the United States exercised its control over the affairs of Western Europe, France had begun to withdraw from active participation in the military structure of the Alliance even while not renouncing the

[7] For a discussion of the withdrawal see Brigadier Kenneth Hunt, "NATO Without France: The Military Implications," Adelphi Paper Number 32, Institute for Strategic Studies, London, 1966. On the other hand, some Europeans have come to the belief that the American nuclear guarantee would extend to Western Europe even in the absence of the Alliance.

North Atlantic Treaty itself, and none of the proposals to broaden
the command and control of nuclear weapons were helping matters
any. The resentment felt from Washington over this situation
prompted de Gaulle to comment:

> Certainly, this independence which we are once more practicing
> in all areas has not failed to surprise, and even to scandalize
> various circles for which France's vassalage was the habit and
> the rule. . . . the Americans speak of Machiavellism, as if the
> clearest conduct did not consist precisely in following our own
> path. They are alarmed at our isolation at a time when there have
> never been more people flocking around us. In addition, the fact
> that we have reassumed our faculty of judgment and action in
> regard to all problems sometimes seems to displease a State which
> may believe that, by virtue of its power, it is invested with su-
> preme and universal responsibility. But, who knows if, some day,
> the advantage which this friendly country may have in finding
> France on her feet will not by far outweigh the annoyance which
> it now feels about it?[8]

Even the inability of France, after 1968, to continue to assume
this posture, has not changed the impact of France's policies. For
example, by 1970 Canada also moved to withdraw its forces, using
similar arguments about the necessity for "independence" vis-à-vis
the United States.

AMERICA'S OWN DOUBTS ABOUT
ITS MILITARY STRATEGY IN EUROPE

An annoyance to all the Alliance members had been the
unilateral announcement in May 1962 by the United States of a
revised strategy for NATO. Instead of "massive retaliation," now
the doctrine would be one of "flexible response." It has been said
that when the new Kennedy Administration had finished looking
long and hard at the consequences of a nuclear war with the Soviet
Union, they recoiled from the logical outcome of massive retaliation.
To sidestep a situation whereby nuclear devastation lay at the fore-
front of any NATO-Warsaw Pact encounter, Secretary of Defense
McNamara and his colleagues contemplated a more gradual esca-

[8] Charles de Gaulle, Press Conference of 27 April 1966.

lation of any conflict in Europe, hoping that before the escalation had reached the nuclear stage, it could be resolved. To them, not to provide for a "condition of pause" before introducing nuclear weapons would be foolhardy in the extreme. This, of course, was just what America's European allies did *not* want to hear. They did not want to see their territory turned into another bloody battleground—one "liberation" had been enough. Nor did they want to put up the more massive land armies which such a strategy would have entailed.

And so, even while accepting pro forma the new doctrine, virtually all of America's allies in fact could not bring themselves, intellectually and morally as well as in pure calculations of their respective national interests, to accept flexible response in practice. The cost in terms of their national survival appeared to be too high. This situation had, it is clear, a rather cruel element of irony: the Americans' search for the greatest security for everyone appeared to be bringing about greater insecurity.

However, after the conflict in Vietnam had begun to demonstrate to the United States some of the pitfalls of graduated or flexible response, and after America's European allies had continued to demonstrate their unwillingness to build up the minimum number of conventional ground forces to make a reality of flexible response, the Alliance began to turn back to massive retaliation, where it is at present. The gradual withdrawal of American ground forces from Europe in the late 1960's and the planned withdrawal of more in the 1970's has not helped to forestall this development.

AMERICA, GERMANY, AND EUROPE

Without a doubt, the major problems of post-war Europe, for which the United States has carried the major responsibility, have been the division of defeated Germany, and the relations of West Germany with its Western allies, and especially France. The French concern about Germany had evolved by the end of the 1950's in four ways. First, the de facto division of Germany still existed which France did not want to see resolved nor, at the same time, see confirmed since this could arouse German desires to bring about unification through their own initiatives. Second, the coal and steel

producing areas of West Germany had been placed under an international authority in which France had a veto. Third, West German armed forces, as pointed out earlier, were integrated into
NATO, which made them subject to French control as long as
France remained a signator to the North Atlantic Treaty, and France
has not denounced the Treaty. Finally, West German membership
in the Common Market has provided a means of keeping Germany
from becoming economically isolated, and any West German initiatives in the economic sphere have been subject to French assent. On
the other hand, West German influence over France has grown
steadily. For example, France will probably pay a high political as
well as economic price for the adjustments in the Market arrangements brought on by French economic difficulties, and especially
by the devaluation of the franc in August, 1969. These concessions
could redound to Germany's benefit. As one observer put it:

> The six-nation European Common Market today took the biggest
> backward step of its 11-year history by suspending its joint agri-
> cultural policy for as long as two years. Emerging at dawn from
> an 18-hour meeting made necessary by French devaluation, Gun-
> ther Harkort of West Germany spoke of the 'burial' of the farm
> policy that had been the Common Market's most significant
> achievement towards political and economic unity. 'We took so
> much time,' the secretary of state of the West German Foreign
> Ministry said, 'because we wanted to put the tombstone in place
> so that it is possible for a resurrection to take place in a reason-
> able time.' Observers believed such resurrection would depend on
> a complete overhaul of the present policy. . . . The French have
> insisted that agreement with their partners on a definitive new sys-
> tem for financing farm products was the precondition for letting
> the British join the market. The fact that France has been granted
> the first across-the-board exemption since the uniform farm policy
> was initiated in 1962 weakens French arguments against giving
> new members special treatment during a transitional period.[9]

This economic crisis in the Common Market, resolved in early
1970, underscored the relative economic weakness of France to

---

[9] "Paris Forces Commart to Scrap Farm Policy," article by Jonathan
C. Randal in *The Washington Post,* 13 August 1969.

West Germany. West Germany's refusal to revalue the mark in the fall of 1968, and then the Germans' refusal to agree to lower the so-called Common Market "unit of account," which pegs farm prices in all Common Market member states against a specified gold amount, underscored at that time to France and the world the growing economic strength of West Germany and the adaptation of its foreign policies in the light of this strength.

One of President de Gaulle's long-range goals had been to keep Franco-German ties as close as possible partly in order to reduce American influence over West Germany. A formal expression of this desire had been the signing of the Franco-German Treaty of Friendship in 1963, which provided for periodic meetings of the two Heads of Government. This arrangement could reinforce French influence over West Germany, presumably at the expense of American influence. The Treaty has never been completely successful in this purpose and therefore it has not been a major political factor in Franco-German relations. It remains to be seen if the Treaty will have a renewed significance as the economic relationship of France to its Common Market neighbors, and especially to the Germans, changes. President Georges Pompidou has attached importance to establishing cordial relations with both his West German and his American counterparts.

THE FUTURE OF THE ATLANTIC ALLIANCE

The strains in the North Atlantic Alliance were thus not only due to changing and differing conceptions of the nature and imminence of the Russian threat to Western Europe, but also to differences in the national interests in Europe of the allies themselves, and especially so between the United States and France, and between France and West Germany. In nuclear affairs, by the late 1960's new consultative machinery had been created in NATO to bolster confidence in the American deterrent and to facilitate inter-allied cooperation after the French withdrawal from the NATO military structure. A Nuclear Planning Group (virtually the North Atlantic Council without France) was formed and has worked effectively. Also, a special NATO report, the Harmel Report, named after the chairman of the committee which drafted it, recommended strengthening NATO's political consultative role, aiming toward negotiations with the Soviet Union and the Warsaw Pact over European security problems, and toward an affirmation of the "bridge-building" tendencies which had already been apparent between the states of Eastern and Western Europe. Unfortunately, the Harmel Report was submitted just as the second post-World War II Czechoslovak crisis was taking place, and so the more conciliatory political aspects of the report, as regards relationships with Eastern Europe, had to be set aside. The proliferation of these Eastern European relationships have nonetheless gone on, with President Richard Nixon's visit to Rumania in July, 1969, underscoring the trend. This was the first occasion since the end of World War II that an American President had visited Eastern Europe.

There was still some question as to whether the political "malaise" in NATO's anti-Communist stance could be forestalled for much longer. Not only had it arisen because of the factors already mentioned, but also NATO had been beset on its southern flank with a bitter conflict, bordering on open warfare, between Greece and Turkey over Cyprus which had to some extent soured their sense of NATO solidarity. Even the expansion of Soviet influence into the Eastern Mediterranean has not altered this situation too much, partly because of Scandinavian hostility to the Greek military-ruled government. Nonetheless the political guarantees of the North Atlantic Treaty, committing the United States to come to the aid of its Western European allies in case of aggression will probably be maintained and honored, but the military structure which had grown up in NATO in the 1950's, and modified in the 1960's, could continue to be modified as changing circumstances demanded. It would seem doubtful that any of the Middle Powers who were signators of the Treaty—Britain, France, West Germany, Italy—would renounce it. Even if perhaps Norway or Denmark would do so (possibly to consolidate a Baltic security arrangement which would perforce have to be more neutralist vis-à-vis the Superpowers), or Greece, Turkey or Canada (which took up the question early in 1969 and then dropped it), the heart of the Alliance would remain.

THE "NECESSITY FOR CHOICE"
IN ATLANTIC AFFAIRS

What of the Anglo-American "special relationship"? Ironically, as the French government under President Pompidou appeared to be taking a less harsh stand toward either Britain or the United States, the difficulties of British entry into Europe appeared no less real. For one thing, the West Germans and the Italians, who along with the Dutch have seen Britain as a useful potential counterweight to French political domination in Western European politics, will now need to show what concessions they, in fact, would be willing to make in the structure of the Common Market to accommodate British needs. To quote again from a political observer on the impact of the French devaluation on the Market: ". . . the gains France's weakness provided for partisans of British entry are qualified by the mood of disarray that could dissuade all members from tackling the inherently disorganizing initial effect of accepting newcomers."[10]

For another thing, any movement for greater Western European political integration appears ambiguous at best. Early in the 1960's, proposals were put forward by a study group chaired by a French minister, Christian Fouchet, suggesting a formalized political dimension to the Community. These proposals died stillborn in the aftermath of the Skybolt episode and the first French rejection of British membership in the Market. By 1965, however, there was formed an amalgamated European Communities consisting of the former Coal and Steel Community, the European Atomic Energy Community (EURATOM) and the EEC. These Communities have a common Commission, accountable to a Council of Ministers, and under the loose scrutiny of the European Parliament. At the present time there is strong sentiment in Britain and in the member states of the Communities in favor of creating a European parliamentary body, the members of which would be elected by universal suffrage. Another joint body is the Court of Justice.

How the future of Western Europe will evolve, and how American interests will be served or injured thereby, are difficult to foretell. One analyst has summarized the situation thus:

[10] *Ibid.*

. . . The conventional wisdom is that the central question about Europe's future is whether the Common Market will be expanded to include Great Britain. The real question is what kind of Common Market Britain will be joining. . . . For ten years, nationalism—or, to put it more accurately, parochialism—has gathered strength in Europe. This sentiment was masked, in some degree, by de Gaulle's towering presence; he was blamed for attitudes which had wider roots. . . . In the economic field, this would mean settling for a customs union, and turning away from proposals to strengthen the Community's role in monetary, budgetary and agricultural matters. In the political field it would mean adopting the Fouchet Plan—a well-worn French proposal for using the Community to exchange national views on political issues, instead of envisaging new institutions to propose common European views about a wider European role. In the nuclear field, it would mean cooperation between the French and British national nuclear forces on terms which would maintain them as instruments of independent national action—doing nothing to ease, and perhaps underlining, discrimination against European non-nuclear nations. Italy and the Low Countries might object, but they are too weak to do much about it without strong German support. The German attitude might be ambivalent: Immediately after the war, a shattered Germany wished to submerge her national identity via European integration; now, some German leaders may believe that, as the strongest state in Western Europe, Germany could protect and even advance her national interests in a loosening European Community. All this has important implications for the United States. Decisions to be made during negotiations about British entry will pose concrete issues for us—on both the economic and nuclear fronts. On the economic front, the United States will have to react to a natural European tendency to solve European economic problems at America's expense. . . . On the nuclear front, U.S. assent would be required for any British sharing of atomic secrets with France, since U.S. technology is involved. The Joint Congressional Committee on Atomic Energy has generally taken a dim view of further nuclear sharing, on security grounds. Again, there is no reason why the administration should push hard on this front, unless clear political gain is in sight. The key question here is, as Professor Bator wrote in Brookings' AGENDA FOR THE NATION last year, whether Anglo-French nuclear cooperation 'engages the Germans, Italians, and perhaps others, on terms consistent with the nonproliferation treaty . . . has built into it the right kind of command and control, and is seen as a good thing by a responsible German government, without any pushing or pulling by the United States, and despite the cross-cutting effects on its eastern policy and the general nervousness on both sides about any German role in nuclear defense.' A scheme which fails this test is not one which the United States should be working hard to help.[11]

---

[11] "Decisions Due Soon on Europe's Future," article by Henry Owen in *The Washington Post,* 8 August 1969. © The Washington Post. Reprinted with permission.

ROBERT RANGER

2 The Political Involvement of the Soviet Union in Europe

The European approach to international politics is traditional and conservative. It is seen primarily as an exercise in the balancing of power, a striving for an equilibrium that would be stable because it would truly reflect the underlying interplay of national forces. Ideology, including Communism, is usually subordinated to state interests, even Russia's, though ideology can influence the way in which these interests are perceived by the rulers. The antithesis between ideology and *realpolitik* is between two different criteria of judgment of success in foreign policy. The two can be reconciled by arguing that the long-term interests of Socialism and the Soviet Union are indivisible.[1]

The European situation when Germany surrendered on May of 1945 was, in systemic terms, the product of a seventy-four year struggle to determine the balance of power in Eastern Europe. Originally, this was between the four Empires of Austro-Hungary, Turkey, Russia and Germany. World War I had destroyed the first two and had caused the temporary eclipse of Germany (by defeat) and Russia (by revolution). The dominant nationalities in the Empires proclaimed their statehood, which was recognized because there appeared to be no alternative way of establishing political order out of the chaos of the war. But their new independence was conditional on the weakness of the two remaining dominant Eastern European Powers. As Germany and Russia were able to reassert their underlying strength,

---

[1] See Raymond L. Garthoff, *Soviet Military Policy* (New York: Frederick A. Praeger, 1966), esp. chapter 4, "Ideology and the Balance of Power," and Marshall Schulman, *Stalin's Foreign Policy* (Cambridge: Harvard University Press, 1963), Chapter I.

the question again became: What sort of balance would emerge and what freedom would it leave smaller states? Denied an alliance with Britain and France, Stalin attempted to accommodate Germany by defining the Russo-German spheres of influence in their August 1939 Pact. This traditional method of preventing expansion from leading to war failed.

Hitler's defeat left unanswered the interrelated questions of the balance of power in Europe, Russia's interests in it, and the means of securing these interests. Since the answers reflected changes in the political environment and the perception of these changes, it is heuristically easier to divide the post-war era into four periods, in each of which existed a distinct interpretation of Russian interests: 1945–1953 (Stalinism); 1953–March 1956 (the Interregnum); March 1956–1963 (de-Stalinization and separate roads to socialism); 1963–1968 (East-West détente and bloc repression). Lest this lead to an underestimate of underlying continuities, it must be emphasized that the changes referred to were always more gradual and never as inevitable as they must seem in such a condensed history. For example, although Khrushchev was deposed in October 1964, few substantive changes in Russian foreign policy were visible until the invasion of Czechoslovakia. The increasing use of conventional forces, especially the Soviet Navy, to establish Russia's right to be a World Power as well as a Superpower, reflected strategic decisions taken under Khrushchev. The difference between trying to halt a trend and moving with it can also lead to confusion between changes in policy and in underlying realities; Khrushchev tried to adapt polycentrism to Soviet needs but did not originate the movement.

STALINISM: 1945–1953

Stalin seems to have assumed that, as Lenin had predicted, the internal contradictions of capitalism would lead to wars between Imperialist Powers, which would unite only to attack the Socialist regime in Russia. The Soviet Union must therefore prepare for war, while trying to avoid it until recovered from World War II. His life had covered six other Russian wars: against Japan (1904–5); World War I (1914–17); the Bolsheviks against the Allies, White Russians and Poles (1917–21); against Japan (1938); indirectly, the Spanish

Civil War (1937–38); and against Finland (1939–40). Any future war would be decided by five permanently operating factors, defined by Stalin as: stability of the rear; the morale of the army; the quantity and quality of divisions; the armament of the army, and the organizational ability of the command personnel.

First atomic and then nuclear weapons had reinforced his respect for American military power and had emphasized to him the need for caution until the Russians had acquired them. Together with the technical developments producing the Blitzkrieg form of warfare, these weapons meant Russia's traditional strategy of trading space for time would require modification, with Europe as a whole providing the space. As one observer commented:

> Stalin was forced to organize and deploy his army, navy and air force so that they could threaten a vital interest of the United States and deter that country from launching a preventive war against the Soviet Union. Since the Russians could not reach North American territory...the best substitute was western Europe.[2]

This strategic background determined the timing of Stalin's European policy. The 1945 Allied Conferences at Yalta and Potsdam had to accept the gains made by the Russian forces, which occupied all Eastern Europe except for Czechoslovakia (where they quickly withdrew) and Yugoslavia. Having retaken the Russian territories lost in 1917, including Poland up to the Curzon line, Stalin had to decide his next step. He wanted control over the largest possible area, including Germany, but to proceed too quickly would mean antagonizing the United States, with unpredictable consequences for the future of Europe, and especially Western Europe.

The compromise of putting Communist parties into genuine coalition governments, such as in Poland, is a reflection of Stalin's uncertainty. With Germany under Four-Power occupation and powerful Communist parties in Italy and France working toward taking power legitimately, he could exercise considerable influence in Western Eu-

[2] J. M. Mackintosh, *Juggernaut: The Russian Forces 1945–53* (New York: The Macmillan Co., 1967), pp. 270–271. Stalin cited his five permanently operating factors in his Order of the Day, 23 February 1942, quoted in Mackintosh, *Strategy and Tactics of Soviet Foreign Policy* (New York: Oxford University Press, 1962), pp. 90–91.

rope, especially as the United States steadily withdrew its forces during this period. The inherent contradiction between striving for gains through diplomacy in Western Europe and maintaining military control in Eastern Europe produced a continuing alternation in Russian policy toward Europe. But the primary concern was— and is—how to retain control over Germany. Hence the ambivalence in Stalin's policy between cooperation with the West and the consolidation of Soviet power in Eastern Europe. Defensive measures in the latter context seemed to contradict moves in the former.

For example, the Soviet government's official line in discussions with the West continued to be that the wartime working relationship should remain. Outstanding problems could be resolved by negotiations, such as those concerning peace treaties with former enemy states, which were signed by 1947 except for those with Germany and Austria. In contrast, the simultaneous removal of non-Communist elements from the governments of Poland, Hungary, Rumania and Bulgaria[3] and the Russian zone of Germany suggested a more hostile approach toward the West, and especially the United States. The result, as so often in Russia's German policy, was to bring about the danger feared most, which was the resurgence of Germany as a Great Power by trying to prevent it.[4]

Instead of the withdrawal of all American troops from Europe two years after the war ended as President Roosevelt had forecast in 1944, 1947 saw a conscious American commitment as the dominant Power in Western Europe, balancing Russia in Eastern Europe. The Truman Doctrine was enunciated in March 1947 and the Marshall Plan the following June. Stalin countered by ordering the French and Italian Communist parties to abandon their constitutional path to power, and instead called for "direct action." The resulting wave of strikes from September 1947 into the fall of 1948 failed to stop the realignment of Western Europe under American leadership and destroyed those Communist parties as popular political organizations for some time. Their re-emergence in the 1960's has been as indepen-

[3] Adam Ullam, *Expansion and Coexistence, A History of Soviet Foreign Policy, 1917–1967* (New York: Frederick A. Praeger, 1968), Chapter VIII.

[4] For an excellent discussion of the place of Berlin in post-war international politics, see Philip Windsor, *Berlin, City on Leave* (London: Chatto and Windus, 1962).

dent national Communist parties, representing more indigenous left-orientated political groupings than the interests of the Soviet Union.

Once the process of defining spheres of influence had started, it created a situation where all Europe would be divided between the Soviet Union and the United States. The cold war thus became a set of self-fulfilling prophecies where virtually all political actions and conflicts were interpreted in ideological terms. The complex of forces behind any political decision were ignored in favor of the assumption by each Superpower that its adversary's aim was ultimate hegemony.[5] The establishment of a Communist government in Czechoslovakia in 1948 and the Korean War in 1950 were taken as signs of Soviet aggression. The United States dropped its budgetary limitations on defense spending and requested its allies to engage in crash rearmament programs, with 1954 as the "year of maximum danger." In fact, Korea seems to have been in the Far East what Czechoslovakia was in Europe—a Communist attempt to round off a local sphere of influence in an area apparently open to the first taker.

Stalin's actions in 1948 represented a response to what appeared to him to be the American consolidation of its sphere of influence in the West. Ideology determined the modality, the establishment of a rigidly conformist Communist dictatorship, rather than a less obvious military takeover. Stalin's main need appeared to be securing this important area before his opponent had a chance to move in.

Czechoslovakia was the one major East European state not then under Communist control or occupation. Its coalition government had included Communists in key posts, but they were certain to lose them in the next elections. If not sooner, the other parties might after the elections be persuaded to ask for American military assistance. Stalin therefore ordered a coup carried out in March 1948, although he did not send in troops, probably because of the risk that the United States might follow suit, producing a direct confrontation. As the events of August 1968 showed, Czechoslovakia's geographical position makes it in Russian eyes an essential part of any system of buffer states. But Soviet attempts to remove Tito from power in 1948 failed, leaving a fiercely independent Communist Yugoslavia. Again,

[5] Contrast George Kennan's "The Sources of Soviet Conduct" (under the pseudonym of "X") in *Foreign Affairs*, February 1947, with his B.B.C. Reith Lectures, printed as *Russia, the Atom and the West*.

troops were not used for fear of American reaction. But a series of purges, from 1947 to 1949, removed any potential Titos elsewhere in Eastern Europe.

There remained the so-called "German problem," whose essence was, and is, the unwillingness of either side to exchange the zone within its sphere of influence for reunification, which might create a unified Germany that at least might favor ideological opponents, and at worst might become itself the dominant Power in Central Europe. But because a commitment to reunification has seemed until recently politically essential to reassure its respective German ally, each Superpower has officially accepted the division of Germany only as an interim step, even while more and more accepting the de facto desirability of continued division.

The Western Powers' decision in 1948 to establish a separate currency in Trizonia (the fused American, British, and French occupation zones) and the corresponding sectors of Berlin was decisive. Stalin was probably aware that this could ultimately lead to the emergence of a West German state possessing most of the former Reich's industrial and military resources and opposing the new status quo in Europe. The Berlin Blockade, starting on 23 June 1948, indicated the importance of Germany in Russian thinking. It attempted to prevent or delay national restoration of the Western zones by showing that the West could not protect the West Berliners. Berlin in Russian hands would be a useful bargaining counter, logically completing their new sphere of influence. Stalin failed because the airlift succeeded in supplying West Berlin and he was not prepared to escalate this conflict by interrupting the airlift, even though there was little the West could have done if he had. When the Blockade ended in May 1949, the Four-Power administration which had been set up earlier, pending reunification, had been divided into Western and Russian zones, soon to become separate states.

Thus by 1949 the scope of the Russian empire in Eastern Europe had been defined on the basis of the 1945 armistice lines. In accordance with Stalin's belief in doctrinal conformity, each member state (Tito's Yugoslavia not included) was ruled by a Stalinist Communist party which adhered to his policy of collectivizing agriculture and selectively building up heavy industry. In fact, if not in name, they were Russian "colonies" of exploitation, providing raw materials, labor, and military bases. The exceptions were Yugoslavia, Finland,

and Austria. The Finnish government was too vulnerable to invasion to allow its territory to be used again against Russia, so its limited internal independence could be tolerated in exchange for the influence it gave Stalin on the politics of the Baltic subregion. Under the Austrian occupation agreement, a unanimous vote of the Central Council was needed to veto the government's laws. So when it proved to be anti-Communist instead of Communist after the November 1945 elections, the Russians had to choose between partition or continued occupation. Because it had little real or symbolic value a decision could be postponed until the Russians saw how events elsewhere developed. These suggested that this marginal addition to Russian control would not be worth the diplomatic loss of imposing political conformity. Therefore, Austrian reunification and neutralization, achieved in 1955, was offered as evidence of Russia's good intentions toward Europe, thus pointing an alternative to West German Chancellor Konrad Adeneuer's concept of German reunification via integration in West Europe and membership in NATO.

Between 1949 and his death in March 1953, Stalin's concept of Russia's European interests apparently remained unchanged in essentials. But his tactics altered. Realizing hostility breeds hostility, he took up the idea of "peaceful coexistence," stressing the absence of any conflict of interests not resolvable by diplomacy, using the divergence between American and Western European interests and outlooks to inhibit the American response and to buy time, hence, the Stockholm Peace Appeal of March 1950 and the follow-up peace ballot in France. Stalin's solution to Western nuclear weapons in 1946 had been a Russian bomb (exploded in September 1949) and at the same time proposals for the prohibition of nuclear weapons.

Despite the start of the Korean War in June 1950, this more flexible policy continued, culminating in the Soviet Note of 10 March 1952 proposing immediate Four-Power discussions on a German Peace Treaty and conditions for forming an all-German government. Whether it offered a basis for negotiations remains debatable. Its main aim was clear: to delay a decision by the West in favor of West German rearmament. As pointed out in the preceding chapter, this had been a major American objective after the Korean War broke out. The war was interpreted by the Americans as a prelude to Russian aggression in Europe which could be forestalled with the help of a rearmed West Germany. Stalin had delayed action himself,

hoping European, especially French, opposition to West German rearmament would suffice. In his last year he saw the main Russian effort directed against West German rearmament. It failed when West Germany became a member of NATO in 1955.

THE INTERREGNUM: MARCH 1953–MARCH 1956

Any nation's foreign policy is more likely to be a series of reactions to events in the light of certain preconceptions than the imposition of "grand designs" on a receptive world. From 1953 onward this ever-present aspect of diplomacy became increasingly dominant in Russian foreign policy. Stalin's successors never established a comparable personal autocracy, removing the coherence imposed by a strong-minded individual. Later under Nikita Khrushchev it reemerged only periodically, on particular issues and never for very long. With the increasing rate of change in every aspect of the international political scene, it meant Russian interests could no longer be seen as clearly articulated goals and corresponding modalities. Instead, the wish to preserve existing political and territorial gains became separated from defensive security needs as these were adapted to developments in military technology. Dominating, because linking both, was the German question, concealing the underlying tension between Russia's quest for security via stabilizing a favorable status quo in Eastern Europe and its methods of maintaining Soviet domination.

Georgi Malenkov initially headed the collective leadership, which started by relaxing the most extreme elements of Stalinist terror. The contradiction of running a Stalinist empire without Stalin was the keynote of their rule, and this was soon evident. On 17 June 1953 the raising of production norms in East Berlin produced worker riots similar to those that had occurred in Czechoslovakia the previous year. But these turned into a limited East German rising which was, however, quickly suppressed by Russian troops. Tragically, this ended the very real possibility that the political weakness of the East German Communist regime headed by Walter Ulbricht might have led the new Soviet leadership to negotiate reunification in exchange for the neutrality of all, or at least the Eastern part, of Germany.

The decision then had to be made whether the concessions needed

to prevent further riots would jeopardize Russia's security needs. The choice was made to permit limited relaxation, and it has remained the basic post-Stalinist policy toward Eastern Europe, even though there has been periodic difficulty in retaining the controls thought necessary to prevent too much political liberalization or economic independence. Allowing *some* freedom is much harder than forbidding *any*.

In 1954 Malenkov claimed that a new world war would mean "the destruction of world civilization."[6] His opponents, including Khrushchev,[7] feared that too-open acknowledgement of a balance of deterrence might mean foregoing the possibility of further political advances at the expense of the United States. In a compromise decision of the leadership, it was decided that the conventional military forces of the Soviet Union and its allies should remain in Eastern Europe as the main deterrent to the United States and its allies. But Stalin's expectation of their *use* and the consequent need to prepare continually for war, was replaced by an expectation of the *avoidance* of war. This was more important and more realizable because of an emerging implicit understanding with the West that the Soviet-imposed status quo could be preserved in Eastern Europe. Internal political upheavals were therefore considered undesirable because they would be potentially destabilizing and would encourage the West to think that they could gain more from challenging than from accepting the status quo, as they had done earlier by not intervening in East Germany during the riots.

Accordingly, from 1953 to 1956 modified Stalinism in Eastern Europe was complemented by détente between Russia and the West. Within Eastern Europe the changes were very limited but they at least offered the hope of improvement in living conditions. Furthermore, limited cultural contacts with the West were promised. The main political event was the establishment of the Warsaw Pact on 14 May 1955 between Russia, Poland, East Germany, Czechoslovakia, Hungary, Bulgaria, Albania, and Rumania. It was a nominal counterpart to NATO, but did not disturb the bilateral treaties binding the other member states to the Soviet Union. The Pact consolidated Rus-

---

[6] Arnold M. Hoerlich and Myron Rush, *Strategic Power and Soviet Foreign Policy* (Chicago: University of Chicago Press, 1966), p. 19.

[7] By the Fall of 1950, Khrushchev was claiming that a world war would "lead to deaths of hundreds of millions of people." (*Ibid.*, p. 79.)

sian influence over Eastern Europe by legitimizing the Red Army's control over the subregion's arrangements for defense against external and internal threats, thus reinforcing a status quo which included a divided Germany. The Pact was explained in part as a response to the threat to Eastern Europe posed by the incorporation of a rearming West Germany into NATO.

The parallel switch from Stalinism to a "Socialist Commonwealth" in the economic sphere was carried out by reviving COMECON (Council for Mutual Economic Assistance). Established in 1947, it had been irrelevant when Stalinist autarchy and Russian exploitation of Eastern Europe were the guiding principles of Socialist economic relations. But it offered considerable potential for less obvious control as it theoretically coordinated its members' national plans to avoid unnecessary duplication, regulated their trade with each other, and regulated bloc trade with third states.

The Cominform had played a similar but more active role in the ideological sphere, ensuring that the world Communist movement followed Stalin's line. Also founded in 1947 as a successor to the Comintern, its dissolution in 1953 thus marked a major shift in Russian attitudes. The significance lay less in the actual changes in the political situation than in the evidence of Russian readiness at this time of political relaxation to permit a process of political readjustment in which the Soviet Union would be predominant but in some ways dealing with sovereign equals.

Outside the bloc this was called détente, which was the theme of Soviet policy in 1955. On 15 May of that year, as already mentioned, the four former wartime allies signed a peace treaty with Austria, establishing its independence in exchange for permanent neutrality and the prohibition of Anschluss (union with Germany). Attempts to link the treaty with Western concessions had failed, while in West Germany rearmament was imminent, and the American Secretary of State, John Foster Dulles, was making bellicose noises about "rollback." The Russians therefore had more to gain from playing this moderating card at that time than retaining it. Certainly it helped promote the "Geneva spirit" of the Superpowers' Summit Conference held in July of that year, whose importance to Russian leaders cannot be overemphasized. For the first time since the Russian Revolution the Communist leaders of the Russian state were being received as equals by the major Powers that seemed at last to be recognizing the victors of war and revolution. Important enough in itself, it was doubly so because it represented a quick triumph for Nikita Khrushchev and Nikolai Bulganin who together had forced Georgi Malenkov's resignation the previous February.

But the Geneva Conference also accentuated the dichotomy between inter- and intra-bloc relations, symbolized by Khrushchev's visit to Yugoslavia a month before the Summit. He apologized to Tito for previous Soviet hostility, blaming it on Laurenti Beria (the symbol of Stalinist terror), and he sought to resume normal relations between the Yugoslav and Russian Communist parties. By rejecting Stalin's insistence on ideological conformity, Khrushchev implied that there was the possibility for greater political flexibility within the Communist world. This was a reflection of the inevitable Politburo debate between those who felt changes had gone too far and those who, like himself, argued that they had not gone far enough to meet Russia's changed international political position.

SEPARATE ROADS TO SOCIALISM:
MARCH 1956–1963

Khrushchev's resolution of the internal Soviet debate on leadership and policy in his favor, resulting in the eventual ouster of Bulganin from the top leadership, triggered a series of changes in Eastern Europe which forced a parallel redefinition of the Soviet Union's interests in the area.

In March 1956, at the Twentieth Congress of the Communist Party of the Soviet Union (CPSU), Khrushchev denounced Stalinism and the cult of the individual. This indicated to Eastern European Communist parties that their Stalinist leaders could no longer rely on Soviet support against pressures for changes. The leaders in Bulgaria and Hungary quickly fell in April and July.

In Poland the industrial workers rioted in Poznan at the end of June for "bread and freedom," and the national police force and army refused to suppress them. The Polish choice between instituting internal reforms and requesting Russian help was largely decided by traditional Polish hostility to Russia and two Soviet blunders. On 20 July Bulganin arrived in Poland to announce that Poland could not endanger bloc solidarity, offering ten million pounds' worth of consumer goods as a palliative. This, combined with Chinese support, led to the decision on 13 October to form another Polish Politburo, including, however, Wladyslaw Gomulka, who had lost power in Stalin's Titoist purges. A Russian-supported coup by Polish Stalinists on 18 October was foiled and the next day Khrushchev arrived in Warsaw with a Soviet delegation.

The alternatives facing him here, as in Hungary, can only be understood in the context formed by the interaction of events and his broad concepts of Soviet interests. For the first time, the Russian leaders had to choose between accepting the full implications of de-Stalinization or trying to restore Stalinism under much less favorable conditions for the Soviet Union. Gomulka and Ochab (the former First Secretary of the Polish Communist Party) explained that de-Stalinization was essential to the survival of Polish Communism; there was no possible compromise. Political liberalization, they argued, would not jeopardize Poland's position in the Warsaw Pact or Polish relations with the Soviet Union because it had no significance anywhere else. If the Russians used force, on the other hand, the Polish Army would fight. Khrushchev gambled on the Poles' being able to keep their promises to stabilize de-Stalinization and to prevent any spill-over, which would have created a situation in which Communist China could intervene politically. If this gamble failed, it could always be met by sending in Russian troops later, whereas to do so at that time might have brought on an uncontrollable spread of conflict in Europe, given the deteriorating Hungarian situation.

By 24 October riots in Hungary had turned into revolution, with the Hungarian Stalinists requesting the intervention of Soviet troops. The Stalinists had been unable to prevent the destruction of the Hungarian internal security apparatus, the main system of political control, and on 1 November Imre Nagy, the new Premier, repudiated the Warsaw Pact and declared Hungary neutral. This challenged the fundamental Soviet interests the Poles had guaranteed: maintenance of Communist party rule and the military integrity of the Warsaw Pact. Within three days the Russian troop buildup was strong enough to accede to the request from Janos Kadar's newly-formed Communist government to re-establish politically reliable Communist rule.

But was this to be on the Stalinist or Polish model? Khrushchev, having staked his political career on de-Stalinization, produced a solution in the policy of "separate roads to Socialism" which led to a withdrawal of Soviet troops from everywhere except East Germany, Poland, and Hungary. The full implications were not apparent for some years; the essentials were evident from the first. Political difficulties would be dealt with by political means to make Russian domination more acceptable as a long-term prospect, though a differentiating approach to problems and states would offer room for individual national disputes on particular issues. This policy ignored fundamental questions, raised in 1955, of whether the East European Soviet empire would have a continued validity once the cold war would cease and German reunification would become obviously and openly non-permissible by both East and West.

Khrushchev preferred not to raise such long-range questions. He needed to preserve deterrence from the United States by increasing Western Europe's hostage function which to him was more important in the short run, given his belief in the inevitable victory of Communism. The contrast between his and Stalin's views of the role of ideology on national policy shows the importance of individual perception; they were largely incompatible. Unlike Stalin, Khrushchev almost never sacrificed realpolitik to ideology. But he saw Communism triumphing in the long run because of its superiority as a form of social organization. As he said:

> When we say that the socialist system will win in the competition between the two systems—capitalism and communism—this by no means signifies that its victory will be achieved through armed interference by the Socialist countries in the internal affairs of capitalist countries. Our certainty of the victory of communism is based on the fact that the socialist mode of production possesses decisive advantages over the capitalist mode.[8]

To Khrushchev the task of the existing Communist bloc was to demonstrate this while maintaining its defenses against the West. Increasing military costs, however, made it desirable to reduce Pact manpower in favor of qualitatively superior forces, reinforced by the introduction of 700 Russian intermediate-range ballistic missiles. These could function in a counter-value role against Western European cities

---

[8] Report of the Twentieth Party Congress, 14 February 1956, as reprinted in Robert A. Goldwin, (ed.), *Readings in American Foreign Policy* (New York: Oxford University Press, 1959), p. 361.

or as counter-force weapons against American Strategic Air Command bases in and around Europe. But they could not deal with the greatest danger.

This was, to the Russians, West Germany's rearmament combined with its increasingly strong position in NATO, in which West Germany was becoming the European lynchpin. The Germans' indispensability ensured that the Americans would always have to support them in a crisis, even if objecting to specific German policies. Given West German hostility to the status quo of partition and presumed German irrationality (shown, in the eyes of the Russians, by Hitler's attack on them), West Germany could play a catalytic role in a Superpower confrontation. (Russian fears here anticipated those of American strategists concerned with the catalytic potential of Nth powers.) American deterrent policy, envisaging a Soviet first-strike once hostilities started, accentuated this potential instability. It could only be removed by an understanding with the United States which its European allies might be persuaded to support, provided all of the Western states were convinced that Russia was not aggressive. Polycentrism in the Eastern bloc, which was the outcome of Khrushchev's calculations, demonstrated this and therefore became the best means of preserving the Soviet sphere of influence from internal stresses and external threats.

From 1957 to 1961 the Soviet Union's major interests in Europe thus lay in stabilizing the German situation through agreement with the West. There were three distinct, though interrelated, elements of this problem. Ulbricht's regime in East Germany could not survive the loss of skilled manpower to the West for an extended time, which required that the escape route via West Berlin be barred, resulting in the erection of the Berlin Wall.

The Russians had been opposed to this move by Ulbricht. To do so, in their eyes, Ulbricht ran the risk of the very confrontation involving West Germany that Russia wished to avoid. Unless this danger could be reduced, a permanent solution of the Berlin problem was impossible; yet the longer the manpower drain remained unsolved, the greater was the likelihood of a unilateral East German solution, which was the Berlin Wall.

The motives behind Soviet initiatives are often misunderstood, because the West never has grasped fully the extent of Russian fears concerning Germany. Likewise, Britain and France have remained suspicious of West Germany but have been unable to persuade the

United States that what it regarded as its one reliable ally might be seen as a potential danger to its neighbors. Consequently, the United States has tended to see Russian moves regarding Germany in isolation instead of placing them in the context of the more general European security situation. Any solution to the Berlin problem has thus become impossible, since no solution has been negotiable for Berlin outside of the general question of German unification.

In 1958, the first of three Russian approaches to the German problem was tried: European security through disengagement, embodied in the series of plans starting with Polish Foreign Minister Adam Rapacki's proposals in February. Being a Polish initiative it was ensured a favorable reception, especially as it echoed George Kennan's B.B.C. Reith Lectures of the same period. These proposals for a German settlement would have limited or reversed West German rearmament, and would have prevented West German access to American tactical nuclear weapons under what were regarded as inadequate safeguards (the two-key system). Western superiority in these weapons was probably regarded as less important than their catalytic role, since Soviet military doctrine at that time held that rapid escalation would inevitably follow the first nuclear explosion.

What really mattered were not the proposals of men such as Rapacki or Kennan, but the attempt to get the West to talk about the dangers inherent in the German problem. Hence Khrushchev accepted (Marshal Bulganin having been deposed early in 1958) President Eisenhower's suggestion for a Conference of Experts on the Prevention of Surprise Attack. Preliminary negotiations revealed the Russian fear that instead of discussing what the Russians saw as the real problems, the West would concentrate on the to them non-existent threat to strategic stability from the dangers of a pre-emptive strike on either side's strategic bomber force.

In fact, the Western fear that Russian missiles would cripple the Strategic Air Command were unfounded. Their deployment had been very slow, giving the Russians only a minimal deterrent even as late as the Cuban crisis in 1962. Nor were the Russians likely to launch an attack on the probability of success, as American thinking implied. But, equally, the Soviet Union's nuclear weakness meant that they could not agree to any inspection which might reveal it and thus tempt the United States to attack them first. So when the Conference opened in October, Western delegations of technical experts, forbidden to discuss more than controls on theoretical threats to stability in hypothetical cases, faced Eastern representatives apparently sent to negotiate on West Germany's role in the Atlantic Alliance and its implications for European security. The delegations from the Soviet bloc, consisting of forty-two experts and advisers (as compared to 108 experts and advisers from the West), apparently included no scientists, but was composed of diplomatic and military personnel.[9]

William C. Foster, then heading the American delegation, commented: "We have sought to promote technical discussions and understanding. You have sought discussions of a selection of political proposals, for the most part not susceptible of technical assessment."[10]

Shortly beforehand, Khrushchev had started his second approach: direct negotiations, to include European problems. To insure a favorable context, he undertook three diplomatic offensives. The main one was directed against Berlin; it opened with his Note of 27 November 1958 threatening to hand over access arrangements to the German Democratic Republic within six months, thereby ending the four-Power occupation status. The alternative offered was a free city. This tried to force the West to discuss Berlin, perhaps in the Surprise Attack Conference, by implying (correctly) the alternative of a unilateral solution once the existing situation was intolerable (which it was not, yet). A separate German Peace Treaty was threatened in the follow-up Note of 1 January 1959. The original ultimatum expired uneventfully on 27 May, having been formally withdrawn in March when Khrushchev accepted the Western invitation for a Foreign Ministers Conference.

This lasted until July, giving Khrushchev grounds for optimism. He was to visit the United States for bilateral talks with President Eisenhower prior to a full-scale Summit the next year, while the West had made concessions that brought recognition of East Germany (and therefore of the Oder-Neisse line) much closer. The difference between East Germany's de facto and de jure existence was vital, because it was the only part of the Russian bloc not acknowledged by the West, suggesting it was not part of the accepted status quo.

Psychological pressure on the West was reinforced by Khrushchev's

[9] Bernhard G. Bechhoefer, *Post-War Negotiations for Arms Control* (Washington: The Brookings Institution, 1961), p. 470.

[10] *Ibid.*, p. 471.

advocacy of Atom-Free Zones for the Baltic, the Balkans and the Mediterranean, in the first half of 1959. These proposals succeeded in bringing out the latent Western European antagonism to West German access to nuclear weapons. Khrushchev then concluded his visit to the United States by embracing the concept of General and Complete Disarmament (GCD) before the United Nations General Assembly (functioning as the UN Disarmament Committee). Hailed as evidence of the Russian desire for peace and a major step forward, Khrushchev's ebullient presentation completely eclipsed the previous day's GCD proposals by the British Foreign Secretary (Selwyn Lloyd, now Lord Holyoke).

Khrushchev's speech to the Supreme Soviet on 14 January 1960, announcing cuts in the armed forces from 3.5 million men to 2.5 million, indicated his confidence in a settlement by negotiation. It must have been shaken by two major speeches in April by Christian Herter and Douglas Dillon (the American Secretary and Under-Secretary of State respectively). They rejected any agreement concerning establishing West Berlin as a free city and recognizing East Germany; no interim solution was deemed acceptable without Soviet withdrawal from Eastern Europe. Far from recognizing the status quo, the United States appeared to challenge it. Whether this led Khrushchev to order the shooting-down of the U-2 spy plane to provide an excuse for breaking off the Paris Summit in May is uncertain. Offering President Eisenhower the diplomatic excuse of ignorance, while asking for an apology, suggested a desire to preserve their personal relationship and the Summit. It seems at least as likely that Khrushchev's opponents, strongest in the Army, secured authorization for the interception, which he could hardly refuse, in order to torpedo his policy. The Summit was destroyed less by the U-2 incident itself, however, than by President Eisenhower's statement that he was fully aware of the flights and supported them.[11]

Designed to contain West Germany by negotiations with the West, Khrushchev's policies had doubly failed. The Herter and Dillon speeches had been made under pressure from the French and West German Chancellor Konrad Adenauer, so the Soviet policy, instead of dividing Western Europe, had strengthened the opponents of a settle-

[11] See Michael Tatu, *Power in the Kremlin* (New York: The Viking Press, 1961), Part I, Chapters 1-3.

ment, especially West Germany. Circumventing them by direct agreement with the United States had become impossible after Eisenhower
justified the U-2 flights as vital to American security: they could have
provided the basis for an American first-strike against the handful of
Soviet ICBM forces they had revealed. In summary, in three years
Russia had seen West German rearmament become a reality, its dominance over NATO policy increase, and a vast expansion of the
West's strategic and tactical nuclear capabilities.

The third and final phase of Khrushchev's German policy, a unilateral settlement, paradoxically arose from an attempt to play down the
German question. Instead, a separate crisis built up, transforming
West Berlin from a long-run irritant, useful as a lead-in to the German
problem, into an immediate threat to East Germany.

In January 1960, Ulbricht had engaged in a drive to collectivize agriculture, involving intense indoctrination and even tighter political
controls, to prevent his regime collapsing if the Summit produced a
German Peach Treaty and confederation. Now Khrushchev, en route
from Paris, announced that the crisis caused by the peace treaty was
off and that he would wait until the new American President was in
office before taking it up again. In other words, Russia would once
again try for a diplomatic solution, under less favorable circumstances.
Ulbricht could no longer afford to wait: his government's survival had
become equated with Stalinism while the resulting flow of refugees
threatened his entire economy. He therefore set out to exacerbate relations with West Germany, building up a cycle where every rise in
tension increased the refugee flood, making it more likely that Russia
would impose a solution, thus increasing East-West tensions. Weakness was his trump card against the Russians: they could not replace
him without risking another Hungary.

The separate West Berlin crises fell into two stages, reflected in
the refugee figure. Prior to his June Summit with President John F.
Kennedy in Vienna, Khrushchev issued his customary threats, but in
a low key. During this period East Germans were fleeing at a rate
of 17,000 per month, about half as much again as before Khrushchev's
1960 East Berlin speech. This outflow increased internal pressures in
East Germany. After June 1961, when he issued the ultimatum of an
all-German peace treaty or a separate treaty with East Germany,
the figures doubled in response, to 34,000 per month, which was recognized by both East and West (for different reasons) as an intolerable level. The crisis quickly spiralled. On 25 July the President

announced a series of military measures to demonstrate Western firmness, NATO following suit. East German police, after being turned back by Russian troops on two previous occasions, were then allowed to erect the Berlin Wall on 12 August. It was the only solution meeting the Russians' minimal goal of keeping Ulbricht in power without risking a war in Europe. Hence, it was accepted by the Western allies, who recognized the lack of alternatives left the Russians by Ulbricht's maneuvers.

The immediate crisis had been solved, but there still remained the original Soviet concern about West Germany's threat to the post-World War II European status quo. So long as Germany remained divided but with some Germans refusing to acknowledge the fact, the Federal Republic would seek reunification. If successful, this would alter the balance of power in East Europe against Russia. If denied, West Germany could try to bring it about by pressure on Russia via the United States, or Eastern Europe, or both. Having built up momentum on the Berlin question, Khrushchev therefore tried to link this to a German settlement, directly or indirectly. Western confusion promised concessions which, however, never materialized. As with West Berlin, neither side could give the other what it needed through negotiations without compromising its own position. Furthermore, American plans for an international access authority were wrecked by Chancellor Adenauer leaking them in April. By June 1962 Russia and the United States were in a deadlock, though Russia clearly had the initiative and seemed to be gaining. Four months later the Cuban crisis transformed the situation.

To assess its effects, the Soviet Union's position in Eastern Europe must be considered. Its policies were still those formulated in 1957: national independence for the satellite states, but within limits that preserved Russian political control and bloc military security. In the increasingly global context of Soviet foreign policy this had proved successful. By making Communism compatible with nationalism, Khrushchev began an appeal to the newly independent Afro-Asian states, and also gained acceptance for the Soviet sphere of influence in Eastern Europe. Internally, the Russians had acquired increasing bloc strength and cohesion, with the Warsaw Pact armies adding appreciably to Soviet conventional forces. On the other hand, there were developments raising questions about how far the polycentric process should continue unchecked.

The Russian split with Communist China, made public in 1963, could be defended as inevitable. China's rulers had rejected Russian control since the 1920's, and the two states had little in common. Nevertheless, China's challenge to Russia's ultimate authority on the interpretation of Marxist-Leninist thought could, and did, split the world Communist movement, previously an instrument of Russian foreign policy. But China was supported by Albania's Stalinist rulers (who were to defeat a pro-Russian coup in 1965). Also, Rumanian Stalinists were asserting their independence in the economic sphere, building up a balanced economy through expanded trade with the West, while promoting Rumanian nationalism. At the same time, attempts at integrating the bloc economies through COMECON were symptomatic of the general failure to improve national economic performances, raising the problem of economic reforms, with the inevitable political spin-off.

An important psychological change had also occurred. The series of crises over Germany from 1958 onward had given governments in Western and Eastern Europe a heightened awareness of their mutual vulnerability to Superpower policies that they could not directly affect. The result was a mutual adaptation between the two halves of Europe, based on a growing sense of the possibilities, however limited, in favor of beneficial cooperation. In 1962 these were perhaps embryonic tendencies, but the potential challenge to the existing concept of Russian interests was real, especially as these challenges were at that time so vague. Russia was an imperial Power with an anti-imperialist ideology, justifying an empire as a temporary necessity to defend Communism against an increasingly improbable threat. Its maneuvers over Berlin had shown an interest increasingly defined in terms of this dilemma.

Yet while Eastern Europe was still useful to Soviet defenses, the area was increasingly irrelevant to the direct Superpower strategic balance. This now depended on ICBM's and FLBM's, bringing about a return, with nuclear instead of conventional weapons, to the immediate post-war situation where Russia could destroy Western Europe without affecting the American retaliatory capability. This situation explains in part the attempt to place IRBM's in Cuba, compensating for the lack of second-strike ICBM's. Though the missiles had to be withdrawn, the crisis convinced Khrushchev and President Kennedy of two things: the balance of deterrence was more secure than they thought and, within this, they must establish a better modus vivendi, recognizing each other's genuine interests.

DÉTENTE: 1963–1968

With the Partial Nuclear Test Ban Treaty in August, following the June Hot Line Agreement, 1963 became the year of détente. Because it came to describe a fallacious optimism about the extent of relaxation, the Soviet concept of détente, as it emerged in internal debates after Cuba, must be defined. Between the Superpowers it signified a more pragmatic, less ideological, approach to their relations, accepting their common interest in avoiding unnecessary confrontation by differentiating their various interests and conflicts. Within the European context, it meant that the development of separate policies by the East Europeans would continue and even broaden, without affecting Russian security (now more dependent on the bipolar relationship). Increased trade and contacts with the West would further reduce the chance of internal upheavals.

While strengthening the status quo in Eastern Europe, détente offered chances for political advance in Western Europe.

West Germany's stranglehold on Western policies toward Eastern Europe had been weakened by the removal of Berlin as a focal point of conflict and had been destroyed by the American adoption of détente with Russia as the major policy goal, symbolized by the burial of the MLF proposal in favor of the Non-Proliferation Treaty in 1965. With improved controls over tactical nuclear weapons, this removed the other aspect of the German threat to Russia: catalytic war. The consequences were that the states of Western Europe began to pursue uncoordinated policies toward the East, offering generous trade arrangements, and that West German or American attempts at policy coordination aroused resentment and accentuated centrifugal tendencies. Since the Soviet Union dominated all the Eastern bloc economies except Rumania's, it could veto any developments threatening this control, while Western technology might permit postponement of bloc economic reforms with, in Russian eyes, undesirable political consequences.

Perhaps the best evidence for the success of détente for the Russians was acceptance of détente by the collective leadership under Brezhnev and Kosygin, who had deposed Khrushchev in October 1964. It should also be noted, however, that the American involvement in an Asian war its European allies regarded as unrealistic, unwinnable, and insupportable had combined with General de Gaulle's policies to reduce the Atlantic Alliance to what was euphemistically described as disarray.

The sole drawback to détente was West Germany's adoption of a positive policy toward the East after 1963. The new *östpolitik* sought to isolate East Germany by establishing economic and diplomatic links with the rest of Eastern Europe, making full use of West German economic strength. Essentially a long-term policy, it was regarded with a curious ambivalence in Moscow. Paranoic suspicions of German cunning reinforced opposition on political grounds. Yet, Russian political and military controls were able to contain any such German advances in the bloc, since they served as a useful reminder to Poland, Czechoslovakia, and Hungary that they needed Russian protection. The ghost of Rapallo could be invoked by both parties to the 1922 Russo-German Treaty. True, the West German Government had gained an important diplomatic victory by establishing relations with Yugoslavia in 1967 and Rumania in 1968. But the rest of the bloc was forbidden to follow suit (as Hungary might have) by the conditions that were laid down at the Karlovy Vary meeting of European Communist Parties in April 1967.

This meeting represented the most advanced development of Soviet détente policy, emphasizing the individual Communist parties' responsibilities for their own policies and calling for a European security conference. The Warsaw Pact Declaration after the Bucharest meeting on 5–8 July 1966 claimed: "The convocation of a conference on questions of European security and co-operation could contribute to the establishment of a system of collective security in Europe."[12] A German peace treaty was no longer needed to preclude political stabilization, but rather to form part of a much wider European settlement, perhaps including the removal of military blocs. Utilizing the obvious advantages in playing off Western European states against each other and against the United States, the Russians were attempting to secure their status quo through a multilateral approach toward the West conducted under their overall direction.

The underlying assumption of stability in Eastern Europe rested on the premise that inherent tensions between economic reforms necessary for "goulash" Communism could be reconciled with maintaining essen-

---

[12] Point 7, The Warsaw Pact Declaration, reproduced in abridged form in *Survival*, September 1966, Volume VIII, Number 7.

tial political controls by a series of pragmatic adjustments. In Czechoslovakia this was done between 1958 and 1962, but thereafter this reconciliation became increasingly difficult, posing a choice between growth and Stalinism. Czechoslovakia's President Novotny could not resolve the deadlock, whose affects became greater as the polarization made any change a test of strength, with reformers opposing Stalinists. His removal from office in January 1968 took place after a visit from Brezhnev, who apparently decided that within the context of détente, Czechoslovakia's internal cohesion could better be sought by controlled reforms.

The subsequent events have been subject to many interpretations, for the full implications are by no means clear. Like the previous European crises, it forced a redefinition of Soviet interests and policies, exacerbating divisions within the Politburo. Arguably, the actual invasion of Czechoslovakia was consistent with those aspects of Russian policy that had dropped into the background, as there was an increasing emphasis on détente. Without military forces in the country, the Russians were dependent on the Czech Communist party to guarantee continued obedience. Because Alexander Dubcek's internal reforms jeopardized this, his assurances of conformity in external politics became questionable. To the Russians, incapable of understanding democratization, he was a Soviet vassal unable to command his subjects.

The subsequent enunciation of the "Brezhnev Doctrine," that all Socialist states (i.e., the Soviet Union) have a right to intervene when the achievements of Socialism (i.e., Soviet Communist party control) are threatened in another Socialist state, reformulates an established Russian view. Originally stated in *Pravda* on 26 September 1968 (as translated in *Survival*, November 1968): "The sovereignty of each socialist country cannot be opposed to the interests of the socialist world." Gomulka put it thus: "When the enemy mines our house, the community of socialist states, with dynamite, it is our patriotic, national and international duty to obstruct this by using the means that are necessary."[13] The reformulation thus suggests a return to Stalin's insistence on doctrinal uniformity. So at its November meeting, NATO member states warned against any Soviet implementation of this im-

[13] Brezhnev quoted in Robert Ranger, "NATO's Reaction to Czechoslovakia: The Strategy of Ambiguous Response," *The World Today*, January 1969, pp. 19–26.

plied threat to Yugoslavia and Rumania. The collective leadership thus remains in an impasse: it had a policy of retaining control, but for what ends, and therefore to what extent, it could not decide.

CONCLUSION

Russian interests in Europe have been consistent inasmuch as they have comprised three basic elements. The original security requirement, linked with political ambitions, dictated a defensive position as far westward as possible in 1945, forming the basis of the only deterrent strategy available: holding Western Europe as a hostage. With the emergence of a direct Superpower deterrent balance in the 1960's, this became less important in preventing an all-out American nuclear attack, serving instead to restrain such lesser actions as might be possible within the overall balance, and so the difference between Western European and American strategic requirements became more sharply defined. The system of bloc political control also secured for the Soviet Union a major addition to its total resources, military, diplomatic, economic, and ideological. Western Europe is an area over which Soviet control would be desirable but unobtainable; however, the area's utility to the United States must be minimized, as must any Western European threat to the status quo of Russian domination in East Germany and Eastern Europe.

The interpretation of these principles has undergone considerable change, partly in response to and partly causing adjustments in the policies furthering them. These have fallen into two categories: Soviet unilateral action within the bloc; and negotiations outside it with the United States and Western Europe. The emphasis between the two categories varies with the Russian leaders' perceptions of where the greatest dangers or opportunities lie at any particular time. This alternation will continue, but without resolving the central dilemma: is the fundamental Russian interest in stability in Central Europe and its denial to outside political or military intervention (including a divided Germany), compatible with its chosen system of political control over the bloc, whose military functions are now secondary to the Superpowers' strategic balance of deterrence?

PART II

The Central Problem
of Central Europe

If we are to assess the practical significance of the
national minorities protest in international politics,
we have to remember the goals of these movements
and the prospects before them. Was the objective
independence or merely autonomy?

—*Pierre Renouvin*

INTRODUCTION

The end of World War II brought with it a fundamental rearrangement of the political pattern of Europe. Not only were the historic European Great Powers no longer Great Powers, they were not even Middle Powers. Europe was in a shambles, and the beneficiaries lay outside of Europe proper.

Part II focuses on Central Europe because the major wars of the twentieth century have had their origins and conclusions there. Small wonder, then, that in the post-World War II period Central Europe remains the potential "cockpit of war."

The division of Germany has been looked upon by many Americans as a tragedy both for the German people and for Europe. In feeling this way, however, we should remember that Germany was not united as a modern state until the mid-nineteenth century, and immediately thereafter the first of the three Franco-German wars of the modern era took place. The German people for a thousand years had survived without the advantages of territorial integrity, and for many German-speaking groups, such as those in the Austro-Hungarian Empire, without separate political independence.

To German political historians, and to many other European students of politics (in the classic sense), the greatest achievement of Western civilization over the past three centuries has been to forward the concept of the national, territorial state. Nowhere was this evolution more welcomed than among the German people, for they came to this stage of political development much later than the English or the French, and even later than the Italians and the Belgians. If there is any element of historic tragedy at all in the present division of Germany into two dependent states, each challenging in various ways the political legitimacy of the other even while negotiating with each other, it is the fact of Europe being divided between the Superpowers, and thereby disrupting long-standing and potentially beneficial relationships among Europeans east and west of the Elbe. In other words, the contemporary division of Germany is a reflection of the greater division of Europe.

If, in some way, it were possible to reestablish the trans-European ties which were destroyed by World War II and by the consequent Soviet-American competition in Europe and throughout the world without bringing about a reunited, militarily aggressive Germany, then we might witness in the final quarter of the twentieth century a reformulated Europe that could complement the world role of the Superpowers. Whether this restored Europe would challenge the Superpowers is another question; it would seem unlikely as long as the nuclear dimension of warfare remained firmly in the hands of the Superpowers. Economic competition, both among the states of Europe and between them and the Russians and Americans, would probably not be injurious to the various vital national interests, even though annoying to secondary national interests. In this sense, the notion of competitive coexistence has considerable merit.

Pierre Hassner, in the following two chapters, has written about the political patterns of Europe looked at from the Center, which is a very useful antecedent to the special essay by Waldemar Besson in Part III on the problem of Germany itself.

PIERRE HASSNER

3   Europe East of the Elbe

IS IT EASTERN EUROPE OR EUROPE EAST OF THE ELBE?

Does Eastern Europe exist? The question may seem awkward or at least rhetorical, yet it goes beyond the general problem of definition and regional delimitation. Before 21 August 1968, one could begin to wonder whether one still knew what Eastern Europe was and whether it still constituted an intelligible field of investigation. Then, the Soviet troops supplied us with an answer.

In a way, this answer had been obvious ever since 1945. The term "Eastern Europe," even though it has been rejected by many persons situated east of the Elbe who nevertheless belong much more to Central Europe and to the legacy of the Austro-Hungarian Empire than to the East and to the legacy of the Tsars, has since World War II always had one common element: the Soviet army. The union of a geopolitical specification of the term—European states that are weaker neighbors of Russia—and of a political specification of the term—regimes which are ruled by the Communist Party—is explained by a central and definitive factor: those states which are either occupied by the Soviet army or are liable to be so without causing a shake-up of the larger European and/or global international balance.

In turn, this factor, whose test and symbol are given by the 1956 events in Hungary and by the 1968 crisis in Czechoslovakia, gives the key not only to the external position of the states in Eastern Europe, but also to the fundamental political configuration within each of these states. Each government in Communist Eastern Europe essentially plays a balancing game between its own population

and the Soviet Union; it bases its authority on its mediating position, i.e., on its claim to be alone in being able to avoid the rebellion of the former and the military intervention of the latter. (A
brief historical summary of the various "nationalities" and "nationalisms" of the Eastern European and Balkan states is in Chapter 6.)

But because this double relationship of the ruling party with its
own population and with the imperial Power has taken so many different aspects since Stalin's death, and because these many aspects
seemed so closely linked to an evolution which went beyond not only
the framework of the subregion but that of the Communist world as
well, it has seemed in many respects that "Eastern Europe" has
been both much more and much less than "Europe East of the Elbe."
To understand the subregion, we must look not so much to the subregion itself as to each specific state and to the world at large.

Today, each state has acquired or recovered its own history and
national physiognomy. From beneath the imposed uniformity of
Stalin's time, national traditions and conflicts have tended to re-
emerge. Essentially, in each state there has been a shift in the critical
political balance by a decrease in submissiveness to the Soviet Union
and an attempt by the government to gain popular legitimation. Some
regimes have tried to satisfy their population more by economic
concessions; others have put the stress on national independence;
others still on domestic freedom of expression and criticism. Hence,
the various evolutions have diverged or converged in sometimes unexpected combinations between the two major phenomena of domestic de-Stalinization and external de-satellization. They have led
to liberalization or de-Stalinization in Yugoslavia; to de-satellization
without de-Stalinization in Albania; to de-Stalinization without de-
satellization in Hungary; to parallel progress followed by parallel
regression in de-Stalinization and de-satellization in Poland; extreme
prudence in de-Stalinization and de-satellization in Bulgaria; economic reform without de-Stalinization and an active foreign policy
without de-satellization in East Germany; to spectacular de-satellization leading to a cautious beginning of de-Stalinization in Rumania;
and to spectacular de-Stalinization leading to a cautious (and short-
lived) beginning of de-satellization in Czechoslovakia, which is
leading toward re-Stalinization.

The relations of Eastern European states with states other than
the Soviet Union are even more influenced by specific situations

linked to geographic location and historical conflicts. In particular, the most decisive elements for understanding the position of the East German and of the Albanian governments in relation both to their respective populations and to the Soviet Union, obviously, are the respective relations of East Germany with West Germany and of Albania with Yugoslavia. This has led these two states to doctrinal positions which in turn have prevented them from following the general trend toward a détente with the West. But the general tendency favors a search by these governments, relying sometimes more on diplomacy, sometimes on economics or on cultural life, for a counterweight to the Soviet Union and for a contact with the West which is made necessary by the modernizing evolution of their societies and by the economic and social aspirations of their populations.

But, in order to avoid misunderstandings and false expectations, we must take into account the complex interplay between the geographic dimensions, whether national, subregional, or universal, and certain aspects of international reality, and in particular strategic, diplomatic, and societal aspects. Only thus can we understand how the recent history of Eastern Europe is one of the most striking illustrations of what might be called the paradox of our time, i.e., the double trend toward the interdependence of societies and toward the independence of states; toward the universalization of social and economic realities and the renationalization of political concerns; toward the diffusion of industrial society and mass communication and the reassertion of exclusive particularities; toward the erosion of old ideologies, blocs, and alliances, and the contagious influence of new trends and links.

The more the cold war seemed to lose its intensity and the East-West struggle its priority, the less "Eastern" and the more "European" has Eastern Europe appeared to be. In fact, what has seemed to emerge more and more is on the one hand a clearer level of national identity and on the other hand a global level of international politics. Predictions about the political evolution of Eastern Europe have been based on identifying, accurately enough, social and economic trends among the states that might have led toward convergence; identifying various national diplomatic attempts at playing a more independent international role; and identifying popular aspirations for self-expression and for contacts with the West. What the predictions failed to give proper weight to was the likelihood of

Soviet reaction, and of the provisional victory of the side that com-
manded the big battalions and whose presence was one of the pillars
of the European power and security structure. The Soviet Union
can suppress in its satellites neither the desire for national independence nor the aspiration to participate in the worldwide spiritual, cultural, technological, and economic dialogue. But it *is* able
to slow down these desires and aspirations, to repress them, or to
silence them, and by so doing, to make clear to the world that the
ultimate limits both of Eastern Europe's global involvements and
of the initiatives taken by its various states are still set by the
Kremlin.

More than ever, Eastern Europe has submitted to its old fate of
being that "other Europe"—that peripheral subregion whose fate,
whose nature, whose very definition are dictated from outside because of its geographical situation, or because of the ambitions or
the indifference of the empires which surround it. The fact that today it includes states like East Germany and Czechoslovakia, who
by their tradition and culture belong to Central Europe or indeed
to the West, strengthens even more the fact that Eastern Europe's
self-consciousness and aspirations are themselves the expression of
an arbitrary and imposed situation. More than ever, and more than
anywhere, we must, when we speak of Eastern Europe, recognize
the primacy of international political relationships and within these,
of the territorial and military dimension: in this case, of the role of
the dominant imperial Power.

CONDITIONS OF THE SOVIET
DOMINATION IN EASTERN EUROPE

While ultimately it was the Soviet Union which determined
the situation by its initial action of 1945–48 and by its reaction to
later developments, over the years the Soviet Union has been cast
more and more in an essentially conservative role in international
politics. This does not mean that the Soviet Union does not take the
political or military initiative. Just as a revisionist Power is not
necessarily aggressive, a status quo Power is not necessarily peaceful. Just as Czechoslovakia in the first half of 1968 can be considered from the point of view of international politics as the classic

case of the unwitting revisionist, challenging by its domestic reforms the subregional organizations to which it intended to remain
faithful, so the Soviet Union, in Eastern Europe, is the classic case
of the aggressive conservative, taking military initiatives for the
purpose of protecting a status quo which was not subjected to any
external military challenge. But it does mean that while the presence
of the Soviet Union is the essential element in the fate of the Communist regimes in Eastern Europe, since it alone has brought about
their birth and can produce their death, it is only their *own* action
and their *own* political evolution that give this situation its ultimate
meaning. Once this basic situation is recognized, the real problem
lies in the partly unexplained diversities that have enabled West
Berlin or Finland to escape the dictates of a geopolitical location
not so different from Czechoslovakia's in 1948, and enabled Yugoslavia, Albania, and Rumania to avoid, for the time being at least,
the fate of Czechoslovakia in 1968.

But this margin of tolerance, which sometimes enables some Eastern European states to preserve what is essential for them as long as
it is not essential to the Soviet Union, is due precisely to the second
qualification, which is that Soviet domination is the key factor only
in decisive situations at decisive places and times. And what is
decisive in the eyes of the Soviet Union seems to be determined
less by a global and permanent price attached to Eastern Europe
than by something both more general and more subject to changes
in time and place: the effects on the power relation between the
Soviet government and its competitors or challengers, actual or potential. These competitions or challenges could be on the domestic,
European, or world scene; within Soviet society; with the international Communist movement; or within the international political
system. Even if one assumes, as one must, that the Soviet Union's
wish to maintain its domination over Eastern Europe is as permanent and unchangeable a factor as any in world politics for the
foreseeable future, the character and extent of this domination,
the choice and efficacy of the means endorsed, of the risks and costs
accepted by the Soviet Union in order to maintain it, will vary according to the state of these various balances and competitions.
They could range from domestic trends in Russia to relations with
China and the United States.

After every attempt of an Eastern European state to achieve more autonomy or independence, and after every reaction of the Soviet Union, there has been a scramble to establish criteria, to remain valid until next time, of what enables a state to go its own way and of what makes the Soviet Union tolerate this evolution or put a stop to that evolution.

Are conditions more favorable to an independent policy in states where the Communists have gotten into power by themselves like Yugoslavia and Albania, or in states where they were brought in directly by the Soviet army like Hungary and Poland, or indirectly, like Czechoslovakia, but where at least they could rely on a pre-existing Communist tradition and force? Are conditions more favorable in a state like Rumania where the Communist party, completely imposed from the outside, has created for itself a new legitimacy by striking national roots? Does change occur when the ruling elite is divided, as it was in 1956 in Hungary and Poland, or when it is united, as it is in Rumania? Does change occur from below, under pressure from intellectuals and workers, as in the cases of Hungary and Poland; or from above, through the control of the Party, as in the case of Rumania; or from a combination of pressure from outside groups like writers and economists and a crisis within the ruling party itself, like in Czechoslovakia? Does it help to have a common border with the West or not to have one? And what about a common border with the Soviet Union? Is the need for reform and the potentiality for revolution related to the level of economic development? But then why is it that rebel Czechoslovakia and submissive East Germany, rebel Rumania and submissive Bulgaria, are at comparable stages of growth?

If the key is more in the nature of the new policy itself, especially in its effects on attitudes toward the Soviet Union, here again the criteria for Soviet toleration have a strong flavor of generalization based on a single case or on prophesy after the event. From the experience of Poland and Hungary, it had been concluded that the Soviet Union could tolerate an original road in domestic affairs on two conditions: that it should not affect foreign policy, and that it should not set itself as a model for other states. But Rumania did precisely that by its emphasis on national independence and on an international role. From comparing the limits which are respected both by Rumania and by Poland but which were ignored by Hungary in 1956, one tended, then, to deduce two criteria: the non-

renunciation of membership in the Warsaw Pact and the leading role
of the Communist Party. Czechoslovakia was particularly careful to
emphasize its good behavior in these two respects, but the Czechs'
protestations of good faith obviously did not carry enough credibility in Moscow. Since, at the time of the invasion, Czechoslovakia
was engaged in introducing reforms which made a qualitative transformation more likely domestically than externally, we can draw
the conclusion that what Moscow cannot tolerate is the abandon-
ment of the Leninist party structure and role.

Moreover, in this same set of national conditions that so far
Czechoslovakia has lost and Rumania has won, we also can read
the victory of the Rumanian priority (de-satellization before de-
Stalinization) over the Czechoslovak priority (de-Stalinization before
de-satellization). And, indeed, we are right. Getting away from
Stalinism and a portion of Leninism is by itself a challenge to the
Soviet Union which makes it impossible for the Russians to evade
the issue of de-satellization. Conversely, Rumanian Premier Ceausescu's iron hand both in not allowing any spontaneous domestic
forces to interfere with his delicate political acrobatics, and in always looking for external opportunities and backing (whether in
Peking, Paris, or Washington) to protect him seems more realistic
than the former Czechoslovak leader Dubcek who trusted the moderation both of the Czechoslovak population and of the Soviet leadership to let his reforms give Socialism a human face. However,
Rumania might very well have been invaded in the stride of the
21 August action if the passive resistance of the Czechoslovak people had not complicated things for the Soviet Union. The differences
in treatment may reflect differences in the time of the challenge and
in the location and importance of the respective states, as much as
in the strategies they adopted.

Finally, if tomorrow Rumania is invaded, we shall look to Hungary which, while keeping a stronger party control than did Czechoslovakia during its brief "spring," still follows, in a much more
cautious way, a road closer to what Prague attempted than to what
Bucharest has achieved. Hungary combines complete external political submissiveness with far-reaching economic reform and some
genuine intellectual liberalization. The Hungarian government,
taught by experience, combines the best feeling for the limits of
Soviet toleration with the most genuine desire for improving the

fate of its population, as distinct from scoring points in the international game.

In fact, none of these criteria is misleading; but what *is* misleading is the notion of a clear-cut choice between "to tolerate or not to tolerate." In each case and in each point in time, the available means, the other problems at hand, the experience of past successes and failures, the foreseeable reactions in the Soviet Union and the satellites themselves and in the international system at large (above all, with the other Superpower), influence the level of Soviet toleration and the nature of Soviet action.

It would be wrong, for instance, to say that while the Soviet Union did not tolerate the trends in Czechoslovakia, it had tolerated those of Yugoslavia, Albania, and Rumania. In each of these cases, the Russians found themselves confronted by developments which they disliked and which they attempted to stop. In each, they tried at various times and to various degrees, containment through multinational institutions, persuasion, intimidation, division of the ruling group, domestic revolts, murder, economic sanctions, and ideological excommunication. In some cases these means may have achieved their purpose (as perhaps in Bulgaria in 1965) or else led to a compromise (as in Poland in 1956). In most, they failed. In the majority of cases, the Russians seem to have reluctantly reconciled themselves to this failure, at least in the short run—in East Berlin they resorted to military action after a few hours; in Bucharest after a few days; in Prague after a few months. Does the difference lie in the conditions of the local balance or of the global one; in the character of the evolution of the given state or in the general situation of Soviet authority; in the possibilities of guerrilla resistance or of American reaction? We cannot really answer these questions but they force us to go beyond the bilateral relations between the Soviet Union and Eastern Europe, and to put them in the framework of European international politics, of East-West relations, and of the general crisis of the Communist world.

EASTERN EUROPE IN WORLD POLITICS

Before being anything else, Eastern Europe is part of the Soviet empire. But this empire is not immune to centrifugal pressures, both from inside and outside. If this basic assessment is true, then Eastern Europe's relationship to the Superpowers and to the East-West conflict is essentially an indirect one: the relationship between the Superpowers affects Eastern Europe to the extent to which it affects the policies toward the subregion of one Superpower, namely the Soviet Union. The East-West conflict is important to the extent to which it modifies the intra-Eastern European conflict between the imperial Power and its satellites. It is important to keep the distinction in mind precisely because it is at the heart of the main issue posed by such events as the invasion of Czechoslovakia, President Nixon's visit to Rumania, and the simultaneous affirmation by the Soviet Union of its right to defend the integrity of the "Socialist camp" even against domestic change in other Socialist states, and of the Soviet Union's desire for détente and for dialogue with the West, even with West Germany.

What the Soviet Union is trying to do is to separate the two issues—to isolate the relations within the Socialist camp both from the evolution of its own relations with the West and from the political evolution of the world at large. The continuation of détente after the invasion of Czechoslovakia shows that this is possible to a certain extent. President Nixon's visit to Rumania shows that this extent is limited; that complete isolation is impossible. In the dialectics between Eastern Europe's domestic evolution and its relationship with the Soviet Union and the outside world there is always a limit, if only an indirect one. But the example of Rumania looking to the United States, after having looked to China, for outside reassurance to protect its independence, and the motivations of American and Soviet behavior themselves, bring into play yet another element: the triangle constituted by the two Superpowers and the third, potential one, China. The Sino-Soviet conflict has played, to a certain extent, a role analogous to the East-West role in the relations of the Soviet Union with Eastern Europe. Hence, if the main location of "Europe East of the Elbe" is on the map of the "world Socialist system" or rather of the "Socialist commonwealth" determined both by geography and by ideology (which is another name for the Soviet empire), the limits and nature of this commonwealth must be found in the situation of its different states in relation to a given phase both of the international political system (and in particular of East-West relations in Europe) and of the world Communist movement (in particular of the Sino-Soviet split).

From the point of view of East-West relations, we can distinguish three phases: the preparatory years of 1944–47, the years of the cold war between 1947 and 1962 (with, of course, the two essential thresholds of 1953 and 1957), and finally the new era of the "post-cold war" or of coexistence within a more complicated international political system (with Khrushchev's fall and the invasion of Czecho-slovakia being again important landmarks). In each of these periods the various elements of the Superpower relationship, the domestic realities of the various states involved, and the world Communist movement combined differently, bringing different consequences on the central, Soviet-East European relationship. (See the Chronology for a review of the major political developments being analyzed.) The basic idea of the system has always been the maximum feasible centralization or the maximum feasible primacy of the center, or of the vanguard over the periphery, i.e., the primacy of the apparatus over each Communist party and of each Communist party over each state; and further, of the Soviet party over the other Communist parties, and of the Soviet Union over the other Communist states. Nonetheless, the version promoted by Stalin in Eastern Europe between 1944 and 1947 relied on a relatively great measure of di-versity and on a relatively indirect form of control. This was certainly due to the various degrees and forms of national specific features and resistances, and to the provisional character of the whole phase. But the external framework also played a double role. Stalin did not want to jeopardize the long-rang chances of domi-nating Germany and, if not dominating Western Europe, at least of keeping the subregion from organizing. He also did not want to provoke the Anglo-Americans, especially in the Balkans.

After 1947, we enter at the same time into the period of the cold war and of Stalinization proper. Stalinization was, in a sense, pre-pared from the beginning of Russian wartime influences. But its timing, its harshness, and its extreme character were a reaction to the fact that Eastern European leaders tended to take their "do-mesticism" too seriously and to transform it into national Commu-nism by believing in national roads to Socialism and by attempting to create groupings like a Yugoslav-Bulgarian federation. Tito's exclusion in 1948 was the signal of the bloc's *Gleichschaltung,* which took place over several years, with certain differences in speed and results according to the importance, the zeal, or the resistance of the various states. The Rajk, Kostov, and Slansky trials appear today as instruments both of the anti-Tito campaign and of the elimination of national Communists in order to complete Stalinization.

But external elements also played a role in the campaign. The combination of American demobilization and then in rapid succession of the Truman Doctrine for Greece and Turkey, of the Marshall Plan, of the creation of Trizonia in Germany, and of the failure of the Berlin blockade, showed that the West was ready to resist any further Soviet advance but not to exert pressure in order to avoid or to mitigate the Sovietization of Eastern Europe even though its economic aid could endanger it. At the same time, within the Soviet Union, the brutality of the Zhdanov phase contributed to the combination of hardening inside the bloc and of prudence outside, at least in Europe.

The resemblance of this period to certain aspects of the present period is striking. More generally we find in four cases the succession of first a certain loosening in Soviet authority, then the rebellion of an Eastern European state which in retrospect will appear to have overstepped the bounds tolerated by Moscow, and finally a Soviet effort to restore discipline in the bloc. We can see this pattern in the cases of Yugoslavia (1948), Hungary and Poland (1956), Rumania (1962–64), and Czechoslovakia (1968). But the types of action adopted on both sides differ from case to case according to the domestic, Soviet, and international situation.

The 1947–53 period is, in this respect, the time of minimum complexity. The Iron Curtain having fallen upon Europe, the relations between its two halves were minimal. Contrary to certain myths about Yalta, there was no agreement to divide Europe or the world but rather the formalization of a kind of static trench warfare (*guerre de positions*), each side trying to make life difficult for the other, while waiting for the other's break-down. In Eastern Europe the monolithism of the bloc led to the suppression of international relations proper, whether with the Soviet Union whose direct authority was exercised everywhere in the bloc; within the respective states through the party and police or through the economy; whether with the external world (which represents the class enemy) or with the other states of the bloc that lived in isolation from each other and had almost exclusive bilateral relationships with the Soviet

Union. In spite of the differences we mentioned in degrees of terror or of Russification, the overriding reality has been the total and exclusive character of the bloc. Only East Germany remains the sign of the unsettled and unsettling character of the German problem, through which the cold war remains open and the two Europes communicate. The East German institutional situation was adapted only later, in the 1950's, and only incompletely to that of the other states, even though it is subject, in fact, to the same military, ideological, and political conformity.

Both aspects take on an increasing force and importance after Stalin's death. In particular, after the reconciliation with Tito and the revolutions of 1956, a double process of internal dislocation within the bloc and of opening toward the outside are the result of Khrushchev's attempt to make the Soviet control over the satellites more flexible and multilateral. This attempt itself is connected with the effort at a transformation both of Soviet society and of Soviet foreign policy. As early as 1953, a certain trend toward emphasis on domestic consumption within the Soviet Union and the "new course" promoted in the People's Democracies but applied only by some of them, indicate a common plan. Here again, however, Germany is the place where changes are the most quickly stopped because it is the place where they run the greatest risk of going too far. This is the meaning of the explorations apparently conducted by the "Malenkov-Beria" leadership on the German problem in 1953, of Ulbricht's reluctance to apply the "new course," of the 17 June 1953 revolt and of the subsequent consolidation of Ulbricht's regime and authority.

Khrushchev, through his reconciliation with Tito, his offensive toward the Third World and even more, through the Twentieth Party Congress and de-Stalinization gave to the new course a more global and dynamic inspiration. The link between a more far-reaching or long-distance ambition and a more relaxed control (in contrast with Stalin's tighter control limited to the territories actually or potentially occupied by the Red Army) is clear. But so are also the difficulties it raises, since the 1956 Hungarian and Polish explosions drive Khrushchev to use Stalinist means to control the empire he wanted to de-Stalinize along with the Soviet Union.

The two revolutions of 1956 originated in the conjunction of domestic discontent (linked both to the regime and to the economic situation) and of the hope produced by Soviet de-Stalinization. The international influence is absent, except to the rather weak extent to which the roll-back policy, proclaimed by John Foster Dulles four years earlier, may have raised false hopes in Hungary. Rather, the external influence appears on the opposite side, through the Anglo-French-Israeli Suez expedition which made intervention easier for the Soviet Union. But conversely, the characteristically Khrushchevian combination of world-wide détente and offensive certainly contributed (along with his attempts at a certain dynamic reformism in the Soviet Union) to keeping him from choosing a pure and simple Stalinist freeze or restoration in Eastern Europe. While conservatives (as East Germany's Ulbricht was and Rumania's Gheorghiu-Dej seemed to be) were strengthened, so was their relative autonomy. It is in 1958 that Gheorghiu-Dej is able to persuade Khrushchev to withdraw Soviet troops from Rumania, a move which was followed by increased authoritarianism and terror within the country but which also laid the foundation for its future independence and autonomous evolution. The reconstitution of the bloc is attempted not so much by brute force and unilateral action (as with Hungary), as through the multilateral road both through the creation or revitalization of institutions like COMECON and the Warsaw Pact, and—with the help of fear of China—through a more flexible ideological control at the level of the parties.

If the logic of détente has had an influence on the methods of controlling the bloc, the other face of the Khrushchev offensive, the logic of competition and of challenge to the West expressed by the success of the Sputnik and by the second Berlin crisis, were bound to have even more direct consequences. As with everything concerning Germany, it is difficult to know whether this offensive was designed to destabilize the West or to stabilize the East, to isolate West Germany and to create a means of pressure over the United States or to stop an emigration which was making East Germany economically non-viable.

In the same way, the attempts to revitalize COMECON and to initiate the beginnings of a cooperation with the Common Market are in part a reaction or a defense against the Common Market's success, in part an effort to imitate its efficiency, and in part an attempt to use COMECON to promote economic specialization and political centralization within the bloc.

This is indeed how Rumania—the new rebel that wanted to resist both specialization and centralization—interpreted them. But if the immediate cause of Rumania's rebellion is the difference in economic development and interests between the Soviet Union and its allies, and between the industrialized states among them and the others, Rumania is also the rebel for whom international conditions have played the greatest role. This is so because to a certain extent, it imitated Gaullist policy with which it had in common the affirmation of sovereignty, the struggle against supranational institutions, the opposition to the suggestions of the leader for reforming yet maintaining the international military organization, the search in the short run for a spectacular role on the world scene and in the longer run for a real change of the status quo in Europe through the demise of the two military alliances. Rather, the basic factor is that, by acting when they did, the Rumanians were, as S. Fischev-Calati remarked, betting on two features of the international game—the Sino-Soviet conflict and the East-West détente—which would protect them from a brutal Soviet reaction.

It will always remain controversial whether the Rumanian rebellion has to be read as far back as 1954 or, more classically, can be seen to begin in the early 1960's. But it is very likely that, at any rate, the moment chosen by the Rumanians to come out into the open was strongly determined by external conditions. At the very least, the Rumanian rebellion was only possible in a bloc which was affected by the beginnings of a de-ideologized Europe and of a decentralized Communist world. Geographical regions like Central Europe and the Balkans were beginning to become significant again because of proposals for denuclearized zones, wherein traditional links could be recreated and where new presences could begin to be felt.

This would apply especially to the United States, through its economic aid to Poland, and to China, and through its influence in 1956–57. This would also apply to France under de Gaulle and to West Germany under the *Östpolitik* of the Grand Coalition, and the successor SPD government of Chancellor Willy Brandt. A complex game had become possible, with the Soviet Union trying to maintain the unity of the various central authorities, knowing that a challenge to one brings danger to the others, while the various actual or potential rebels make use unwittingly or deliberately of their differentiation. An Eastern European state may look for a counterweight to the Soviet Union either in the Chinese direction or in the Western direction, according to its geographical situation, to its ideological orientation, and to the nature of the two conflicts.

Albania, which is essentially hostile to Yugoslavia for national reasons, was driven into opposition to the Soviet Union by the reconciliation between Khrushchev and Tito. Since this took place under the stigma of de-Stalinization and of concessions to right-wing revisionism, Albania was driven by its anti-Yugoslav and anti-Soviet stance toward Stalinist and left-wing diplomatic positions. This in turn led Albania to seek a counterweight not in the direction of the West but in the direction of China, within a balance which is absurd from a geographic, economic, or military point of view, but is based on the peculiar structure of the Communist world. On the other hand, the specific dynamics of the conflict with the Soviet Union after the invasion of Czechoslovakia brings Albania today into an objective alliance with Yugoslavia, i.e., with the number-one enemy without whom the Albanians would not have gotten into conflict with the Soviet Union in the first place.

Rumania did not choose, like Albania, to identify with China. Indeed, the Rumanians tried to look for counterweights and economic or diplomatic support in every other possible direction: toward the United States (primarily in 1964–65 and in 1968–69 after the invasion of Czechoslovakia), China, France, West Germany, and Israel, as well as toward Balkan or small-state cooperation. Probably, at the time of the Sino-Soviet crisis between 1962 and 1964, they saw in this conflict the major chance for their independence. They tried at the same time to exploit it and to limit this conflict, knowing that, as in any triangular situation where a small Power tries to exploit the rivalry of two big Powers, both a total reconciliation and a total break between the Powers would be against their interests.

Poland, Hungary, and East Germany, with some nuances and with some discrete and timid attempts at reinforcing their position vis-à-vis Moscow by hinting at a Chinese overture, have chosen to enlist unequivocally in the Soviet camp. As for the Czechoslovakian leadership of 1968, they chose the opposite of the Albanians' position and even of the Rumanians' tactics, by trying to compensate their attempts at domestic reform and economic independence through showing perfect discipline toward the Soviet Union in the debates of the international Communist movement. As they were also very discreet in their attitude toward foreign policy and East-West issues, they banked everything either on trusting the Russians or on not provoking them, thereby being left (with the exception of the Yugoslav and Rumanian solidarity) in the position of a direct confrontation with the Russians without outside backing. This is precisely the position which the Rumanians have always tried to avoid.

Again, nobody can say whether or when external involvement is more likely to provoke the Russians into action against their reluctant satellites or to deter them from it. What we do know is that in the period from 1964 to 1968 the Soviet reaction, at the level of the bloc, was rather to look for *indirect* means of reestablishing control without giving up intra-bloc détente. Khrushchev's efforts for the reform of COMECON in 1962–64, those of his successors for the reform of the Warsaw Pact in 1965–69 toward greater coordination and centralization, failed because of Rumania's obstinate resistance. The result was a kind of draw. Rumania was not followed on the road of directly challenging the Kremlin, nor on that of reforming the Warsaw Pact, but more discreetly, other Eastern European states expressed similar criticisms within COMECON. They put forth views on security matters concerning, for example, anti-ballistic missiles or nuclear non-proliferation which were not completely identical with Moscow's; at the same time, they continued to reorient slowly their trade toward the West and to cooperate with various Western states that were ready to throw economic and cultural bridges eastward. While COMECON was clearly in a condition of permanent crisis, Eastern Europe and the Soviet Union, although divided by classical claims of national interest, were following parallel economic paths in the direction of cautious reform.

Similarly, the organization of the Warsaw Pact seemed to evolve, after the failure of the conflicting Soviet and Rumanian designs, again very slowly and cautiously, toward a more balanced and classical alliance. The "Northern triangle" of the three states which, politically, strategically, and economically, were most essential to the Soviet Union (East Germany, Poland, and Czechoslovakia) and the unalterable faithfulness of Bulgaria, seemed to limit to a minimum the risks of disintegration. On the other hand, the East Germans, who had always served as a crucial indicator, seemed to acquire more and more stability and self-assurance.

Hence the Russians could, while maintaining the Khrushchevian post-Cuba détente, lay lesser stress on the acceptance of the European status quo by the United States and put more emphasis on trying to exploit the tensions which the Vietnam war and de Gaulle's policy created within the West. They could campaign for a European security conference, for the end of NATO in 1969, etc., with a certain degree of confidence in the stability of their own zone.

In 1967, developments in all three relevant areas—in the Soviet Union itself, where a definite freeze and hardening against liberalization was taking place; in Eastern Europe, where Rumania, by establishing diplomatic relations with West Germany and by refusing to take an anti-Israeli stance in the Six-Day war was pushing its independent policy beyond intra-bloc matters; and in Western Europe, where the West German Grand Coalition was pushing its opening to the East—brought on a definite hardening of the Soviet position. Bilateral treaties were concluded with the Eastern European states. An "Ulbricht doctrine" (or Hallstein doctrine in reverse) was accepted which, in effect, gave East Germany a veto right over Eastern European relations with West Germany. And Ulbricht and Gomulka were upgraded as keepers of the orthodoxy. The Czechoslovak "spring" of 1968 could not fall on less favorable soil.

The Czechoslovak crisis itself was due more to domestic, economic, national, and cultural causes which, in turn, were influenced by international or transnational factors like the general economic crisis of Communist regimes or the gap between bureaucrats of the Novotny type and an intellectual youth ever-more open to Western influences. Nonetheless, the international dimension proper did play a great role in the crisis itself. While the Western Powers (to begin with the United States, but including West Germany) showed little warmth toward the new Czechoslovakia, either to avoid compromising the Czechs or to avoid antagonizing the Soviet Union, and while Czechoslovakia proclaimed its wish to remain faithful to the essentials of the Socialist camp's foreign policy, the change in atmosphere at the very least was weakening the credibility of Soviet anti-West German invectives. Also, the prospect of further westward commercial reorientation was affecting the interests of the Soviet Union, and the prospect of an accompanying political evolution could, in the long run, raise the question of the solidity of the Warsaw Pact organization.

By the beginning of 1969, the Soviet Union already had completed the switch of emphasis begun in 1967. While in 1965 and 1966 the Vietnam war and French opposition to NATO enabled the Soviet

Union to take the diplomatic offensive toward the West, in 1967 and 1968 the conversion of West Germany to a more active détente policy in Eastern Europe and the changes taking place in Czechoslovakia were pushing the Soviet Union toward the defensive. The first preoccupation for the Russians was the consolidation of their own bloc, and for this the attempt to disintegrate the opposite bloc was temporarily sacrificed. The campaign against NATO and for a European security system was downgraded, to be revived in 1970.

The choice between a posture of defensive stabilization vis-à-vis Eastern Europe and a posture of offensive de-Stalinization vis-à-vis Western Europe is never made once and for all by the Soviet Union, since the Russian conception of a dynamic status quo (on the basis of: "what's mine is mine—what's yours is negotiable") consists in trying to achieve both. Likewise, the choice between a bipolar, global, or strategic dialogue with the United States and the search for a regional advance on the European continent by using America's allies against the Americans, does not have to be made as long as it is possible for the Soviet Union to have it both ways, as in the bipolar campaign for the non-proliferation treaty and the continentalist campaign for a European security conference. But in both cases, the choice may have to be faced in the long run, and even in the short run circumstances do impose priorities. In the context of its difficulties with Czechoslovakia on the one hand, and with China on the other, the Soviet Union must give priority to Eastern Europe over Western Europe. The priority also must go to the bilateral dialogue with the United States, which alone is capable both of being a threat and a partner, over the attempt to divide the West.

THE SOVIET UNION, EASTERN EUROPE, AND THE UNITED STATES

To a certain extent, these two priorities have their counterpart in the policy of the United States. The defense and stability of Western Europe has always had a priority in American concerns over influencing events in Eastern Europe. If anything could challenge this priority, it could only be the bilateral relationships with the Soviet Union, once that the overriding need to avoid nuclear war appeared to call for cooperation with the Soviet Union even on issues, like non-proliferation or the status quo in Europe, which might bring the Superpowers into a conflict of interest with their respective allies. The policy toward Eastern Europe is either a consequence or an instrument of the policy toward Western Europe and toward the Soviet Union. The policy toward Eastern Europe would also be subordinated to them, if and when these two primary priorities happened to be in agreement. Hence, as long as Soviet behavior in Eastern Europe does not appear as a threat to Western Europe, a strong impulse exists toward a policy of partition or of spheres of influence.

This tendency is still very powerful today because it is grounded in structural features of the international system. It seems to have reached its climax at the time of the Czechoslovak crisis, and of the very weak (probably not acquiescent but certainly very passive) American reaction. The Johnson Administration's wish for Soviet help out of the Vietnam entanglement and the Soviet's wish to legitimize their Czechoslovak action were added to the other permanent factors of US-USSR convergence: nuclear war and China.

More generally, two basic conditions had previously limited the sphere of influence temptation and had made a conscious partition by the Superpowers impossible. One was ideological and the other was the problem of Germany. The United States could neither acquiesce in Stalinist terror in Eastern Europe, nor renounce its responsibility for the reunification of Germany. It could do so even less when the Sovietization of Eastern Europe appeared as one step in an attempt to spread Communism to the whole continent and the whole world, and when the effort to impose it on East Germany led to offensive actions against West Berlin. With the less dynamic and more conservative post-Khrushchev leadership, Soviet rule in Eastern Europe, including Eastern Germany, has appeared linked more to a Superpower's security preoccupations or to an imperial Power's desire to maintain its sphere than to an expansionist plan. Hence for the first time, the possibility of a de facto division of the world has been present, with American passivity in Eastern Europe responding to Soviet passivity in, for instance, Latin America. This is all the more so since Eastern Europe itself has seemed more diversified and since, on the Western side, the hope of German reunification has seemed to be receding in West Germany itself, thereby reducing the pressure for an active policy on the part of the United States.

No real change of policy has been involved, since the United States, precisely because of the subordinated nature of Eastern Europe from its point of view, has never had a coherent, long-range Eastern European policy. In this sense neither the accusations that the Americans at Yalta were consciously dividing Europe or the world, nor conversely, that John Foster Dulles was trying to "roll back" Communism, were justified. American policy has always been empirical and most of the time passive, reacting to changing circumstances and fully (perhaps excessively) aware that the United States could not do much beyond the Iron Curtain, while hoping for things there not to go too badly. However, changes have taken place along the lines indicated: of recognizing first the extent of Soviet primacy, then the rebirth of some East European diversity, then again the inevitable and not altogether negative character of Soviet presence and influence.

The Americans made feeble attempts in the early years at resisting the Soviet take-overs through diplomatic protests. After a policy of resignation tempered by verbal non-recognition, strategic embargo, and some CIA activities at the height of the cold war, they helped Yugoslavia after 1948 and Poland after 1956, when situations which they had not initiated gave them the opportunity to do so. On the other hand, after 1961 the Americans were the first of the Western states to initiate a program of active détente in Eastern Europe but without any coherent vision. President Kennedy's peace strategy was above all global in scope, bilateral in method, and applied primarily to the German problem.

The policy of "peaceful engagement" in Eastern Europe and of bridge-building, first formulated by Professors Zbigniew Brzezinski and William Griffith at the beginning of the Kennedy Administration and officially adopted by President Johnson in his 6 October 1966 speech, was an attempt to put Eastern Europe more in the center of a coherent policy which would ultimately transform Soviet-American relations and the German problem. But its fate testifies to the increasing trend toward the acceptance of the status quo and the primacy of the dialogue with the Soviet Union. Peaceful engagement first meant to try to detach the Eastern European satellites from the Soviet Union. Then, in 1964–65, it meant pursuing a multilateral détente starting with Eastern European states but progressively including the Soviet Union while excluding East Germany which the policy aimed at isolating. It ended by including both the Soviet Union and East Germany in a grandiose process of multilateral rapprochement based on technological trends, and supported by a mostly bilateral dialogue with the Soviet Union within which Vietnam and non-proliferation have enjoyed a constant priority over a European settlement.

As far as Eastern Europe was concerned, the policy followed met only with limited success because it was advertised too much in words and applied too little in practice—too much publicity, too little priority. But beyond these faults, the United States (like all Western Powers, including de Gaulle's France and the Grand Coalition's German Federal Republic) was caught in a dilemma which is still the major stumbling block of any policy toward Eastern Europe. Too much eagerness toward the satellites runs the risk of compromising them and of provoking a Soviet reaction; an exclusive dialogue with the Soviet Union runs the risk of consolidating its domination and of betraying both the populations and the governments of the states of Eastern Europe. Rather than trying to anticipate the contradiction by tying the two aspects in a diplomatic dialogue, by building umbrellas rather than bridges, thus protecting Eastern Europe's evolution away from the Soviet Union by diplomatic commitment aimed at moderating both sides, the United States has tended to lose on both sides by passively letting events in Eastern Europe run their course while sometimes claiming credit for it without attempting either to protect the states or to channel the events into mutually acceptable directions. It was thus led to react in contradictory ways before and after the invasion of Czechoslovakia, and toward Czechoslovakia itself, as well as toward Yugoslavia and Rumania.

In turn, these contradictions were to a great extent the mirror image of the contradictions of Soviet policy. The two divisive elements—the ideological drive and the struggle for Germany—while attenuated, were still present enough in Soviet policy to prevent the hostile partition of the cold war going all the way into the cooperative partition of a détente based on spheres of influence. Ever since Stalin's time, the Soviet government could easily have obtained the latter if on the one hand the brutality of its rule in Eastern

Europe and in the Soviet Union itself had not given to the word
"influence" a sinister meaning, going much beyond Soviet security
requirements and even beyond the imperial ambitions of a Great
Power. If, also, the Soviet Union had not always, even in predominantly defensive or conservative phases, wanted to maintain
at least in words a potentially expansionist or destabilizing ambition beyond its sphere. This is particularly striking vis-à-vis Germany, where Western acceptance of the division, desired by the
Soviet Union, would have been made much easier if the regime in
East Germany had been allowed to be liberated and to have shown
a measure of autonomous stability, and if, through various channels, the Soviet Union had not reserved the right to interfere with
the stability of West Germany.

Something similar occurred in the aftermath of the Czechoslovak
invasion. The Soviet Union could count on United States approval
for wanting to maintain the Warsaw Pact, and on its tacit acquies-
cence combined with mild moral disapproval for using military
pressure to that effect. But while the actual use of force was moderate, its political and ideological justification and exploitation were
a clear case of overkill. The proclamation of the Soviet Union's
right to intervene wherever Socialism seemed threatened, domestically or externally, and the dismissal of any restraints coming from
the rights of sovereignty or the requirements of coexistence could
not fail to be rebuffed both by the West and by those states which
were threatened with the application of the doctrine. The practice
was nothing new. Its doctrinaire and boastful proclamation made
it impossible to gloss over what had just happened and not to worry
about where it might lead in the future.

The Soviet Union encouraged these worries by seeming to extend
some version of its right of intervention doctrine to West Germany
via two clauses of the United Nations Charter pertaining to World
War II enemies, and via the East German statements that a war
between the two Germanies could be a "just war" since it would
be based on the class principle. It also encouraged these worries by
refusing to give assurances of the doctrine's non-application to other
European states (neutrals like Austria and Finland, and even more,
Socialist neutrals like Yugoslavia and Socialist maveriks like Rumania and Albania). To the revival of cold war militant rhetoric
was associated, then, the accentuation of a more aggressive diplo-

macy, particularly toward "gray areas" territorially adjacent to the Soviet Union. This was bound to prompt the West into more defensive and deterrent actions and into the discovery of those European gray areas themselves and of the security problems they raised. On other security problems, like Vietnam and the Middle East, the Soviet Union did not choose to buy further Western passivity toward Eastern Europe by being particularly forthcoming or helpful.

Finally, and perhaps most importantly, the small Communist states themselves refused to be left to the tender mercies of cooperative partition. The passive resistance of the Czechoslovak people, by delaying, complicating, and publicizing the Soviet takeover, especially during the crucial first week, and by depriving it of any face-saving semblance of legitimacy, made it impossible for the United States and for all other Western governments except the French, to minimize the 21 August event as a mere incident. The Rumanian and Yugoslav reaction proclaiming their readiness to fight if invaded accentuated the prospect that further application of the "Brezhnev Doctrine" might lead to an even more prolonged and more painful conflict which might damage more seriously the prospects for East-West détente and into which, at least in the case of an invasion of Yugoslavia, the West might be drawn.

Hence, starting with President Johnson's San Antonio speech on 30 August, warning against an invasion of Rumania, the United States took several steps during the fall of 1968 to express interest in the security of the "gray areas" in Europe, and especially of Yugoslavia. While the Soviet threat seemed to subside, Soviet rule in Eastern Europe and particularly in Czechoslovakia seemed to reassert itself slowly but heavily. If anything, external influences were going in the same direction, as the Soviet Union was trying to use the Chinese menace (dramatized by the Ussuri incidents) as a means to call for bloc solidarity. While Rumanians continued to resist on this and other essential issues, they seemed to be more and more aware of the narrowness of their margin of action, and to take protective steps toward a more orthodox line toward the Soviet Union.

As East-West relations were resuming their natural course, centered on Vietnam, the Middle East, and arms control (with the Non-Proliferation Treaty ratified by the U.S. Senate and SALT talks undertaken in 1969) it appeared that the two external preconditions of Rumania's independent venture—the Sino-Soviet split and East-West détente—had gone too far. They had become too irreversible to be used any longer in their deterrent function toward the Soviet Union. The latter seemed to be able, as after 1956, to reestablish the unchallenged rule, with the faithful satellites Poland and East Germany (who were also, in the case of action against Czechoslovakia, the "hawks" favoring intervention) firmly united behind it and extolled as models which the other East European states, including both Czechoslovakia and Rumania, would sooner or later have to come back to.

However, in the spring and summer of 1969, two relatively unexpected developments, both originating in the Superpowers, seemed to have reintroduced some uncertainty and hence some mobility in Soviet relations with Eastern Europe and to have broken or at least diminished the subregion's isolation from East-West relations.

On the one hand the Soviet Union, after having copiously used the West German ploy in connection with the events in Czechoslovakia, and while continuing to use it to a certain extent, inaugurated a phase of apparent flexibility toward West Germany. For the first time in many years the Russians seemed, at least tactically, to differentiate between the various West German domestic political forces (in favor of the SPD) and were not excluding West Germany from their appeals for détente. This led to a revival of the campaign for a European security conference.

The new turn seemed to have led to some disarray among the two Communist governments most concerned with West Germany and most faithful to the Soviet Union: East Germany and Poland. Rumors have it that both governments made tentative counter-moves toward a more flexible Chinese policy and toward some encouragement of Rumanian resistance in matters like COMECON. But one certain fact is that they adopted divergent lines on the main issue. Poland followed the Soviet Union into the adoption of a new tone toward West Germany while East Germany openly manifested its resistance and its displeasure, but by early 1970 was willing to engage in a "dialogue."

From the other end of the spectrum, President Nixon's visit to Rumania in August 1969, whatever its motives and whatever its indications for American support of Rumania in the event of a Soviet attack, both of which are unknown, still could help to convey at least two messages. To the Soviet Union, it meant an American repudiation of the Brezhnev Doctrine, and a message to the effect that détente must mean mutual concessions or else it could include mutual harassment by the Superpowers in each other's spheres. Whether meant as a tactical pressure to elicit greater Soviet cooperation elsewhere or as a permanent stand to induce greater Soviet moderation in Eastern Europe itself, at least the visit introduced an element of reciprocity, breaking the "what's mine is mine, what's yours is negotiable" pattern. For Rumania it meant that, the Chinese card being largely spent, they found again, at least for the purposes and for the period of its diplomatic acrobatics (a mixture of shadow-boxing and of poker-playing) the partner which had been sought in 1964–1965 and which had failed it largely because of the Vietnam war and the emphasis on U.S.-Soviet bilateralism.

The lesson is clear and must be seen by the Rumanians as a confirmation of the premise of their policy: freedom of movement for smaller states is possible only when the relationships of the Superpowers are in the intermediate situation of a somewhat friendly competition. Both complete hostility (cold war or quasi-war) and complete reconciliation (condominium or partition) make for the freezing of the status quo and the consolidation of the rule (separate or joint) of Great Powers over Small Powers. The only hope of the latter when their geographic or strategic situation does not permit them to find safety in isolation, lies in playing the Great Powers (or in this case the Superpowers) off against each other.

Whatever the results in each particular case, it seems that the initiatives of Small Powers like Rumania, the resistance of populations like the Czechoslovaks and the mixture of convergences and conflicts of interests between the Superpowers, make both bilateral solutions, a complete return to the cold war and the two-bloc system, and a complete agreement between the Superpowers for the status quo, unlikely.

But the impossibility of stabilizing the status quo does not mean that the prospects of transforming it through peaceful evolution toward a settlement are any better. Here we find again the three aspects mentioned in the Prologue—the security system, the diplomacy of states, and transnational technological economic, social, cultural, and psychological forces or trends. If the Superpower does not hold the key to a satisfactory peace for Eastern Europe, the political maneuvers of states and the aspirations of populations are powerless to do so by themselves. Rumanian tactics can win a perpetually precarious margin of independence—they are unable to challenge the system itself. President de Gaulle's policy, relying on similar principles, attempted such a challenge through the break-up of the two alliances, the military disengagement of the two Superpowers, and the agreement by the Soviet Union to replace its direct rule over Eastern Europe which had as its counterpart American rule over Western Europe, by a more relaxed and moderate influence on Eastern Europe, to be compensated by a greater influence in Western Europe. Understandably, the Soviet brand of conservative power, inspired or rationalized by ideological dogmas, was immune to the doubtful temptation of giving up, so to speak, two birds in the hand for one bird in the bush.

But the last remaining road—relying on broad social and technological trends and on the force of popular aspirations to lead both the Soviet Union and Eastern Europe together toward a community of developed states—does not seem less illusory. As soon as the process of détente and convergence sets in, Eastern European states with a democratic or Western tradition and an urgent need and thirst for the outside world will tend to go too far for the comfort of the Soviet Union. There is a real gap between a country like Czechoslovakia and the Soviet Union when it comes to Europeanization or modernization. A law of uneven political development emerges, by which contacts and national evolution, insufficient for Czechoslovakia, are already too much for Brezhnev and Ulbricht. In other words, national evolution may never go far enough out of fear of its going too far.

The tragedy is that the least open society (besides Albania, the exception to every generalization) is also the strongest. It is not Eastern Europe which drags the Soviet Union into Europe; it is the Soviet Union which keeps Eastern Europe out of Europe. On the other hand, a system based on cycles of liberalization and repression must lead to explosions, the more so since the same type of contradictions that exist between the Soviet Union and the satellites exist also within the Soviet Union itself, between the party leadership and several social groups impatient with the essentially reactionary character of its rule.

What the outcome of these various struggles will be cannot be predicted, except to the extent that a harmonious evolution can be excluded. Beyond that, one can only reassert the two basic limiting conditions. As long as the character of the Soviet regime and that of the international political system remain the same, Eastern Europe cannot change fundamentally. Any change which risks undermining the international power structure by its effect on Germany, or by its contagious effect on segments of the Soviet population, is doomed. To that extent, states like Rumania which are situated in the Balkans and keep their intellectuals in line have a better chance than Czechoslovakia, whose proximity to West Germany and whose trend toward freedom has made it particularly dangerous in Soviet eyes.

Beyond that, the fate of Eastern Europe is not in Eastern Europe but within the Soviet Union and in the outside world. It would take both a domestic transformation of the Soviet Union (which would make it interpret its security interests or its concept of its sphere of influence in a more moderate or flexible manner) and a change in the structure of East-West relations (through Soviet relations with China, with the United States, or through the emergence of a new political and military reality west of the Elbe) for a subregional structural change or a basic Eastern European-Western European realignment to take place. To evaluate its chances, we must now turn to the other Superpower and to the other Europe.

PIERRE HASSNER

4   Europe West of the Elbe

IS IT WESTERN EUROPE OR
EUROPE WEST OF THE ELBE?

Throughout this book so far, we have been asking about Europe as a whole and about Eastern Europe: do they exist? And if they do, what are they? About Western Europe, the question arises a little differently.

While Europe as a whole is, on the one hand, a geographical expression and, on the other, a distant political dream, and while Eastern Europe is a collection of states under Soviet domination, Western Europe stands out as having a degree of reality, identity, and cohesion. Of course, it shares to some extent all the imperfections and the difficulties of the two other notions: it does not have a common political authority or will; its limits have been drawn by the Iron Curtain rather than by geographical determinism or self-determination; it lives under the protection and influence of one of the Superpowers.

Yet the degree of homogeneity in social and economic regimes and levels of development, in broad cultural and political attitudes, in the degree of communication, and in travel and trade, are greater than in any comparable subregion. The division of Europe has excluded states which would naturally belong to this cultural and economic area. But in spite of the differences between Nordic prosperous democracies and Mediterranean poor dictatorships, all the states on the Western side, especially in the central area, do share at least some common features and experiences. Finally, even though some Western European states belong to NATO and others are neutral, and even though in some respects the individual links of these states with the United States is greater than their mutual solidarities or influences, on the whole the relationship between both sides of the Atlantic ocean is a fairly coherent one of diversity within a common framework and with the stronger side being clearly the North American.

The question, however, is that of the direction in which the winds are blowing: are these various aspects tending to cohere even further, and to give Europe West of the Elbe a common sense of the reality of its purpose and of its relations with the outside world; or do the goals or interests of the Western Europeans, and their relations with the outside world, particularly with the Superpowers and with Eastern Europe, tend increasingly to differ from state to state and from issue to issue?

The answer probably lies in the distinction, as made in the Prologue, between the three levels of strategy, diplomacy, and society, and in historical terms, the distinction between the period of the primacy of subregional construction, then of the broadening of the international horizon to global or all-European perspectives, and finally of the turn of the states of the subregion to domestic problems and interests.

In terms of the military balance, the decisive element for Western Europe is still the American presence and protection. But while this was almost exclusive until 1962, first the American preoccupation with Asia and with the bilateral (or "détente") dialogue with the Soviet Union, and then the inclination against foreign involvements, have tended to produce a separation of perspectives between the United States and Western Europe.

The diplomatic efforts of the Western European states were first designed to end their traditional rivalries and to promote integration (this is described in the Epilogue). Then, with President de Gaulle, came a preoccupation with the outside world—the challenge to the "two hegemonies," and the emphasis on a continental Europe from the Atlantic to the Urals. The post-de Gaulle era (and already the post-May 1968 and post-Czechoslovakia Gaullist policy) have given up those ambitions. But they seem, rather than returning to the unity of the first phase, to be turning toward a rivalry within the French-

German-British triangle moderated by the necessities of practical cooperation.

Much of this evolution is explained by the social and economic level of analysis. While the Common Market retains its importance, clearly the need for the states of Western Europe to develop world-wide ties, and particularly ties with the United States, has increased. Also the influence of the national bureaucracies continues to vie with the bureaucracy of the European Communities. Similarly, on the level of ideology, the unity and originality and role of Western Europe are challenged from both sides—by the world-wide relatively unpolitical international unrest of modern youth, and by the tendency of governments (in response to this challenge and to others, such as that of ethnic minorities), to concentrate on the everyday handling of domestic affairs.

The impact of this threefold evolution on Europe's bifurcation and on the region's relations with the Superpowers is made primarily, as usual, through one central element: Germany—which remains the problem, the pivot, and the prize in European politics. If West Germany no longer feared Russia or no longer trusted the United States, if it abandoned all thoughts of reunification and bet entirely on Western European integration; or conversely, if it returned to a more Central European than Western European concept of its destiny, and to a greater emphasis on West German reassociation with East Germany than on its association with its Common Market Powers; if, finally, it dispensed with both long-range dreams —that of German reunification and that of European federation— to become a state like every other state, exclusively preoccupied with everyday diplomatic and economic rivalries and with everyday social and economic domestic crises, then the elements of the European problem would decisively change.

The twin goals of providing an international political counterweight to the Soviet Union and a political frame of reference for West Germany were the core of post-war Western policies, and resulted in NATO and the Marshall Plan as well as Western European integration. There was a desire to create in the West a pole of strength solid enough to balance the Soviet Union without being dominated by a restored and reunited Germany, and to channel the potential and energies of the German people in a constructive direction. While this framework was essentially Atlantic at first, it was thought it could become progressively European while the second, primarily positive, objective of solving the German problem would progressively replace the first, primarily negative, problem of avoiding Soviet domination.

But then the question, "What kind of Germany in what kind of Europe?" was bound to become essential. Was the objective to provide an all-European framework for a reunited Germany, as a consequence of German and European reunification, or a Western European framework for West Germany, as a consequence of German and European division? Or would the re-emergence of Central Europe as a special demilitarized or denuclearized zone provide the framework for a more or less reunited Germany, isolated and supervised both by its neighbors and by the Superpowers? Were integrated institutions the best way to prevent German domination or would they accelerate it? Similarly was the presence of the Superpowers a consequence of the German problem or the cause of German division? Did the integration of Western Europe in an Atlantic partnership and of West Germany in a Western European one act as a help, an obstacle or a substitute for their reunion with their respective other halves?

These questions were raised when the Atlantic and the Western European international institutions were being formed. They were revived every time a decisive military-security-threat threshold was about to be crossed—at the time of German rearmament in 1952–1955 and today—usually accompanied by Soviet initiatives favoring a European security conference. But the distinguishing feature of the present situation is that both in the Western and in the Central European direction, the level of hope is rather low. Especially in West Germany there is no overwhelming body of opinion either against the Atlantic Alliance or Western European integration, or against German and European reunification; yet there is very little optimism about the prospects of either course.

At the same time, this outlook on distant objectives has not precluded a rising disagreement in West Germany on priorities, which had receded in recent years. For example, the Christian Democrats are again giving priority to ties with France and to strengthening Western Europe; the Social Democrats are giving priority to the "opening to the East" and to the widening of the Common Market.

But while in principle everybody would agree that the two directions are far from being contradictory and can only succeed if they are combined, they can also give the impression of blocking each other or of serving as mutual alibis.

The question for the future is whether, after the failure of the attempts to give exclusive priority to one or to the other direction, their mutual links can be converted from stalemate into a positive program of action which might be seen as aiming at a Third Europe. This Third Europe would probably arise out of the failure of the Monnetist and the Gaullist conceptions—i.e., the one based on Western European integration and on the interdependence of societies, and the other based on all-European reassertion and the independence of states.

THE MOVEMENT TOWARD WESTERN EUROPEAN INTEGRATION

In the first post-war years there was a feeling in Western Europe of impotence and of hesitation between different possibilities for Germany and the other states of Europe, and their relations with the Superpowers. The United States was "bringing the boys home." France wanted to divide Germany and aimed first at a bilateral understanding with the Soviet Union, and then at a kind of intermediary role between West and East. Britain was living its last years with quasi-Superpower status. In the deliberations and planning, especially in the American government, for the post-war recovery of Europe, the all-German and all-European perspectives were given their chance in the first instance, even though it looked more and more probable and to a certain extent more and more desirable, that both the economic help to Europe and the reorganization of Germany would first have to be limited to their Western halves. After the Soviet rejection of the Marshall Plan, the Prague coup, and the Berlin crisis of 1948, it was obvious that the Iron Curtain and the cold war were imposing on Europe their boundaries and their alignments, and that whatever German reintegration and European unity was to be hoped for would have to be sought west of the Elbe and in close alliance with the United States.

What was, in the minds of the architects of Western policy, the degree of permanence of this framework and its relationship to the alternative one of a continental Europe from which the Superpowers would have disengaged? The appraisal of the East-West struggle, and hence of the relationship to the United States, was certainly different from state to state. France and West Germany were probably the two extremes—West Germany taking the Soviet threat and the American alliance most seriously, while France, even before de Gaulle, has always had a certain tendency toward neutralism. On the other hand, as regards the larger dimensions of Europe, Germany (which was most eager to find a new identity and respectability in a united Europe) was also the state which could least forget about the division. France, while it was subjected to the centrifugal pressures of its colonial troubles and later to de Gaulle's nationalism, did not have this Central European dimension and could even welcome—in a smaller Europe based on the division—the chance of an organization in which the comparative weight of West Germany would be reduced.

In a broader perspective, the American and Western European statesmen of the cold war put primary emphasis on Western solidarity, without really having to decide on its ultimate effects on reunification with the East since this perspective was closed by the Soviet Union. The extent to which Secretary of State Dean Acheson *really* believed in negotiations from strength, Secretary of State John Foster Dulles in roll-back, and Chancellor Konrad Adenauer in reunification based on building up Western strength, is debatable. But the real issue was whether the reunification perspective which could only be unpredictable, should keep the states of Western Europe from doing what *was* possible in what was clearly the only existing framework. After 1965 this was recognized, both for NATO and for the German problem, by the West German Social Democrats who had been the most vocal exponents of the alternative of negotiations with Russia on German reunification and a European security system.

The problem was not exactly the same for NATO and for European integration. It could be argued that NATO as an integrated political/military organization, while valid against a Soviet military threat, could not form the basis of German and European reunification; yet it could, perhaps, consolidate the division by facilitating (and helping to legitimize) the presence of the Superpowers in Europe and the separation of the two Germanies. The only possible answer, if one wanted to maintain the perspective of reunification, was and still is to regard NATO as a passing instrument which could become a bargaining card in the event of East-West negotiations and which, meanwhile, would progressively be Europeanized. This would contribute to the creation of a Europe standing on its own feet which, while more natural, was made impossible in 1949 by the weakness and division of the Europeans, together with the rivalry of the Superpowers.

The European idea, on the other hand, appeared during this period (beginning roughly around 1947–1950 and ending around 1962–1965) as obvious—as having the nature of modern society and the tide of history running for it: between nation-states incapable of providing for the prosperity and security of their citizens, and an inaccessible World State, the trend of the times seemed to lead toward regionalism or more closely knit subregional arrangements. Those persons who wanted to start from the "Europe of the Six" in order to go beyond the nation-state were in the same relationship to classical internationalists as the scientific socialists were to utopian socialists as Marx saw them: they felt they were not only working for an ideal which was preferable to reality but in the same direction as reality itself.

It was Jean Monnet's creative intuition to make use of this dynamism in order to link the political objectives of a Franco-German reconciliation, an East-West détente and a general European revival with the economic needs of European reconstruction. He wanted to link them by institutions conducive to progress—and progress leading to new institutions. It was this feeling of being carried by a vital drive, by a creative inspiration, which had to be used and channeled but whose very essence was to go beyond the classical historical dichotomies and to refute implicitly, by its very movement, the objections based on them.

Of course, questions about the ultimate ends and geographical dimensions of the enterprise always did cast their shadow upon it: was building a "small Europe" to be limited to the Six or was it to be a starting point for a wider construction? Was one to aim at a new political unit, as the federalists advocated, or should one, as the functionalists maintained, try to empty the state of its content by integrating specialized sectors for specialized functions? Did one want to create a new Great Power to restore Europe to something like its past role, or did one want to suppress power politics and sub-ordinate the independence and nationalism of states to the inde-pendence and prosperity of societies?

The answer was that the first task to tackle was to get Europe go-ing, and that the more the process could be made to advance, the more the original questions would appear in a new and unforeseen light. It was, in this view, more important to know whether one could "make Europe" than to predict what the foreign policy of this Eu-rope would be. One did not have to choose between the Six and a wider Europe; one had to start with the Six and hope that the Brit-ish, the Scandinavians and the East Europeans would follow in due course. One did not have to choose between federalism and func-tionalism; the only realistic way toward federalism was a sector-by-sector functionalism, and by the same token, the logic of functional expansion called for a federalizing process. One did not have to decide whether Europe should play the game of international poli-tics or abstain from it; what one had to hope for was that by intro-ducing a new factor—a new spirit, hence a new style and new rules —the ground rules themselves would undergo change. Of course, one knew that large states bound together by a network of func-tional interests would still constitute an international political sys-tem with its inherent risks. But one could reasonably hope that these risks would not be the same as those of a system dominated by a bipolar confrontation or by the conflicting interests of a multitude of new and jealous states.

While a united Europe would introduce a new factor, and in a sense create a "third force" in the world, the nature of this force—its relationship with the United States and the Soviet Union—would clearly depend on what kind of Europe emerged in what kind of world. Hence, in the years after World War II priority was given to the internal construction of Europe over its external role. Speaking of Europe's relations with the Soviet Union, Jean Monnet used to say: "First let us have faith in ourselves, let us succeed and let the Soviet Union adapt to this new reality." It was always expected that the phase of mutual adaptation with the external world would come, but that it would follow the internal consolidation of an increasingly united Europe, and not jump ahead of it.

Around 1962 the bet seemed to pay off. The Kennedy "grand design" for an Atlantic Community made of two pillars, one European and one Atlantic/North American, the British application for membership in the Common Market, the obvious impression which the success of the Common Market made in Eastern Europe and which prompted Soviet Premier Khrushchev to want both to imitate it and to cooperate with it—all this seemed to justify the Monnetist hope that, starting from the center of the Six, a zone of stability and cooperation was spreading to include Great Britain, then the United States, then Eastern Europe and the Soviet Union (of course, in various ways and with various degrees of association). The cold war divisions, including the unsolved problems of Central Europe, appeared to be on their way to being solved through institutionalized cooperation within a larger whole.

Yet by that time it may already have been too late. A few years later it appeared retrospectively that the internal construction of the European community may well have been losing a race against time. The political evolution of certain of its member-states and of certain aspects of the international environment may have caught up with it in such a way that the question, "Europe for what?" came to be asked before Europe had had enough identity to constitute an answer by its very existence.

THE MOVEMENT AWAY FROM
EUROPEAN INTEGRATION

First, the minimum agreement on goals which was necessary in order to bet on the building of institutions prior to the elaboration of a specific foreign policy was broken because of France. Paradoxically, Charles de Gaulle, who was the most insistent on the necessity of first agreeing on foreign policy was precisely the partner who was breaking the relative agreement which had existed before he came to power. To the integration of Western Europe, which was to be built within the Atlantic framework before being able —once united—to become more independent of the United States and to open itself in the direction of the East to a degree which would have to be seen, he put up the concept of a Europe of cooperation between sovereign states, with the primacy of detachment from the United States and of an opening toward the Soviet Union. He placed the latter over the creation of that united force which alone, according to the orthodox conception, could have given an effective meaning to this detachment and to this opening.

But this Gaullist challenge to European priorities (expressed in such gestures as the veto against British entry into the Common Market in 1963, the initiatives toward the East on the German problem and on the theme of "Europe from the Atlantic to the Urals," the "empty chair" policy in NATO after 1965, and the withdrawal from the NATO military structure in 1966) could not have been possible or at least would not have had once-important consequences if, both within and outside Western Europe, new conditions had not appeared which made the road of integration appear less obvious and which gave increased plausibility to alternative paths. Long-range trends of history lend themselves to manipulation only under specific constellations of events.

After World War II, there was no realistic alternative to Europe: nationalism was discredited; the economies and national bureaucracies of European states were weakened; their military force was negligible; the United States was friendly and encouraging; the Soviet Union was hostile and looked threatening; Eastern Europe and East Germany were inaccessible; Germany, reduced to its Western part, seemed for the first time in history neither too strong nor too weak to be fitted into a larger European framework. All this seemed to be showing that Europe could not recover its security and prosperity unless it went beyond its structure of nation-states, yet it could not hope to be united in a framework larger than that of Western Europe.

By contrast, once prosperity had come back (partly through integration and certainly through international cooperation, starting with the Marshall Plan), states were resuming their former importance and self-assurance. Nationalism was becoming respectable again as memories of World War II were fading and examples of nationalistic policies were flowing from newly-independent states, from Communist states or from Gaullist France. National interest and, even more, the self-preservation instincts of national bureaucracies were gaining the upper hand again. As security and prosperity no longer seemed absolutely to require a change of dimensions, governments no longer felt bound to work in a direction which, naturally enough, was repugnant to them anyway but which had appeared under the post-war circumstances as the only legitimate one, but which would if carried to the ultimate conclusion, lead to their own demise.

With the transformation of the international political and economic environment, the opportunities for this reassertion of separate interests were decisively encouraged. The United States was no longer as obviously interested in European unification, nor was the Soviet Union as obviously threatening as ten or fifteen years before. Earlier the influence of both Superpowers had combined, whether negatively or positively, to drive Western Europe toward uniting. With the decline of the cold war both influences, without disappearing, had lost much of their force, while other external influences were acting centrifugally: the trend toward polycentrism and contacts with the West in Eastern Europe meant a broadening of the horizon for Western Europe. Although still separated, the two Europes could no longer be unaware of each other and could not be discouraged from dreaming of a common future. At least as far as West Germany was concerned, the fact that integration in the West had proved slower and more limited than expected and détente with the East seemed to have been quicker and more far-reaching, was bound to encourage any West German government to re-examine its priorities and look again toward the East in the hope, if not of reunification and of a resumption of Germany's traditional role in Central Europe, at least of some progress in its relations with East Germany and with the Soviet Union.

This started to happen with the foreign policy of Dr. Gerhard Schröder, and was confirmed and extended by Willy Brandt when he was Foreign Minister during the Grand Coalition's "opening to the East." The commitment to Western European integration remained, but obviously the sights were set on a wider horizon than the Six.

This was also the case in the Western direction. As Great Britain no longer looked hostile or inaccessible, and as the United States increasingly stressed the necessity of an open European Community, other members of the Six, beginning with the Netherlands, increasingly gave priorities to their ties with the Atlantic world. This was also apparent in the Erhardt-Schröder policy. But, after Chancellor Ludwig Erhardt gave way to Chancellor Kurt Kiessinger, while the Grand Coalition again emphasized ties with France, its Social Democratic components insisted on the importance of widening the Community. While the Christian Democrats have agreed, the differences between the two parties in the concept of Europe's role and of West Germany's role in it are increasing.

Domestic concerns are more and more important both in the discussion about Europe within European states and in the bargaining between them and within European Economic Community institutions like the Common Market. This "renationalization of politics," to use Helmut Schmidt's expression, does not prevent national interests from converging, in particular under the influence of transnational economic trends which push toward the opening of boundaries and the prevalence of free trade. But then, both in commercial and in diplomatic terms, what seemed in the years 1965–1967 to emerge as the trend of the future could also be seen as a trend toward a return to the pre-1914 world.

The combination of political independence and of economic interdependence points to a European concept of balance-of-power on the diplomatic level, fulfilling the wishes of General de Gaulle, and to generalized free trade on the economic level, fulfilling the wishes of West German businessmen or those of the maritime states. From both points of view, the framework of the Six and the Community method appear to have distorted a natural trend which, rather, would have led to the economic interpenetration of industrialized states (at least of Western or capitalist ones)—and hence to an economically Atlanticist Europe, from the Elbe to the Pacific Ocean, and to the political balance of continental states, hence to a diplomatically "European Europe" from the Atlantic to the Urals, both being based on the rivalry and cooperation of states.

THE RAMIFICATIONS OF
THE "NEW NATIONALISM"

However, every year after 1965 was to demonstrate that the Gaullist pattern was leading neither to a genuine broadening of Europe to the East, nor to a genuine independence from America, nor to a political solution of the German problem. Rather, it led to an increase in the very dangers it was meant to avoid; i.e., to an increase in American economic domination, an increase in Soviet military superiority and political power, and an increase in West Germany's economic weight and political potential.

One of the reasons is that, as the classical Atlantic and European frameworks were challenged or reformed, what tended to replace them was not a concerted search for a Gaullist Europe but a rivalry between differing conceptions resulting from differing interests.

France itself wanted to change the post-war status quo in the sense that it wanted to replace the bipolar division of Europe by a new continental system in which it would have a central place by playing a balancing game between Russia and Germany. But it wanted to keep some crucial elements of the status quo, like its own sovereignty and Germany's inferiority. The problem was that by undermining the collective structures of the West, it was jeopardizing the special situation it wanted to preserve.

At the other extreme, most of Europe's medium and small states were predominantly in favor of the existing balance. The Benelux and the northern NATO states have welcomed the Anglo-American presence not only as a security against both Germany and Russia, but as a countervailing influence against French or Franco-German hegemony in Western Europe. Yet they have had an element of revisionism in their policies in that they would have liked Western European integration to bring about a change in the nature of international relations, whereas the Gaullist philosophy assumed and welcomed the permanence of power politics. But this change would, at the same time, have given Western Europe a greater voice within the Atlantic Alliance and the international political system, and have given these states a greater voice as compared with the larger Powers—two objectives which find their parallels in French policies.

Nowhere is this competition between attachment to the present system on the one hand, and growing dissatisfaction with the place of the European states in it on the other, more evident than in the case of the West European Middle Powers other than France. Britain, a pioneer in attempts at more security, more trade, and more détente between the two blocs, has always tended to regard these efforts and their possible outcomes in status quo terms, both from the point of view of American strategic leadership in the West and from that of "accepting realities" in Eastern Europe, including, implicitly, not only the Oder-Neisse line but also East Germany. Britain, like the Benelux and the Scandinavian states, is the advocate of more détente, more East-West trade and more East-West contacts within the present framework.

But at the same time, the turn toward Europe necessarily means a turn toward a greater self-assertion vis-à-vis the United States, if only on the technological issue, where Prime Minister Harold Wilson had spoken of the danger for European states of becoming "industrial helots." And the trend toward a British-West German understanding and cooperation on strategic matters may lead to a less orthodox Atlanticist position and to attempts, at least, toward a common Anglo-West German position on East-West relations.

The same goes for Italy, always a model of "Atlanticism plus détente" and of attachment to Western European integration. The Italian political right-of-center, with ideas for a specifically European point of view on defense and hence being critical of the Nuclear Non-Proliferation Treaty, paralleled the concerns of Franz Joseph Strauss of West Germany. In contrast the Italian political left-of-center, with initiatives for détente, especially, under Socialist Foreign Minister Pietro Nenni, on the issue of a European security conference, were expressing the same attitude as West German Foreign Minister and now Chancellor, Willy Brandt.

Of the three basic directions of the Gaullist alternatives to postwar Atlantic and Western European orthodoxy (greater independence of states within Western Europe, greater separation from the United States, greater opening toward the East) various components were adopted or practiced by various states or political parties within them, before or during de Gaulle's tenure of office. But the divergence between the various combinations as well as the inner contradictions of each of them has prevented the adoption of the common alternative desired by France, which is that the French should play the central role in the complex maneuvering which, as a consequence of the combinations and contradictions, has taken place both on the Western European and on the wider East-West scene.

This has been especially so because of the central role of West Germany and of the contradiction into which West Germany was, and still is, forced by its special condition. West Germany is the state most wedded to the status quo at the level of the post-war European international political system, because of its conscious need for security and hence for a close tie with the United States. At the same time West Germany is the state which is most interested in challenging the status quo, if not on a territorial basis by recovering its lost provinces, at least on a political one by desiring to change some of the undesirable human aspects for Germans brought on by the division. Equally, it is both the state which, besides the Superpowers, has the greatest actual economic and potential military and political weight, yet the state which has the narrowest freedom of international political action, not least because of this very weight. For instance, proposals and policies undertaken by all the other Powers in the West, and recommended to West Germany (like a policy of détente toward Eastern Europe), or actions by the other Powers that could lead to multilateral arrangements that would limit the danger of West German preponderance and adventurism (like proposals for a European nuclear force) have been met with distrust and counterreaction when they have come from West German sources.

The hardening of the Soviet bloc and the intervention in Czechoslovakia would have occurred even if West Germany had not existed. But the sensitivity of the Soviet rulers to any signs of a détente between West Germany and their satellites underscores that the opening to the East, whether it hears the French label of "*détente, entente et cooperation,*" the American one of "peaceful engagement in Eastern Europe," or the German one of "Östpolitik" cannot solve the problems of Central Europe nor even lead to a genuine broadening of Western Europe by a genuine Europeanization of Eastern Europe, as long as the structural problems connected with West Germany's relations with the two Superpowers have not been solved. For example, the Polish non-committal attitude to General de Gaulle's visit in 1967 showed that the Franch conception of Europe could be used by the East against West Germany and the United States, but would not be accepted as the basis for a new settlement.

WESTERN EUROPE'S RELATIONS WITH THE UNITED STATES

Similarly, in Western Europe's relations with the United States, we see a double movement which, again, seems to lead to a stalemate. During recent years the economic presence and superiority of the United States in Europe has increased, while a political and psychological gap has developed. This was due to the unpopularity of the Vietnam war in Europe, particularly in the years 1965 to 1968, and to the increasing priority of Asian over domestic problems for the United States. The coincidence of these two developments with each other and with the real or apparent decrease of the

Soviet threat caused the Western European consciousness to take an increasingly anti-American character. The substitute for the feeling of resistance to the Soviet military threat has tended to become feelings of resistance to the American economic and cultural threats or at least challenges. But this feeling for a "European" or Gaullist Europe, defined by its opposition toward the United States, has never succeeded in going beyond negative (and unequally shared) resentment.

Nonetheless, the only matters that have produced a common feeling or position among the Six have been those common matters cemented by opposition to the United States: the "technological gap," American investments in Europe, etc. The only one of these matters where a real result was reached was the Kennedy Round of tariff negotiations, because Community institutions enabled the Six to speak with one voice. In every other case, the perennial calls to consultation or coordination of national policies have produced only a cacaphony of discordant voices. Meanwhile, the Western Europeans have been less and less holding their own in the economic and technological competition with the United States.

A final aspect of the relationship between the attempts at organizing Western Europe and the United States within an Atlantic framework is defense. The consequences of the Vietnam war, of the invasion of Czechoslovakia, and those of the strategic balance between the United States and the Soviet Union and of their new strategic dialogue on nonproliferation and arms limitation raise again, to a certain extent, the problem of Western European defense. The Soviet threat is far from being again taken as seriously as in Stalin's time, but the American protection, too, is no longer as reliable as when the United States enjoyed a nuclear monopoly or clear-cut superiority, and when the United States was not submitted to growing domestic pressures for withdrawing militarily from Southeast Asia.

This is why it would seem desirable to create a Western European defense capability, eventually including a nuclear force, either in order to contribute, one day, to the reunification of the European continent by a certain mutual Soviet and American withdrawal or troop thinning-out, or, more modestly and negatively, in order to contribute to the balance of the continent by substituting to a certain extent the Western European force for a declining American presence and protection. The United States itself has recently indicated less hostility to the idea than during recent years. But here again we find the dilemma between the multiplicity of states and their integration into a Community. Even more than other technological ventures, a European defense force would be costly and ineffective if it consisted only of the coordination and (more likely than not) duplication of national efforts. It would be considered a danger in the eyes of the national participants themselves and even more in the eyes of the outside world (especially the states of Eastern Europe and the Soviet Union), if it were nuclear and included West Germany. Once more, the "Gaullist" objective that Europe should have its own defense is impossible to reach if one does not appeal to the opposite, "Monnetist" inspiration. A nuclear force which would not belong to a federal or integrated Western Europe governed by a common political authority could neither include West Germany nor dispense with it.

The attempt to solve first the problem of Western Europe's relations with the outside world—East of the Elbe and West of the Atlantic—has increasingly brought us back, then, in the years 1967 to 1970, to the problem of its inner structure (inter-state or supra-national) and of its inner balance, i.e., to the place of West Germany. The central problem of providing a framework for West Germany had already increasingly come to the fore in the earlier 1960's, as the Soviet threat seemed to be receding and détente seemed to be taking precedence over defense. The Gaullist solution, by loosening multilateral ties in the West but broadening the Western European perspective toward the East, tended to replace a narrow and rigorous Western European framework by a broader and looser Continental one, within which West Germany could hope to obtain a loosening-up of its division vis-à-vis East Germany while remaining in a kind of permanent subordination to France and to the Soviet Union. Here again, the positive perspective was nullified by the Soviet reaction in Czechoslovakia in August 1968. But the relative emancipation of West Germany from Community ties has already begun, and the counterweight provided for by the Gaullist concept, that of a bilateral control of West Germany by France, has also started to give way. The French have been losing the seductive appeal attached to the ambiguous perspectives they were suggesting —now for Western defense, now for Eastern détente—while the West Germans have begun, following the French example, to behave as a nation-state in a game where economic and demographic strength, without being decisive, weigh more and more heavily.

So the long-term orientation of West German foreign policy is more uncertain than ever. Because of Gaullism, West Germany has lost a Community but has not found a role. Because of Prague, West Germany has seen the role it was beginning to find, jeopardized at least in the short run through Soviet military intervention, without however regaining the lost Community. But within the framework of Western Europe which is of necessity regaining priority, its role, as shown by the Franco-German monetary crisis of 1968, is greater and greater. France, which has been fearful of losing its primary position in Western Europe, has become increasingly worried by this growing West German weight.

Hence, on the one hand, there is some risk of the Community perspective not being revived, as the West Germans may not want to forget either the Eastern perspectives or their own new power; on the other hand, within a Western Europe dominated by a multinational arrangement and by a West German-French-British triangle, the West Germans could play an essential role, as indeed they would within the wider perspective of continental Europe and of East-West relations in a Europe dominated by an American-Soviet-West German triangle.

FRENCH POLICY IN EUROPE

This explains the French tendency to de-emphasize creating an exclusive bilateral relationship with the West Germans and then trying to isolate them, both by a certain acceptance of Superpower hegemony and by a certain opening toward the British. In the last phase of his policy—after the French domestic crisis of May 1968, after the events in Czechoslovakia, and after the monetary crisis of November 1968—General de Gaulle was clearly seeking a reconciliation with the United States, without abandoning his special cordiality toward the Soviet Union. It was, in a sense, a clear case of "If you can't beat them, join them." But what gave this policy its specific character was its counterpart in the French attitude toward other European states. The enthusiasm toward Eastern Europe had receded, but the enthusiasm toward the Common Market had not increased. An ambiguous opening was made in the direction of Great Britain but without any concession on the Common Market issue. Indeed, the more positive attitude toward Britain was clearly linked to the more negative one toward the West Germans, who were almost openly made responsible by the French both for the Czechoslovak tragedy and for the monetary crisis.

President Georges Pompidou's initial policy was a continuation of this last phase of his predecessor's, with a difference in the accentuation of domestic considerations and in a more positive external attitude. But this only underlines what was already so striking in de Gaulle's last phase, namely that the state that had stood most vigorously against the European status quo and the bipolar order of the two hegemonies, preferred, once its enterprise had failed, to reconcile itself with its two great opponents rather than to embark on the only long-range policy which could challenge them but at the cost of sacrifices to French sovereignty—further Western European integration based on intimate collaboration between France, West Germany, and Britain.

The result of the return of France to a preoccupation with national interest in the name of French independence from Europe, and European independence from the Superpowers, appears to be a Europe dominated economically by the United States, and militarily and hence politically by the Soviet Union. From the points of view of both Superpowers, West Germany would be the leading Middle Power and hence could produce unpredictable anxieties and reactions among all the states of Europe—East or West. Nothing is certain, however—not even this picture of unpredictability. The trend toward the increase of the American and West German economic weight and of the Soviet military presence, and the uncertainty about the political significance of all this, is bound to continue. But, particularly after the departure of General de Gaulle, the reactions they may cause can go in a variety of directions.

THE POSSIBILITIES FOR
THE FUTURE IN WESTERN EUROPE

It is likely that the problem of a divided Germany, which has been central to this discussion because of past European conflicts and the creation of a post-war power vacuum in Germany, may become central again, but for the opposite reasons: because of potential conflicts and an immediate excess of West German power. The difficulties of achieving Western European integration were first caused by Britain (through its initial non-participation), then by France (through its opposition to British participation), and finally by the United States (through lessening support) and the Soviet Union (through becoming less threatening). In the future, if as seems likely, in spite of possible reversals particularly in the British case, the political relations of these four Powers evolve favorably, the difficulties will probably be caused by West Germany. Either, having discovered wider horizons, the West Germans will refuse to follow their nearby European and Superpower guides and models back into the fold; or, returning to the Community home, they may find that it has become too small for them because they have become too powerful for their partners.

But for the time being, it is from West Germany (through Franz Joseph Strauss) that is heard the most pressing appeals for this Western European federation leading toward integration which alone could channel and limit this power. Conversely, while feelings of fear and distrust toward West Germany exist both in France and in Britain and have motivated the initiatives of the former in the direction of the latter, these feelings were also provoked by the first serious beginnings of Anglo-German collaboration in such sensitive fields as nuclear strategy and weapons production. A debate has been taking place in Britain as to whether the road to Europe was passing through special relations with France or with West Germany.

Hence two possible patterns may be emerging: either competitive bilateral relations, with each of the three Powers trying to put pressure on each of the two others by showing that it can get together with the third one, or an attempt at genuine tripartite cooperation without preferential relations. The first pattern could result in the break-up of the Common Market and emergence either of a free-wheeling West Germany, or of a bitter and isolated one. The second pattern could result in a new beginning of a Western European subregionalism, provided the agreement of the three Powers, by choosing multilateral stability over bilateral flexibility, leads to multinational institutions which encourage this stability through integration and guarantees the participation of the other Western European states.

These two possible directions in the relations among the states of Western Europe are of crucial importance for their relations with the outside world. In the short run, by playing their respective national games, they probably can obtain more tangible results in their relations with the two Superpowers and with Eastern Europe. The United States, happy with France's de facto reconciliation with NATO under Pompidou and with the absence of any neo-Gaullist challenge, is sincerely disposed to consult with its allies on matters like nuclear planning or strategic arms limitation talks with the Soviet Union, but is not disposed to push them toward the unity which would alone enable them to exert a decisive influence and eventually to take the lead in their own defense. The Soviet Union, in order to prevent a post-Gaullist resumption of movement toward Western European unity and a defense arrangement which it feels would be dominated by West Germany, is ready to offer bilateral gestures of détente which would include West Germany itself. The Eastern European states, especially Rumania, find it both less compromising and more favorable for their independence to enter into multiple informal bilateral relationships with individual Western European states than to enter into an institutionalized multinational European structure which might be intolerable to the Russians if they were excluded, and dominated by them if they were included.

In the long run, however, the events of the last years in both Western and Eastern Europe have shown the limits of polycentric contacts, competition and combinations. It is more and more clear that the alternative to the rule of the Superpowers can only be the appearance, if not of a third force and of a third way, at least of a third institutional structure and of a third voice. The chances of a real broadening of multilateral European relationships, as of real European national independence as well, are inseparably linked to the prospect of real European unity.

Today, however, equally obvious Western European trends seem to point in two possible directions. On the one hand, Western European international politics is clearly being conducted according to inter-state diplomacy rather than according to multinational Community diplomacy. On the other hand, the limits of the power of the Western European states and of their independent enterprises have been shown to all, especially from the economic and the technological points of view, and there is a general aspiration toward getting together in a tighter and more stable grouping, more centered on Western Europe itself. The question is, first, whether notions like "grouping" and "stability" have any meaning unless they imply a minimum use of common institutions and authority; and second, whether the governments of the states of Western Europe will have the will and the energy to go beyond vague declaratory aspirations to engage in a real building effort, and in that case, which of them would lead out in taking the necessary initiative.

Here the domestic political evolution of the various states would seem to be crucial in two different ways. First, even if—between Mr. Heath and Mr. Wilson, Mr. Strauss and Mr. Brandt, Mr. Debre and Mr. Schumann, between Italian left-wing Socialists and right-wing Christian Democrats or right-wing Socialists and left-wing Christian Democrats—there is a general agreement in favor of Western European unity and independence, there clearly are in each state and among the various political parties crucial differences about priorities which can become decisive when attempts to make a new beginning actually take place. In particular, the respective roles of defense from anticipated aggression and détente, the attitude toward a Western European nuclear force and toward an all-European security conference, are obvious bones of contention within each state, and most of all where it matters most, in West Germany.

Second and most decisively, whatever the result of the various contests in the various states, what matters is that all seem to be caught up in what might be called the new European instability, typified by student rebellions, widecat strikes, monetary crises, political division. All are in a condition of domestic political, economic, or social uncertainty. The various crises may lead to contrasting results at a time when the global orientation of Europe is itself uncertain. The two phenomena are linked: in the absence of external constraint or of a common will, the various states are thrown back on their respective domestic preoccupations. These, in turn, make a new Western European or an all-European initiative more difficult by tending to monopolize the attention of governments and by creating or magnifying their differences in situations and in interests. Domestic crises have tended to replace external temptations as prime obstacles to multinational institutional cooperation. Just as American preoccupation with the Vietnam war created a gap between the United States and Western Europe which will probably be succeeded not by a renewed American attention to Western Europe but rather by a tendency to disengage world-wide and to concentrate on the domestic American crisis, so in Western Europe what may be paralyzing creative multinational cooperation may be less nationalism than *domesticism.*

Paradoxically, this domesticism is itself in great part the effect of world-wide or transnational trends like free trade, modernization, urbanization, mass-media, and the contagion of student revolts. The new internationalism, if there is one, is partly apolitical, and partly centered on the Third World and is directed toward and is composed of the rising generation. The reactions to these universal phenomena are bound to increase the domestic role of national governments rather than the multinational role of regional or subregional institutions. But the reactions are bound also to influence the relationships of national governments and multinational institutions to each other.

Everywhere one finds the same paradox: never have domestic situations and problems been so similar—ardent minorities challenging the social system; conservative backlash and majorities; ethnic minorities rebelling or fighting each other; political institutions and personnel in crisis, etc. But this community of problems and worries does not produce a community of action but rather a tendency for rising domestic entanglements and for an increase in the role of the state. Finally, however, precisely when they are turning inward, these states, by their mutual domestic preoccupation, and by the ways they are attempting to cope with their domestic crises, are influencing each other almost as much as they would through diplomatic or military endeavors.

This primacy of the two extremes of specific problems of individual states and of world-wide trends can lead to uncontrolled and unpredictable results which are highly dangerous to the existing international structure and to any contemplated structures. The task of a European "third force," or of a neo-regionalism, would be to bridge the gap between national domestic preoccupation and universal transnational trends.

Just as economically the institutions of the European Communities, which have been created during and for a period of relatively self-contained and regular growth, must adapt themselves to a more outward-looking and more irregular growth, more exposed to national crises and to clashes of interest among member states, so politically the justification of regionalism will be to respond to the contradictory character of a world simultaneously dominated by trends toward unification and toward fragmentation. European regionalism, or Western European subregionalism, can introduce some balance and some dialogue into the chaos of localized and world problems, of subcultures and Superpowers.

A renewed Western Europe cannot solve the domestic problems of its member states nor become a nation-state itself, nor absorb a divided or a reunified Germany, nor replace the Atlantic Alliance or the bipolar balance. But it *can* offer a structure which can contribute to the positive evolution of each of these realities toward greater domestic satisfaction and external security. By providing the beginning of a Western European defense within NATO, of a common Western European economic and monetary policy within the Common Market, of a common framework for West Germany's dialogue with East Germany and the Soviet Union and for the cooperation of Eastern European states with Western European states, it can pave the way toward a Europe which would be more independent and reunified without being less stable and prosperous. The question which remains is whether "providing a beginning" or "paving the way" is a positive accomplishment in itself or whether it can only be justified by the ultimate success of the whole enterprise, and in that case, whether taking the first steps on that road makes it much more likely that the ultimate goal will eventually be reached. What we face then, is the problem with which we started —that of the relation between what is done in one half of Europe with what is done in the other half, and the resulting consequences for the center and the whole of Europe, including the Superpowers.

CAN EUROPE UNITE?

The most familiar dilemma in human affairs is between what seems necessary and what seems likely. No matter how hard one tries to avoid utopias and blueprints, it seems impossible to find a solution to the European problem which would not be less stable and safe than the bipolar division unless it is a Europe which would be united, would extend to the whole of the continent, would be tight enough not to leave a united Germany a free hand yet broad enough not to leave the Germans in their present state of rigid division, and would enable the United States and the Soviet Union to withdraw the bulk of their troops because the Germans would be strong enough to ensure a certain regional balance in front of the latter. Yet, as we have seen, Eastern Europe has no foreseeable way to attain even the limited degree of independence and unity of Western Europe in order to join the West.

Even if it could, there is likely to remain a basic difference between the West and the East of the continent. Without the Soviet Union, the East would be much weaker than the West. With the Soviet Union, the East is much stronger than the West. Even if Western Europe does make significant advances in institutionalized multinational cooperation, these do not seem to be likely to lead in the foreseeable future to the diminishment of the nation-state which alone would solve, at the same time, the problem of Germany and that of European defense. Finally, even if Western Europe has the resources, it is not, given the domestic problems and moods of the various states, likely to have the will to build a strategic force capable of securing its own defense. Hence the Europe whose revival seems possible, and even likely, is a Europe limited to its Western half; a Europe which, even if it becomes tied by institutional links, will still be a "Europe of the states"; and finally, a Europe whose military power will only be a supplement, not a substitute, to that of the United States.

The crucial question is then: does building a half-way house to the true solution lead to it or away from it? Does the organization of Western Europe increase or diminish the division of the continent which the organization of Europe from the Atlantic to Brest-Litovsk (rather than the Urals) would abolish? Does an inter-governmental economic organization increase or diminish the intra-European subregional disparities? Does an inter-governmental military organization increase or diminish the danger of an independent West German force, which, in either case, a true federation would help to prevent? Does not opposing the United States or even trying to act more independently without being able to take its place, increase the very dangers connected with the diminution of the American commitment or protection which Western Europeans oppose?

In each case, the answer involves difficult choices on priorities and bets on the future. It is likely that, in the short run, the negative answers are more plausible, but that in the long run the positive ones might have a better chance of paying off. If one wants to keep open the possibility of reaching a true European peaceful order or a true United States of Europe, it is likely that for the time being, the domestic and international environment being what they are, the only practicable positive steps to this possibility are those leading to an economic, political, technological, and military organization of Western Europe, even though in the short run they are likely to raise fear and misgivings both in the East and in the West without really solving the problems to which they are addressed. The important caveat is never to lose sight either of these external reactions or of the ultimate goal—to try to progress toward the latter while reducing the former to an inevitable minimum.

This third, post-Monnetist and post-Gaullist Europe, has to be created by pragmatic calculations as well as by a stubborn effort of the will, since neither determinism nor idealism seem to have been sufficient to get it off the ground. It must have in common with de Gaulle's Europe the desire for independence from the United States and for a broadening to the whole of the continent. From Monnet's Europe it must preserve the lesson that independent multinational institutions representing a Community point of view and organized around the convergence of national interests are needed immediately, and that the ultimate goal should be a structure which, whether or not one calls it federal, will result in a more stable and cooperative continent than would be possible through the classical concert of Powers, because it would be based on more solid ties than those of a diplomatic or political character.

As this third Europe would be based on imperfect compromises between contradictory requirements, its various advocates must necessarily differ as to methods and priorities. In various Western European states, a school of thought which might be called "para-Gaullist or post-Gaullist Europeanists," or of "Europeanists with a Gaullist twist" and represented, as mentioned earlier, by Franz Joseph Strauss in Germany, Edward Heath in Britain, Valery Giscard d'Estaing in France, is emerging in favor of a Europe which would energetically pursue its independence in front of American economic and Soviet military might, but would do so by emphasizing technology and functional cooperation. Others, like Willy Brandt or Pietro Nenni, would work for a concept which would be less oriented toward the unity and cohesion of Western Europe and more toward the opening to the East and a European settlement.

Which, if any, of these two directions will prevail is impossible to predict today. Each of them would depend on broadly like-minded governments emerging in two or three of the crucial states. For the time being, the domestic uncertainties of post-devaluation France, of strike-ridden Italy, and the increasing doubts on the British domestic scene about the European orientation altogether, leave West Germany as the only really motivated state in either direction. The outlook seems rather for the continuation of bipolarity, with mild signs of dissatisfaction and feeble attempts at a united reaction among Western European states. For Eastern Europe, the outlook is for the continuation of Soviet rule and, at the same time, of Rumanian active diplomatic resistance, of Czechoslovak Soviet subordination and of Hungarian or Polish potential diffuse resistance. However, much will depend on the Superpowers themselves and on the character of their relationship.

A complete return to the cold war, with the Soviet Union apparently threatening Europe and the United States taking this threat as seriously as in Stalin's time, would cement the division, increase Eastern Europe's domination by the Soviet Union and Western Europe's solidarity with the United States, but not necessarily spur the Western Europeans' attempts at subregional unity. The "Straussian" direction of a Western Europe united and undertaking to defend itself would be most encouraged by the combination of a freeze in the East (the Soviet Union threatening the West, with Eastern Europe and in particular East Germany, inaccessible) and of American disengagement and/or agreement with the Soviet Union in the West. This is indeed the pattern which many trends of today seem to be foreshadowing, and which would be confirmed if, for instance, the Strategic Arms Limitation Talks were to lead to a reduction in the American strategic forces which are protecting Europe, and if this were to coincide with a reduction in the American troops which are stationed on the continent for the same purpose.

On the other hand, other trends, like post-Czechoslovak Soviet attempts at a new détente offensive in Europe, including West Germany as a target, combined with Western European reluctance to increase significantly their spending for defense, would seem to encourage the other, Brandt-type, direction. Indeed, one of the inspirations of the Soviet campaign in 1969-1970 for a European security conference may have been the attempt to prevent, after de Gaulle's departure, a too-powerful and united Western Europe and a "Strauss-type" orientation. But in order to succeed, this attempt must keep open, with a certain plausibility, something like an all-European perspective, and this in turn presupposes some kind of accommodation between the Soviet Union and Eastern Europe. But this, given the nature of the Soviet empire, seems to be the most difficult condition of all to fulfill.

Our analysis has mainly stressed the possible impact of Eastern developments over Western ones, rather than the other way around. This is so because, from a European point of view, the Western half has a much greater opportunity to react to the evolution of the Eastern half than vice versa. What happens between the Soviet Union and its satellites is something to which the West can react, which can be welcomed or deplored, but over which the West has little or no control. On the other hand, social, cultural, and technological processes travel from West to East rather than from East to West. What produces the tensions in Eastern Europe is that it is submitted to the broad indirect influences of the West but also to the brutal political and military actions and reactions of the Soviet Union.

This is what makes prediction about the influence of Western development on the East so much more delicate than the less decisive but more simple effects of Eastern developments on the West. Basically, two patterns of interaction between the developments of the two alliances or of the two Europes, West and East of the Elbe, have emerged and have been cited in this chapter to support either the integrationist or the nationalist line. The first is the pattern of contrast: the force and unity of one camp promotes the weakness and disunity of the other by depriving it of victories and by attracting its weaker elements. The other is the pattern of mimicry or of symmetry: integration in one camp produces integration in the other; relaxation or polycentrism in the first induces parallel phenomena in the second.

The reality seems to be that neither of these patterns is ever observable in its pure form because of the multiplicity of trends and of the strength of specific structures and developments which give a different meaning to superficially similar phenomena. However, it does seem that the influence of the East over the West tends rather to conform to the symmetry or mimicry pattern, while the impact of Western Europe on Eastern Europe tends more often to conform to the pattern of contrast. The evolutions of the East—détente, polycentrism, hardening, regrouping—tend to be followed, in more or less attenuated or delayed form, in the West, although the latter, due to the decisive factor of its own desire to be concerned with domestic affairs, is much more prone to follow hopeful trends toward relaxation than to return to a more militant posture when Soviet behavior would appear to justify it. In the East, there is a tendency to imitate developments which occur in the West (Khrushchev's attitude to the Common Market, and Rumania's imitation of France are cases in point), but this tendency very quickly provokes a counter-reaction which, more often than not, leads to re-establishment of the former situation only in a more tense or rigid form. Of course, in the long run, the result may still be imitation or convergence, but only through a much more chaotic and unpredictable succession of crises.

The two evolutions—one more discreet and leading to compromises, the other more brutal and leading to abrupt reversals—correspond to the two types of societies and of alliances: the Eastern international society tends toward "all or nothing" confrontations because the contradiction between trends and between interests is much more stark. In the West, while it is true that Europe becomes more Americanized every day, nonetheless France *can* withdraw militarily from NATO and the United States *can* be tempted by neo-isolationism. These contradictory trends are sufficiently moderate or limited as to be able to coexist with each other. There is enough diversity and there are enough ties for neither Americanization nor the isolation of France or of the United States, to be very likely to go to their logical extremes. In the East, the opposition between the general social trends and the interests of the Soviet rulers is so stark, that action and reaction, social change and violent opposition, are likely.

There seems little that the West can do to influence these relatively unpredictable developments in the East, except to avoid both provocation and indifference—a return to the cold war or being drawn into unconditional détente. With the Soviet rulers, Western Europeans must succeed in keeping contacts open with Eastern Europeans even when the Eastern Europeans are not free to make their own choices, and with the Soviet Union even when it tends to isolate itself. Along with the United States, the Western Europeans must make clear to the Soviet leaders that aggressive Soviet behavior cannot be pursued without a cost in East-West relations; that they cannot have both an isolated and tyrannically ruled Eastern Europe and a Western Europe which would permanently be weak, friendly, and passive.

Conversely, a Western Europe which would increase its strength and its unity yet remain open to self-transformation and accommodation if changes in the East make reconciliation possible, is the best contribution possible today to that long-range settlement of German, Central European, and European affairs at large which can only be brought about by fundamental changes in the Soviet Union, and in its actual or potential relations with the other Superpower. The German, Central European, European, and East-West problems can develop in different ways and be lived with in different degrees and at different costs; they can be solved—if at all—only together.

PART III

The Growth of Nationalistic Particularism in Central and Eastern Europe (Including the Balkans)

In the second century after Christ . . . , it is an anti-Christian polemicist, Celsus, who for the first time uses the term "Europeans" in a passage where he declares that it is impossible that "the Asians, the Europeans and Libyans, the Hellenes and the barbarians should ever agree to recognize one and the same law."

—*Denis de Rougemont*

INTRODUCTION

As pointed out in Part II, in terms of East-West relations, it appears that West Germany has gone about as far politically as it can to achieve its national objectives with the West. The major unresolved national concerns for the West Germans now incline them Eastward. Therefore, it is appropriate for us to consider the nature of the nationalisms which have evolved in Central and Eastern Europe in order to comprehend the future major thrust of the policies of the states of this area, and especially those of the two Germanies. The policies would, of course, be constrained by the increasingly complex and fluid rivalry of the Superpowers.

The major characteristic of Eastern Europe and the Balkans, in contrast to Western Europe, has been the extent of the domination of the ethnic minorities, or nationalities, of the subregion, by various imperial regimes and their consequent comparatively recent entry into world politics as national states. The nationalistic evolution of these states is quite different from those in Western Europe, and Germany has been different from both. One of the problems in regard to the relationship of the states (or nationalities) of Europe to the Superpowers is, as discussed in Part II, that they are at different stages of evolution toward their various nationalistic particularisms and toward forms of multinational cooperative arrangements which alter, if not compromise, their political independence.

The settlement of World War I gave a new or renewed lease on life to many of these politically "submerged" peoples. In this area, the Russians (or Slavs) and the Germans have, over the centuries, been rivals. With the bifurcation of Europe after World War II, the Russian domination was complete, and the Germans suffered the consequences of defeat. But as West Germany has prospered

132

and is finding a revived place in the international community, and especially in European international politics, and with the unsettled problems stemming from the failure of the Superpowers to achieve a lasting European settlement acceptable to both of them persisting, Eastern Europe and especially the Balkans might become more important in the 1970's than it had been in the 1950's or 1960's.

Furthermore, the movement of Soviet military and naval strength through the Dardanelles, around the "southern flank" of NATO into the Mediterranean, has created new security problems not only for the Atlantic Alliance, but also for those states in the Mediterranean littoral that may not want to be aligned with the West in terms of the cold war, but also may not want to come under direct Russian political pressures. Political developments in the Balkans can influence Russian political expansion into the Mediterranean.

Lastly, the growth of relationships within the Danube basin among states that have previously been ideologically at odds with each other, represents another dimension of flexibility for European—and especially Central and Eastern European—international politics. For instance, the Balkan Pact between Greece, Turkey, and Yugoslavia obviously cuts across ideological considerations. Also Greece has been encouraging trade and possibly later on, more formal political relations with the Soviet Union.

The final quarter of the twentieth century will witness much greater interactions among the nationalistic minority populations of this area, placing strains on the structure and operation of the political and territorial states that now exist. A contributing factor is that the peripheral Superpowers, the United States and the Soviet Union and perhaps later on China, will continue to seize opportunities to enhance their own interests at the others' expense with these small and weak states; in this sense these states can be both actors and objects of the rivalry of the Superpowers in this part of Europe.

WALDEMAR BESSON

5 The Contemporary West German National Outlook

The national states of Western Europe were the first of the modern nation-states. The national development of England and France can be traced back to the heritage of the Middle Ages. During the nineteenth century the national political evolution of these two states came to be identified with liberal democratic political principles which had developed in response to the dynamics of the Industrial Revolution. Germany, however, did not achieve this degree of national unification until 1871. Historically, the political unification of Germany has most often been seen as a struggle between Prussia and Austria to determine which German-speaking people would effect the unification of the various German-speaking entities. The goal, however, was not just to unify the disparate states of Germany. "Prussian policy under Bismarck was designed to further Prussian, not German interests and to safeguard Prussia's position as a great power . . ."[1]

Since the Congress of Vienna in 1815 the status quo of Germany was national fragmentation. Even at that time, to Austria and France, a non-unified Germany proved less of a threat than a unified Germany. More importantly, Prussia posed less of a threat to the rest of Europe as a particularist national entity than as the head of a unified German "nation." However, under Bismarck, Prussia set out to break this condition of German national fragmentation. Austria, on the other hand, hoped to restrain Prussia by upholding the principle of German nationalistic particularism. Ironically, most of the Germans advocating German unity looked to Austria for leadership, mainly as protection from potential Prussian domination.

[1] Geoffrey Barraclough, *The Origins of Modern Germany* (New York: Capricorn Books, 1963), p. 412.

Bismarck's policy was based on the political leadership of the Junker class in Prussia. The most serious threat to this conservative autocratic regime was the spread of liberal democratic doctrines throughout Europe from England eastward. During this period, nationalism had matured as a major political force in most of Europe, and had become identified with liberalism as a means of combating the conservative-monarchist forces in the Hapsburg and Ottoman Empires. (This is discussed in greater detail in the following chapter.)

Bismarck's success in unifying Germany was marked by his ability to separate nationalism and liberalism, using anti-Austrian nationalism to ultimately defeat the liberal forces in Prussia that posed the main threat to Junker supremacy and then going on to consolidate the other German Principalities under the Prussian monarchy. Ironically then, ". . . the curse of German particularism was expunged only by the triumph of the most successful of German particularisms, which had no intention of disowning its own particular origins and traditions."[2]

The issue of German particularism is especially relevant today in a Germany again disunited. Since 1871 the German people have had a tumultuous existence as a unified national entity and for the past twenty-five years they have had no such existence at all. Within West Germany today the question of particularisms has again arisen in the dispute about the German Federal Republic's future and whether the North German (or Prussian) influence of the Social Democrats under Chancellor Willy Brandt or the South German (or Bavarian) influence of the Christian Democrats under former Chancellor Kurt-Georg Keisinger and especially of Franz-Joseph Strauss, will be the paramount national influence in the future.

THE SPECIAL CIRCUMSTANCES OF THE BIRTH OF THE GERMAN FEDERAL REPUBLIC

The German Federal Republic (or West Germany) has now existed for over twenty years, and few would have predicted this in the late 1940's. It had been an artificial creation, born out of the rivalry of the Superpowers after the collapse of the Third Reich. The prediction of the first post-war German Chancellor, Dr. Kon-

[2] *Ibid.* p. 423.

rad Adenauer, that the rivalry would constantly deepen rather than be ameliorated has proven accurate during most of these years. In consequence, by aligning the future of the new German Republic with the West, and making it a political ward of the United States proved beneficial in hastening, at least for a part of the former Germany, a return of the German people to an active role in world affairs. Also, as Adenauer foretold, the restrictions imposed by the Western allies on the West Germans as a price for the gradual restoration of their sovereignty, have in turn gradually given way as the cold war demanded ever-closer cooperation between the reviving West Germany and its allies and neighbors.

Finally, by the 1960's, West Germany emerged as an equal and virtually sovereign partner in the Western alliance system (with only limited and specified exceptions); but this very achievement meant that the division of Germany into two halves had become more rigid and concretely evident. Nearly all physical movement between the two Germanies had ended with the building of the Berlin Wall in 1961, and political movement was stalemated until the advent of the "Grand Coalition" of the two major West German political parties—the Christian Democrats and the Social Democrats—in 1966.

Although some observers have implied that Chancellor Adenauer's policies were purely opportunistic, or that he was making a virtue out of necessity by aligning with the West, it is also true that he genuinely acted out of personal conviction. The creation of a liberal democratic Germany was consistent with his personal values and his earlier political career. For this reason, it would be inaccurate to regard the West German state as entirely a creature of events. Under Adenauer, although the West Germans' friends and enemies were defined in advance by virtue of the cold war, the German people had moved a long way on their own initiative in restoring themselves to a respected place in world affairs.

Furthermore, as the division of Europe persisted, the West Germans were able to share the vision of Jean Monnet in contemplating a smaller Europe in which former rivalries and hostilities could be muted to a larger integrated purpose. West Germany participated enthusiastically in the formation of the European Coal and Steel Community, the proposed and ill-fated European Defense Community, and the European Common Market. It was a healthy condition in that this participation enabled the West Germans to overcome a lost past with a new *realpolitik*—a national purpose of helping to maintain an equilibrium between an Atlantic approach to the formation of a new and smaller Europe in the West, and a more purely intra-European approach. West Germany had been very self-restrained about its nationalistic ambitions as it had willingly enmeshed itself in multi-lateral arrangements which enabled its Western neighbors to share in that restraint. The one basic disadvantage which this new national purpose had was that as these conditions gradually were realized— the duality of Atlanticism and Western Europeanism—the chances for German reunification were lessened. The hope for an early reuni-fication of the two separated parts of Germany which had been so much in the desires and official purposes of the West Germans in the early 1950's, would, as time passed, appear to be more an illusion than a concrete prospect.

The provisional nature of the West German Republic came to appear as a permanent new state in world politics, and in a sense this development might perhaps have helped to diminish the im-placable anti-German hostility of the Soviet Union, to whom the idea of a "ravanchist" and irridentist Germany was the worst fear of the Russian people. Such was not the case. The disadvantage of the Adenauer policies, as regards the Soviet Union, was that his strong pro-Western posture had left the Russians with little expec-tation of benefit for them from any agreements with the West that might have limited the Soviet presence in the eastern zone of Ger-many. Thus, only if the West emerged indisputably as the domi-nant force in Europe could the West Germans continue to benefit from a lasting affiliation in the Western "camp." When the Russians demonstrated through Sputnik that there was a strategic standoff between the Americans and themselves, thus ratifying to the world the existence of a mutual nuclear deterrent, then the West Germans began to wonder if they in fact could achieve through the Adenauer policies some accommodation with the Soviet Union that might lead toward reunification.

WEST GERMAN CHANGES IN OUTLOOK
AFTER SPUTNIK

A decade and a half after Sputnik, it had become apparent that West German opinion favored new policies toward Eastern

Europe and the Soviet Union, while at the same time not rejecting or even being evasive about continuing the former policies. It became clear to the West Germans, for example, that a "United States of Europe" was not then a possibility, nor was a single unified German state very likely. Furthermore, the crisis which arose in the Common Market after 1968 due to French economic difficulties threw the future evolution of these arrangements into doubt. How, then, the West Germans asked themselves, could they convert their eastern border from one of hostility to one of reconciliation through the old policies? How could the outpost of Berlin become something other than a hostage of the cold war?

When the Superpowers found themselves in an almost total strategic equilibrium, with neither of them capable of moving even a little bit without the danger of a nuclear confrontation, then the less powerful states were consequently encouraged to see the world in more flexible terms. This was the source of Charles de Gaulle's initiatives, which are being emulated by other states, as discussed in Part II. He created the basis for a new French influence in world affairs by bringing France back into Europe through the liquidation of the Algerian conflict and finally by turning France away from any lingering colonial aspirations. France did not possess the capability of a Great Power, but through the stalemate of the Superpowers during the Gaullist era it at least resembled greatness.

Détente became a popular keyword in the 1960's, but it did not mean, as some misguided persons in Germany thought, that the Superpowers would start to fraternize and create a world-wide diumvirate. Instead, it appeared that they would find a common pattern of national interaction: they could divide evenly what they might dispute according to the circumstances and their power relationship, thus deviating only in a measured fashion from the status quo established between them; and they could either neutralize contested areas where it would be unprofitable to do otherwise, or attempt to limit the scope of nationalistic ambitions of the newer states. There is no better example of this condition of détente than the Nuclear Non-Proliferation Treaty. Neither the Soviet Union nor the United States understood the Treaty in the spirit of President Roosevelt's "one world." This fact, plus the fundamental change in global international politics as a consequence of decolonization and the spread of new states, was only belatedly recognized in West German foreign policy. With the CDU-SPD Grand Coalition, West Germany departed from the Adenauer concepts and policies, and with the SPD-dominated government of Chancellor Willy Brandt, attempted to find a new national course.

CHARACTERISTICS OF CONTEMPORARY WEST GERMAN NATIONAL INTERESTS

Thus, at present, we can perceive several leading characteristics of any calculation of contemporary West German national interests with which West Germany must deal if internal political stability and external political confidence is to be retained. One of the consequences of a breakdown on both counts could be a strengthening of the place in West German national life of those Germans who view liberal democracy with disinterest, if not with enmity.

A primary characteristic is, of course, the American attitude toward West Germany. West Germany can be politically strong in Western Europe only if it is subsumed into an American hegemony. Without the American presence, the West Germans would find themselves much more constricted in what they could do in foreign affairs because of the fears of their neighbors. Furthermore, stemming from the constitutional foundations of the Federal Republic, the United States in turn is not yet willing to surrender its World War II "rights" in either West Berlin or in the former Western occupation zones as combined into the Federal Republic. In these ways, Bonn is still dependent on Washington. But at the same time, with the Superpowers in nuclear stalemate, the West Germans are experiencing a desire for more independent and national policies. The central question therefore is: how can the unavoidable recognition of United States influence over the politics of Western Europe be combined with West Germany's quest for a greater sphere of independent political movement? The price of American military protection has been political obedience, which may well become even higher as the United States finds itself faced with greater demands on its political and material resources from other parts of the world. Or, if there is a significant lessening of the American military presence in Western Europe, political strains might develop between the United States and West Germany which might have undesirable political consequences for both Powers as they pursue parallel but not necessarily identical policies vis-à-vis the Soviet Union, Eastern Europe and the Balkans.

No West German should lament too much about the influence of the United States now that the occupation of Czechoslovakia by the Soviet Union, and the Soviet thrust into the Mediterranean area have reminded Western Europeans of the practical value of the American security "umbrella." It is difficult to see how the West Germans can follow the Gaullist path as long as they are not willing to accept the status quo of Europe imposed by the Superpowers and thus create a measure of reconciliation with the Soviet Union. Only if such were to happen, as unpopular as it might be to many West Germans, could West Germany seriously contemplate adopting policies which would bring greater independence from the United States. The degree of West German dependence on the United States might decrease under these circumstances. It goes without saying that this would be a Copernican revolution in West German foreign policy.

But at the very least, West German leadership can contribute to the reformation of the relations between the United States and Western Europe from within the NATO framework. This is a task of the first order for West German policy. NATO no longer exists in the same milieu as was true in 1949, when the states of Western Europe were weak recipients of American aid and protection from a threatening Soviet Union. Today, greater Western European and West German independence are necessary, not only because the conditions in Western Europe are vastly different, but also because America's conduct in world affairs shows evidence of a reordering of national priorities. The dangerous entanglement in Vietnam has challenged all previous United States global priorities.

In addition, the weight of unsolved domestic problems may diminish even further the political will, as well as the resources available, for the United States to continue to play an activist role everywhere in the world. President Richard Nixon's comprehensive foreign policy statement of February 1970 presaged a "low profile" for the United States internationally, and especially in such areas as Eastern Europe and the Balkans. In the light of these changes, it is small wonder that many Western European and West German political leaders have been tempted to devalue the Atlantic Alliance and its organizational hierarchy. In other words, the demand for an independent and more powerful Western Europe has become louder and louder as the American domestic and international posture has shifted. To meet these new needs, the United States has been tempted to ask for greater support in Europe from its Western European allies.

This situation leads us to an examination of the West German approach to Western Europe. Within post-war Europe, West Germany has created a firm place. It has contributed to the political and economic reconstruction of Western Europe, and has supported the various multilateral incentives which have arisen, from NATO through EEC. West Germany has become an equal among equals; this is not true when any of the Western European states contemplate their relations with the United States. In this sense, there is a natural affinity among the Western Europeans vis-à-vis the Americans, which is why the idea of a united Europe acting as a complement to the United States has been so attractive.

Such a united Europe would only be possible, however, if Great Britain were included. But to permit Britain into the Common Market—the best avenue that now exists toward a united Europe—it would be necessary to revise the integrative concept of the Market. The resistance of France to the inclusion of Britain and the changes in Market arrangements (especially in agriculture) brought on by France's devaluation, have given rise to the possibility that forms of Western European subregionalism other than those contemplated by Chancellor Adenauer and the other framers of the Treaty of Rome might be more suitable. Today it appears that a number of different methods and multinational institutions are necessary to do justice to the multitude and complexity of inter-state relations that have grown up in Western Europe. Furthermore, new approaches could help to create that intensity and variety of contacts which alone would allow the Western Europeans to maintain a strong— and strongly self-identifiable—position between the Superpowers. The more pragmatic that West German policies are in this respect, the less possible it will be for West Germany to cling to the dogma that Western European separate national interests are identical with the interests of the bureaucratic establishment of the European Communities. For example, greater pragmatism for West Germany might facilitate new relationships with those states in Western Europe and in the Baltic area which are not members of the Communities.

This change in West German outlook toward Western Europe appears more necessary since it became obvious that it was not just de Gaulle's personal predilections and prejudices that stopped progress toward Western European political union. Gaullism continued to influence the European scene even after de Gaulle. President Georges Pompidou certainly will not return to the Europeanism of the 1950's; the compelling attraction of Gaullism has been and continues to be its proclamation of a will to preserve the historic states of Europe and their national identities. Economic integration has, as the EEC shows, not eliminated the hard core of national substance among the member states. This does not, however, exclude new levels and modes of international cooperation. The nation-state has indeed been most flexible. We are not beyond it, but rather in a new phase of its development.

Furthermore, multiplicity in the forms of cooperation among the states of Western Europe could avoid the primary danger to the Germans inherent in Western European subregionalism. At times since World War II we have heard echoes of an earlier European nationalism—a reborn European giant rising in the western half of Europe between the peripheral giants—in which the Germans could participate again in true greatness. Quite apart from the fact that this new European concept presupposes a truly supranational state in Western Europe, the chances of which are nil since neither France nor Britain nor in fact anyone else in Western Europe really wants it, the Soviet Union would not in any case tolerate such a new monolithic force in Europe. For one thing, such a force, in which territorially non-saturated West Germans would be actively enmeshed, would be seen by the Russians as a dire threat to them. Instead of enabling the West Germans to find ways of reconciling themselves to the Russians and their other neighbors to the East, a strong unitary Western Europe would thus encumber West Germany's chances to accomplish this.

This is the reason why West Germany cannot commit itself completely to a unified, integrated Western Europe even if Western European enthusiasm were strong for it; on the other hand, the enthusiasm for West German participation can never be whole-hearted as long as West Germany refuses to accept the status quo. The attempts by West Germany during 1970 to reassure the Soviet Union and Poland about West Germany's territorial claims concerning the Oder-Neisse, and to strike a political modus vivendi with East Germany, helped to reassure the states of Eastern Europe and the Balkans about West Germany's "revisionist" tendencies, but at the same time they created tensions with West Germany's Western neighbors, and especially with the United States. Nonetheless, the most obvious difference between the West Germans and their neighbors in the West, which remains muted as long as the Soviet Union and the United States stand glaring at each other in a divided Europe and a divided Germany, is their different attitude toward the status quo. It is inconceivable that the French, the Italians, and the Benelux peoples would enter a political union in which they would have to give up their national identities as long as the West Germans would continue, even if only verbally, their quest for a fundamental change in the European scene that would lead to a reunified Germany and a rearrangement possibly of Germany's eastern frontiers.

This leads us to another characteristic of contemporary West German national interests, which is geopolitical in nature. The Germans are in the center of Europe, in spite of many Germans having forgotten this during the Adenauer period of the 1950's. The facts of territorial location and national tradition impose on the West Germans the duty of attempting to find a reconciliation with the states in Eastern Europe and the Balkans. The search for a reconciliation must continue even if it seems a bitter pill for the Germans. The Grand Coalition in Bonn had this goal in mind even while not removing the greatest obstacle, which would have required the renunciation of any West German claims that would change the territorial status quo in Eastern Europe. Moreover, the West German, and especially the Social Democratic Party's, desire for reconciliation cannot ignore the Russian presence in Eastern Europe and the Balkans. The dilemma for West Germany is that as long as its Eastern neighbors are dominated by an anti-German Soviet Union, West Germany cannot move to extricate itself from the West for fear that the Soviet Union might move to extend its influence over them as well. And the Soviet Union will not alter its suspicion of West Germany as long as West Germany would not recognize the Oder-Neisse Line and possibly also the German Democratic Republic (East Germany).

The role which the Eastern European states are willing to play in this situation has become very important. As is well known, they strive for greater independence from Moscow's imperium; Eastern Europe also has had its variant of Gaullism. As a consequence, there is a tendency to visualize a reconstruction of a "cordon sanitaire" of more or less neutral states in Eastern Europe which would protect the Soviet Union from an invasion from the West. But such a concept should not lead us into the wrong conclusions. A new "cordon sanitaire" could not possibly result in any loosening of the connection of the states in the Warsaw Pact with the Soviet Union. Any attempt would be foolish and without a chance of success. It seems possible, however, to contemplate some degree of greater national autonomy in Eastern Europe that would lessen Soviet influence and thus would decrease Soviet military pressure on the West German borders. We only need recall how nervous the West Germans became after the Czechoslovak crisis of August 1968, when Soviet armed forces massed at the West German frontiers, to realize how much West Germany would prefer sharing a border with a Czechoslovakia which is unoccupied even if it remained in the Warsaw Pact. It is certainly not for the West Germans to decide if this is possible, but they could contribute to the independent inclinations of the East European and Balkan states by acknowledging the status quo of their borders.

THE REQUIREMENTS FOR A SUCCESSFUL WEST GERMAN "EASTERN POLICY"

By looking eastward in a conciliatory fashion, West Germany would be following a great German historical tradition; Central and Eastern Europe have long been a field of legitimate German national ambition. For example, the West Germans learned in 1968 with surprise how much they were a part of the events that took place in Prague. Furthermore, it is not merely an idle historical reflection to observe that the German language still plays a role in Eastern Europe that it plays nowhere else any more in the world.

West Germans have only recently begun to notice this historical tradition.

Increasing West German activity in Central and Eastern Europe, however, must not arouse even the smallest suspicion of new German hegemonial aspirations. This area has had to endure for centuries the rivalry of the Russians and the Germans. The Germans have decisively lost the competition and for that very reason, if tactfully handled, they can now establish less biased and strained relationships with the states in the area. A secondary but nonetheless important beneficial result might be a lessening of Soviet hostility toward West Germany.

Such a policy on the part of West Germany would require a re-examination of West Germany's attitude toward East Germany. It is clear that East Germany remains today under the domination of the Soviet Union, even while at times strongly influencing Soviet policy toward Europe. It will continue in this situation as long as the Soviet Union is a World Power or until some other state can offer the Soviets a redeeming prize. No state, however, is capable of offering this, and least of all West Germany. In this respect, post-World War II West German foreign policy would appear to have reached a dead end unless the two Germanies can each become more independent of their respective Superpower even while they grow closer politically to each other.

Chancellor Willy Brandt's formula of an ordered coexistence between the two German states *(geregeltes Nebeneinander),* however, could provide a possible new direction. It might enable the Germans, among themselves, to de-emphasize the legalistic aspects surrounding the creation of the two states in favor of more de facto considerations. The question of the formal recognition of East Germany by West Germany has been blown up out of proportion to the true interests of both states. If coexistence without legal recognition is possible, so much the better, for any compromise on legalistic grounds can encourage a greater degree of partnership. We should note, however, that as long as the present leader of East Germany, Walter Ulbricht, opposes coexistence, formal recognition by Bonn of the Pankow government would not be useful and perhaps might be dangerous since it might create pressures within West Germany for concrete evidences of a reconciliation or for reunification. The negotiations between Chancellor Brandt and East German Prime

Minister Willi Stoph in 1970 only served to underscore how difficult it is for the two states to move toward political reconciliation.

In any event, any projected larger West German reconciliation with Eastern Europe and the Soviet Union would have to include a change in West Germany's attitude toward East Germany. As long as West Germany would deny East Germany any secured international status, the security needs of East Germany would never be fulfilled. It would have little choice but to remain firmly dependent on the Soviet Union. But the leadership of East Germany cannot reject permanently the Gaullist tendencies appearing all around them in Eastern Europe. The real question is: how can the West Germans help the East Germans to diminish their dependency on the Soviet Union and thereby help to improve the standards and quality of life of all Germans? As long as West Germany viewed the East German regime as an enemy state, there was little chance that the East Germans would want to free themselves of the continual massive presence of Soviet troops at the Elbe. In other words, West Germans, as Chancellor Brandt has tried to show in his conciliatory posture toward Eastern Europe and the Balkans as well as toward East Germany, must accept the Communists of East Germany as being also Germans.

By taking this attitude, West Germany would be working constructively with the status quo rather than protesting against it. To relinquish hopeless positions in world politics sometimes wins a new freedom for initiative and action. The West Germans, of course, have had to re-evaluate the notion of reunification. A union of West Germany and East Germany is not possible today. But this does not require either side to wait until other forces bring about a change in the post-World War II European international political situation. No status quo is ever final, just as it would do little good for the West Germans to wait for a miracle—i.e., a change in Soviet sentiment— as long as West Germany would not recognize the Oder-Neisse Line. Of course, if the Soviet Union should no longer be a Superpower, many conditions would change. But that is not likely in the foreseeable future. And even if this did occur, would the West Germans automatically find themselves in an improved situation?

The danger in not acceding to the present European status quo has been that the cultural traditions of the German nation, as viewed historically, might be lost; the present political division of the German people could result in neglect of the common German cultural heritage built up over a thousand years. It should be recalled that although the German people have experienced many territorial re-arrangements ever since tribal times, their cultural homogeneity has survived and flourished.

Central Europe has been, over the centuries, a bridge between the Eastern and Western aspects of European civilization because of the territorial variety, yet cultural homogeneity of the German peoples in this region. A united German state with aggressive territorial aspirations, as Bismarck so wisely recognized, defeats this purpose. When his successors refused to accept the definitions of the Reich created by Bismarck, they threw away the chance for a unitary German national state to survive in Central Europe. It would appear that today public opinion in West Germany is prepared to accept this reality.

WEST GERMANY AND THE THIRD WORLD

A final characteristic of contemporary West German national interests is its role vis-à-vis the third world. The final quarter of the twentieth century will witness greater conflict between the industrial "have" states of the Northern Hemisphere and the non-industrial "have-not" states of the Southern Hemisphere. This conflict could challenge the post-World War II international system more fundamentally than would a divided Europe lying under the balance of nuclear terror of the Superpowers. West Germany might find a constructive new national outlet by directing its resources in manpower and in material goods to assist in the national development of the new states. This would be a challenge that is universal, and which President John F. Kennedy was the first Western political leader to comprehend.

But today in West Germany foreign aid still depends on the amount which appears available from year to year in the budget, much of which is used in attempts to prevent by means of subventions the recognition of East Germany by the newly independent states. By changing the attitude of their government toward foreign aid, and by taking the lead in creating a new spirit of economic interdependence between primary and secondary Powers, the people of

West Germany could play a constructive role in world affairs. An obvious advantage for West Germany, in contrast to its neighbors, is the absence of an immediate German colonial tradition.

A derivative benefit for West Germany from this new dimension of German national purpose would be its greater acceptance at the United Nations; also, through the fund of goodwill which could be built up among the secondary Powers, a new form of worldwide solidarity could be formed within the oversized shadow of the Superpowers. It is not sufficient to perceive an exclusively West German national interest; a dynamic attitude toward the non-European world could create new national attitudes within West Germany that could bring long-lasting security ties in Central and Eastern Europe. In other words, the German people could find their destiny by looking forward and outward from Europe as well as by looking backward and inward toward Europe. We must recognize that from 1945, the world irrevocably entered a new epoque; for Germans especially, the past should be seen only as nostalgia or as teaching unpleasant lessons.

In summary, Chancellor Adenauer's policies possessed an ingenious simplicity in that he abandoned German national rights to the West which he did not possess anyhow, in order to gain some of them back. Now it would be appropriate to build on this new national foundation by turning away from the anti-Communist foreign policy formulas of the 1950's. The Adenauer era left West Germany with the heritage of a close connection with the United States and with a new concept of partnership within Western Europe. From this, in the near future, West Germany has undertaken the more difficult task of reconciliation with the Soviet Union and with the states of Eastern Europe. An essential ingredient in any form of reconciliation must be a realistic plan for peace between the two German states. Looking further into the future, West Germany can, within a secure Europe, play a leading role in closing the development gap between the "have" and "have-not" states. West Germany's clinging to the supposed security of political and ideological immobility might prove to be its greatest mistake, for there is no question that the German people are already back in the mainstream of world politics: the only question is whether they will be able to steer an effective course in it.

VIKTOR MEIER

6 Nationalistic Interests in the Balkans and Eastern Mediterranean

No educated Western European would deny nowadays the fact that the area between Vienna and the Black Sea, including Turkey and Greece, is a definite part of Europe. However, this truth was not always generally recognized and even now many Europeans find it difficult to relate properly to these lands, and are reluctant to consider them as belonging to their world. For the purpose of this chapter, we shall call this area the Balkans and Eastern Mediterranean subregion, or Southeastern Europe.

THE AWAKENING AND GROWTH OF NATIONAL STATES IN THE SUBREGION

On the threshold between the eighteenth and nineteenth centuries, Southeastern Europe was firmly divided between the Austro-Hungarian and the Ottoman Empires. Soon, however, three new important influences appeared in this part of Europe. First, in connection with the Napoleanic wars, liberal democratic ideas became more widespread. Second, the influence of imperial Russia was spreading; for example, the Russians started to act as a patron or protector of all the Christian subjects in the Turkish Empire. In reality, the Russians were not so much interested in these Christian peoples as they were in the control of the Straits of Istanbul, which is the passage from the Black Sea to the Mediterranean. Third, the nationalities themselves of Southeastern Europe began to assert nationalistic ambitions. They "awakened from their death-like sleep" as one

Rumanian patriotic song of that time so aptly described it. They wanted to become independent and to form their own national states again.

Even today historians of the West tend to underestimate the political strength developed by these nationalities in their process of political emancipation. Very often, as earlier in this century, the national aspirations of Serbia have been explained as arising merely at the instigation of Russia, while Bulgaria or Montenegro have been labelled simply as Russian creations. Modern Rumanian nationalism has at times been regarded as a creation of France, and the founding of the modern Greek state has been attributed more to the Great Powers and to the Philhellenes than to the Greeks themselves.

Of course one cannot deny the influences of the outside world, and especially those influences from the strong national states of Western Europe, on the movement of national awakening in the Balkans and Eastern Mediterranean subregion. But it is obvious that the groundwork for this movement had to come from the peoples that lived in the area. They had their traditions which were often preserved by their churches, or as in Serbia by epic folk songs. Each of these nationalities had its own point of departure and its own individual historical development; and each arrived by a different road at its present form of national existence. This is why history plays such an important role in European politics even today.

INTERNAL COHESION OF
SOUTHEASTERN EUROPE

The attempts to create a system of collaboration between the nationalities, or ethnic groups, of Southeastern Europe originated with the emergence of national states out of former large multinational empires. In general, these nationalities attempted to work together to prevent the Great Powers from exercising influence in the Balkans and Eastern Mediterranean area, and to establish an international political equilibrium among themselves. These attempts have more often than not failed because Southeastern Europe has never been a unity; it has always somehow been divided.

The first Balkan alliance was the one founded by Prince Mihailo of Serbia around 1860. It aimed at the expulsion of the Turks from the Balkans. It did not work because the Balkan states were too weak. In contrast, the second such alliance, the Balkan League of 1912, was successful. It even eliminated for a short period the influence of the Great Powers (Austria and Russia) in Southeastern Europe. However, immediately afterwards the victorious Balkan allies fought each other over their territorial gains, and in World War I the battle lines cut across the entire Balkan area.

Between the two World Wars, Czechoslovakia, Yugoslavia, and Rumania—the main territorial beneficiaries of the collapse of the Hapsburg Empire—tried to establish a new internal balance in Southeastern Europe, but it was much more of an alliance of victorious Balkan states with the aim of keeping down the defeated Balkan states—that is, Austria and Hungary—than the representation of a new order. The Little Entente, as the alliance of victors was called, was never able to normalize its relations with the defeated states, and therefore the opportunity was opened up to the aggressive dictatorships of Italy and Germany as neighboring Great Powers to dominate the area. A similar development occurred with the Balkan League of 1934, between Turkey, Yugoslavia, Rumania, and Greece, which was reduced, perhaps against its will, to an instrument aimed at repressing Bulgaria.

The Communist and Socialist movements of the Balkans saw the dangers of "micro-imperialism" in these newly-founded national states. They tried to advocate the principle of federation as an alternative to nationalistic fragmentation. Svetozar Markovic advanced the idea of a "Balkan Federation," but since nationalism was already firmly established as the dominant political force in this area, the federation idea did not gain acceptance, and instead did more to bring the Socialists into political isolation than it did to help them win popular support. After World War II, Tito tried to revive the idea of the Balkan Federation, but for him this represented only a tactical maneuver to extend his personal influence and that of Yugoslavia to the whole Southeastern European subregion. His attempts failed because of Stalin's intervention.

The independent policy of Yugoslavia during the Stalin era, however, was very important for the whole future political structure of the Balkans. As long as Yugoslavia was under strong Soviet pressure it had to align itself rather closely with the West, but after 1955, when Khrushchev and Tito tried to settle their differences, Yugoslavia again tried to take an active interest in the political development of the Communist world. These attempts were curbed, however, after the Hungarian revolution of 1956.

THE POSSIBILITIES FOR COHESION IN THE BALKANS AND EASTERN MEDITERRANEAN SUBREGION

We might therefore safely say that the cohesion, and therefore the possibilities for reciprocal collaboration inside the area of Southeastern Europe are rather limited, and should by no means be overestimated. Each of these states is looking in a different direction and each has different aspirations. For example, most of them have never hesitated to mobilize a Great Power against a neighbor. Interest in the problems and achievements of a neighbor is not strong in any of the states, and the existence of national or ethnic minorities within them has created additional problems. A sense of Balkan "togetherness" has never developed. "The Balkans," on the contrary, has almost always been regarded as a condition to escape from, generally toward the center of Europe. The principles put forward today by Rumania can be characterized perhaps as the only ones which are workable, and in the long run able to give the Southeastern European subregion a certain political stability even if on the basis of purely national states. The Rumanians have limited themselves to the proclamation of the principles of friendly neighborliness, practical cooperation, non-interference in internal affairs, and recognition of sovereignty and of existing borders. It remains to be seen, however, whether Rumania will be able to carry on with these policies.

It may be that, after the 1968 invasion of Czechoslovakia and in view of the extremely strong pressures of the Soviet Union to stifle all tendencies toward political independence in the satellite area, it is hopeless to speak about "reunification" of Eastern and Western Europe, which would include establishing again the extremely close relationship which existed before the Communist takeover between the states involved and Central Europe. The invitation extended to President Nixon by the leaders of Rumania would seem to indicate that the concept of a sort of a European entity standing between the two Superpowers is dead and no longer represents a realistic alternative to the two European blocs, each dominated by a Superpower. However, there are axioms which, in the long run, may affirm themselves in spite of all efforts to the contrary. One of these axioms is the right of every state to determine its own destiny; the second is the deep-rooted sense of "togetherness" inside the larger European world. If it was possible to close the gap between the Western part of Europe and the states of the former Byzantine orbit, it might be assumed that eventually the Iron Curtain, too, might be removed in one way or another.

Thus the Balkans and Eastern Mediterranean subregion may provide the best opportunity for all the areas lying astride the East and the West for "bridge-building," because in contrast to Central Europe, the Balkans are not so much incorporated into the overall confrontation between the two Superpowers. Bridge building, however, can mean different things and can bring on serious dilemmas. It would be foolish if the Western European states, for instance, would abandon or even loosen their alliance with the United States in order to obtain concessions from the Soviet Union leading toward the creation of a European entity comprising both Communist and non-Communist states. The Soviet Union showed in Czechoslovakia that they have not the slightest interest in such a combination.

Another question is whether European bridge-building should be concentrated primarily on the Soviet Union, or on the so-called satellite states. President de Gaulle tried both and failed in both. Today, West Germany shows a tendency to repeat the Gaullist example and is pursuing an active "eastern" foreign policy, perhaps on a more realistic basis because there are German interests which really dictate an accommodation with the Soviet Union. But the West Germans may be holding illusions in regard to what the Soviet Union would be willing to offer in return for Bonn's advances. The French and West German experience shows that Soviet influence over the satellites of Southeastern Europe is sufficient to make it necessary that all approaches to the states in the area must take into account Russian interests.

We should, therefore, examine not only the efforts at mutual cooperation among these states, and their various experiences at the hands of outside Great Powers; we also need to see how each of the states of this area evolved politically according to the unique circumstances of the nationalities involved.

YUGOSLAVIA. Yugoslavia, as the common state of the South Slavs, is not just the outcome of the exceptional conditions in 1918. It is the result of an historical process of almost 100 years by which two peoples, the Serbs and the Croats, were driven together, partially by their own will and partially by circumstances. In language and ethnic background they are closely related, but in religion, history, and culture, they are far apart: the Serbs belonging to the Eastern, formerly Byzantine, orbit and the Croats being formed by the Western background of Austria-Hungary. Yugoslavia therefore is not only a multinational state, but a multi-cultural state, composed almost equally of peoples belonging to either side of the old Rome-Byzantium line of division running through Southeastern Europe. Thus it is not at all surprising that Yugoslavia is still searching for a suitable form of internal political organization.

The so-called "Yugoslavian process" which brought Yugoslavia into existence was mainly the affair of the Serbs and the Croats alone. The Slovenes did not originally participate. Almost until the end of World War I, they conceived of their national existence in a federated Hapsburg Monarchy, in which they could have found national security without being exposed to Balkanization. In 1917, only when all hope for such a reorganization of Austria-Hungary was gone, did they accept the Yugoslavian idea. On the other hand, the Macedonians had historically belonged to the Bulgarian national sphere, and were pushed into Yugoslavia only by the European political and nationality complications of the aftermath of World War I. Even the process of rapprochement between Serbs and Croats was by no means simple and harmonious. On the contrary, these two nationalities each began from different premises and each had a very different concept of the Yugoslav idea.

Serbia departed from a mere concept of statehood. After an unsuccessful revolution initiated in 1804 by Karadjordje, it gained autonomy from the Turks in 1815 by the skillful and realistic political maneuvering of Milos Obrenovic, aimed at a direct accommodation with the Turks. It was a rather precarious basis for independence, but it worked.

The original weakness and insecurity of the new Serbian statehood, however, brought the leaders of the country to the firm belief that in the long run Serbia had to be enlarged into a powerful and strong state because otherwise it would not be able to survive on this central and exposed geographical location in the midst of the Balkans.

The wish to become a great and powerful state kept Serbian opinion always open toward unification with the Croats, while on the other hand, the Yugoslav trends in Croatia prevented Serbia, sometimes against the willingness of its leaders, to contain themselves to the mere consolidation of the Principality, and later Kingdom, of Serbia.

The national exclusivism in Croatia had been politically put aside in 1905, by the purely political Yugoslavism of the "Croatian-Serbian Coalition." This movement came from Dalmatia and was initiated by Frano Supilo, later the chairman during World War I of the Yugoslav Committee in London. The coalition was created in Dalmatia in order to take political power away from the then dominant Italian minority. Afterwards the representatives of the new movement sought to achieve the same goals in Croatia against the Hungarians, and for the first time, a collaboration was established with the responsible leaders in the Kingdom of Serbia, with the long-range aim to break away from the Monarchy and to unite with Serbia.

However, in the negotiations during World War I between the government of Serbia with Nikola Pasic as its head and the Yugoslav Committee in London with Frano Supilo, the fundamental differences between the Serbian and the Croatian conception of the Yugoslav state became clearly evident. Serbia wanted the continuity of its kingdom and the incorporation of the Croatian and Slovenian lands into the already existing state which would then simply change its name. Supilo on the other side insisted on the recognition of a Croatian statehood, and conceived Yugoslavia as a dualistic, later even federalistic, state.

Contrary to the beliefs of some extremists in Serbia as well as in Croatia, the failure of the first Yugoslavia in World War II was by no means the collapse of the Yugoslav idea. The Communist partisans under Josip Broz Tito won the civil war against the nationalistic opponents in Croatia, Serbia, and Slovenia, not because they were Communists, but because they were Yugoslavists. They were able to operate on an all-Yugoslav basis, and to attract all those country-siders and populations which were traditionally in favor of a common Yugoslav state or were, as the Serbian minority in Croatia, driven by circumstances to a Yugoslav position.

The Communists founded the new Yugoslavia as a federal state of six Republics, and within Serbia, two autonomous Regions. This federalism might first have been only on paper, but in later years it had become a reality. The Communists avoided many mistakes from the pre-war period, but they committed others. For years they limited the standard of living and the economic development in the more advanced Republics of Croatia and Slovenia in favor of the poorer Republics to the south. Secondly, they persisted too long in a strong centralistic leadership.

In 1965 and 1966, all these elements brought Croatia and Slovenia dangerously close to a real political autonomism which did not subside even when Alexander Rankovic who was the presumptive heir of Tito, was finally deposed. The national agitation among the peoples of Yugoslavia simmered down only after the Soviet invasion of Czechoslovakia in August 1968, when Yugoslavia felt threatened, too. The economic reforms, greater political liberalization and progressive federalization which Tito encouraged were additional elements in helping to stabilize conditions in Yugoslavia. Dr. Vladimir Bakaric, the Communist leader of Croatia, may be considered to be a main contributor to this healthy and positive development.

In summary, Yugoslavia, as a multinational state in a strategically important position in the center of the Balkans, contains in its borders many of the problems which are in fact common to the whole subregion of Southeastern Europe. It has to struggle anew every day for internal balance and internal cohesion. If it succeeds, Yugoslavia will certainly have made a big contribution to the stability of the whole area, especially if this consolidation can take place under the banner of national independence and non-interference from outside. Because of its independent position, Yugoslavia can exercise its political influence both in the Communist and in the non-Communist world, and thereby provide an important link between the two parts of Europe.

RUMANIA. After the incorporation of Transylvania in 1918, Rumania, like Yugoslavia, became a state with territory on both sides of the historical line of division through Southeastern Europe. However, the main weight of the Rumanian state is definitely East of the Carpathes, and in contrast to Yugoslavia, Rumania is not a multinational state but a national state, with minorities.

Modern Rumanian nationalism, however, originated not in the center of the Rumanian lands, but in Transylvania, at the end of the eighteenth century. It was there that the Rumanian church fought for equality, and because the ancient Hungarian kingdom was structured according to the concept of "nations," the struggle for equality meant struggle for the recognition of a Rumanian nation. It was only after the Napoleonic Wars that Rumanian national consciousness became a real factor in the two old Rumanian Principalities, Moldavia and Wallachia. They helped to organize the resistance against the attempts of Russian domination, and they promoted the process of the unification of the two Principalities into a modern Rumanian state, which became a reality in 1862 after the Crimean War, in which France and England defeated Russia.

Both the intensity of Rumanian nationalism and the centralism in the administrative system proved very helpful when, in 1918, Transylvania had to be assimilated. However, nationalism and centralism also alienated the national minorities. Perhaps even more importantly, they proved to be a major obstacle for the establishment of a workable democratic system of government in Rumania. Between the World Wars, the economic crisis of 1929 and 1930 was sufficient to eliminate the two main political forces who were more or less determined to function on the basis of a real democracy: the Liberals and the Peasant Party. Under the banner of "Rumanian patriotism" and with slogans like "all for the fatherland," the nationalistic Right was able to take over the state almost without opposition. The principle of guided and planned economic development was introduced into Rumanian national life at that time.

Therefore, we might assume that the rigidity of the present Communist system, and the obvious lack of democratic freedoms are perhaps not so much the result of a particularly repressive policy by the present Communist regime, but to a certain extent is inherent in Rumanian traditions, and due to the fact that there just does not seem to be any place for political ideologies that would oppose the aspirations of the present regime. As before the war, the lack of true internal democracy is compensated by a positive European orientation of Rumania's foreign policy. Taking into account all the circumstances, it seems fair to say that the present regime is following the same basic principles in its foreign policy as did the well-known Rumanian Minister for Foreign Affairs in the 1920's and early 1930's, Nicolas Titulescu.

BULGARIA. Modern Bulgaria has an unhappy history, perhaps the most unhappy of all the Balkan states. Since the Bulgarians have lived close to the center of Turkish power, all their uprisings in the nineteenth century failed, and they finally had to be liberated by the Russians in 1877. The Russians, therefore, in the eyes of most Bulgarians, are still the liberators. But even more, the Russians, in the

Treaty of San Stefano concluded with Turkey in the year of the liberation, planned the establishment of a "Great Bulgaria" including Macedonia, and Thracia as far as the Aegean Sea. Russia intended to make this "Greater Bulgaria" its stronghold for the domination of the Balkans and the Straits, instead of Serbia which, as we have noted, was very reluctant to play the role of a Russian tool. By the Congress of Berlin in 1878, the Western Great Powers prevented the realization of these Russian intentions. The borders of San Stefano, however, remained like a mirage on the horizon of Bulgarian national thought and aspirations. From an historical point of view, perhaps not everything in the program of San Stefano was unjustified, but its aspirations were too high for a latecomer on the Balkan scene. They could not be achieved: they hindered internal consolidation and prevented peaceful relations with Bulgaria's neighbors.

We must recognize, however, that there have been many serious attempts in modern Bulgarian history to correct this situation, and to get away both from the Russian influence as well as from irredentism. Alexander of Battenberg, the first Prince who was installed in Bulgaria by the Great Powers, already tried to steer the state on a more balanced political course. In the long run, of course, it did not prove very helpful when the Bulgarians tried to substitute Germany for Russia as the Great Power that would realize their national aspirations. After 1903, when the failure of a great Macedonian uprising against the Turks drove thousands of members of the Macedonian revolutionary organization (IMRO) into Bulgaria, and into the ranks of the Bulgarian army and administration, these irredentistic elements were able to terrorize for more than thirty years all those Bulgarian parties and leaders who favored a realistic approach toward the state's fundamental problems. In 1923 they liquidated the government of the Agrarian Party headed by Stamboliski. In 1934, a similar attempt to normalize conditions inside the state and in its foreign relations, undertaken by a group of officers called "Zveno," was prevented from succeeding by conservative and narrowly nationalistic political elements. Bulgaria remained on the road of revanchism and irredentism, and therefore allied itself with Germany in World War II, coming out as a totally defeated state with completely destroyed self-confidence.

The Communist party of Bulgaria that took over the state also had some factions that did not like the idea of total subservience to the

Soviet Union. Georgi Dimitrov, former Secretary of the Comintern, was largely under the influence of Marshall Tito and thought that a sort of Balkan alliance could provide the instrument for at least a limited independence, and the regaining of national self-confidence. Premier Stalin defeated this attempt in 1948, ironically with the help of other nationalistically-minded Bulgarian Communists who took exception to Dimitrov's pro-Yugoslav orientation. Later, Stalin liquidated this group and its leader, Kostov, under the pretext that they were "Yugoslav agents." Bulgaria became the most loyal Soviet satellite.

After 1965, and the onset of polycentrism, even Yugoslavia tried to intensify its relations with Bulgaria in order to bring this state closer to the idea of friendly Balkan cooperation and away from a unilateral Soviet orientation. In the beginning there were hopeful signs that these attempts would be met by the Bulgarian leadership with a certain appreciation. There were even hopeful signs that Bulgaria had regained some national self-confidence. The regime took successful measures to promote agricultural production, tourism, and foreign trade with the West. Interest in Bulgarian history was revived even though it was inevitable that by this, the question of Macedonia would again begin to trouble the precariously normalized relations with Yugoslavia. However, the participation of Bulgaria in the Soviet invasion of Czechoslovakia brought a serious setback for even this limited process of national emancipation. Again Bulgaria antagonized its neighbors and fell back on a course of complete subservience to the Soviet Union. Even if this does not preclude any hope for the future, it shows the still extremely low degree of national self-confidence in this state after so many severe setbacks experienced in its relatively short history.

ALBANIA. The Albanians are the oldest people but the youngest state in the Balkans. A majority of them accepted Islam under the Turks and they accepted the Turkish Empire, but not always the authority of the Sultan. The Turks, on their part, wisely left the administration of the Albanian mountains to local notables and tribal chiefs. There were, so to speak, "Albanian politics," before there was an Albania.

This constellation more or less gave the Albanians the freedom of movement and the possibility of expansion that they wanted. On the other hand, relative happiness with the existing state of affairs, together with religious divisions, prevented for a long time the awakening of a common Albanian national feeling. The latter came into existence only when the Turkish Empire seemed on its way to disintegration, and the newly-founded Christian states of the Balkans tended to divide its territory among themselves, thereby progressively limiting the area of free circulation and settlement for the Albanian population. It is quite logical that the movement for national unification did not start in central Albania, but rather in the Albanian borderlands, which were threatened by annexations from Serbia, Montenegro, and Greece.

After the first Balkan War of 1912, the Great Powers enabled the creation of an Albanian state which, however, was able to comprise only a relatively small part of all the Albanian lands. In the Serbian, and now Yugoslav region of Dosovo-Metchija, and in parts of Yugoslav Macedonia there remained a "second Albania" outside the borders of the Albanian state, with almost as many inhabitants. It is only since the downfall of the centralistic-minded Alexander Rankovic in 1966, that this "second Albania" again has the opportunity to profess its Albanian patriotism and to communicate, as far as circumstances allowed it, with the other half of the Albanian "nation." How this problem will finally affect Albanian-Yugoslav relations and conditions in the Balkans in general is still hard to foresee.

The solid and not unfounded distrust of the Albanians—the other latecomers of the Balkans—against their neighbors drove their state, between the two World Wars, into close collaboration with Italy and away from participation in Balkan politics. Albania, however, jumped from the frying pan into the fire, and was occupied by Mussolini in 1939. During the war, a Communist movement originating in the southern parts of the country, was able to gain power with the help of the Yugoslav Partisans; but since Yugoslavia, after the war, tried more or less to play the same role in Albania as Fascist Italy had played before, the Albanians, making skillful use of the conflict between Belgrade and Moscow, were able to extricate themselves from Yugoslav control in 1948 and to establish a direct "special relationship" with Moscow. However, this relationship too was strained in the late 1950's and early 1960's, when Khrushchev not only promoted his reconciliation with Tito, but also made some advances toward Greece regarding settlement of the question of the Greek minority in southern Albania. The Albanians again made use of a rising conflict between two other Communist states—this time Russia and China—and switched their sympathies to Peking. This new alliance implied a high degree of self-isolation, and self-chosen hostility toward almost the entire outside world. After the Soviet occupation of Czechoslovakia, however, there was again a turning point in the external policy of Albania. In addition to their alliance with China, the Albanian leaders now have discovered common security interests with the other Balkan states.

GREECE. Modern Greece was founded, after the Independence war of 1821–1827, in a small rural corner of the wide Byzantine-Hellenist world, which at that time reached through the whole Ottoman Empire and beyond, from the Caucasus to Crete and Egypt. The intensity of the Hellenistic feeling in this new state was in remarkable contrast to the ethnic strength of Hellenism. One might safely assume that Albanian and Wallachian were as widely-spoken in the villages and towns as was Greek itself. There were other contradictions and contrasts: between the seagoing population of the islands, and the boyars and landowners of the continent; and between the notables sympathizing with the Turkish Empire, and the nationalistic Greek patriots. Soon there were fervent discussions between those who wanted to make the classic Greek heritage the spiritual foundation of the state, and those who saw Modern Greece as a successor to the lost Byzantine Empire. There were, and are up to this time, some Greeks who will agree with Professor Arnold Toynbee, that it was a mistake to have founded the small Hellenic national state instead of continuing the symbiosis with the Turks in the framework of the Ottoman Empire.

In view of all this contradiction, contrast, and discussion, it is rather amazing, and certainly a respectable historical achievement that modern Greece today is functioning as a unified national state with a basically unified national culture. The only fundamental mistake Greece made was when it tried to have its cake and eat it too—that is, when it tried to reconstruct the old empire under the banner of modern Hellenic nationalism. This was the so-called "Great Idea" borne out of the overheated thinking of Cretian irredentism, and transplanted to continental Greece by Eleftherios Venizelos, who came to power in 1909 by a military coup, and is usually presented as the founder of the modern Greek state. His "Great Idea" ended in 1922 in a national catastrophe, when the Greek armies in Turkey were defeated and the whole Greek population on the Aegean shore were either massacred or expelled. Venizelos was skillful enough to put the blame for the defeat of his policy on his political adversaries, and was wise enough to use the catastrophe of Asia Minor as a point of departure for lasting peace and collaboration with Turkey. Greece again proved its viability in absorbing almost two million refugees.

Greece, as a nation and as a society, has shown through the whole history of modern Hellenism and even up to this date, an exemplary strength and vitality. However, its political system has always been extremely weak, and this, too, has not changed up to now. In the nineteenth century the political parties and their leaders were mostly little more than agencies of the Great Powers which had guaranteed the independence of the state. Since World War I Greece had been divided more or less into the two rival factions of the Venizelositic or "Liberal" left and into the Royalist or "Conservative" right; but these two great factions consisted mostly of clientele of different personalities, and they were by no means united. In the last century, partly by the wish of the guaranteeing Powers, and partly by the wish of the Greeks themselves, a monarchy was established and foreign princes were brought in as kings, with the idea that this would give the state a political institution above the political parties, and a neutral arbiter in internal quarrels. The monarchy, however, was able to play this role only up to World War I, and even then not without difficulties. The political struggle between Venizelos and King Constantine I over Greece's entrance into World War I made the court simply another political party instead of a neutral, national institution. Unfortunately for the political system of the state, the involvement of the court in the day-to-day politics did not cease until the present time. All three leading politicians of Greece since World War I— Alexander Papagos, Constantine Karamanlis and George Papandreou have experienced the open hostility of the Crown, which has engaged in an ambitious policy of its own.

The military coup of 21 April 1967 was, therefore, not the origin of a crisis, but much more the consequence of the irresponsibility displayed by almost all the leading political circles, the court included. The military junta on the other hand proved largely unable to resolve the problems it had found when it took power, but instead it has created a lot of new confusion. In the beginning there was hope that the military government would embrace a similar policy of correcting and gradually re-establishing democracy, as had the Turkish armed forces in Turkey in 1960. It became evident, however, that the Greek armed forces were more a professional army with no ideology of their own except for a strong sense of patriotism, and were by their tradition poorly equipped to play the same moderating and progressive role as was the Turkish army seven years earlier.

It seems that the regime is in Athens to stay, with the danger that it will sink further into a conservative immobilism, or even into a dictatorship of the Fascist type. Both conditions would pull Greece back into the situation of the Balkans prior to World War I, and would reverse the trend of gradual Europeanization. The Western European states have reason to follow the developments in Greece with concern.

TURKEY. Throughout the centuries, Turkey directed its whole power against whatever was called "Europe" at the time, and the symbiosis with the Byzantine heritage did not do much to alleviate this anti-Western attitude. The turning point came in the eighteenth century with the arrival of Russia at the Black Sea and in the Balkans. After being defeated by the Russians several times, the Turks slowly came to the conclusion that, in the long run, they had to accept the more advanced techniques and the generally more progressive system of the West, if they were not to be completely wiped out. It was primarily the army leaders who recognized this necessity and therefore the Turkish armed forces became and have remained always the main promoter of Westernization and progress. All the reforms of the nineteenth century originated in one way or another with the armed forces. The same was true later, with the Young Turk movement and with the movement of Kemal Ataturk who completed, out of the defeat and dismemberment of the Empire in World War I, the transition of Turkey into a modern national state with strong leanings toward Europe and later toward the West in general.

Ataturk's reforms demanded a lot of Turkey; perhaps too much at once. He wanted the Turks to get rid of their old Ottoman traditions and of their Muslim religion, in exchange for Western habits and a laicistic state ideology. The reaction to this abrupt change had to come one day, especially since after Ataturk's death the reform movement lost its strength and found in Ismet Inonu more of an administrator than a new leader. The Democratic Party under Celal Bayar and Adnon Menderas which also originated from the Reform Movement won the first democratic elections in the state in 1950, because it promised to bring some changes to the established Kemalistic system. The attempts at correction, however, failed by their own contradictions.

On one hand, the Democrats favored an exaggerated economic liberalism, which was popular in the developed lands bordering the Aegean Sea and among the urban milieus of Istanbul and Izmir. On the other hand, they not only permitted but favored the revival of religion and other traditional trends, the abolition of which by Ataturk was still resented by large segments of the population, especially in the countryside. By this, the Democrats created the impression that they wanted to eliminate completely the achievement of the Reform. The state and its issues became so confused, and the internal struggle so embittered, that in 1960 the army had to intervene. The operation was successful, and today the forces represented by the then Democratic Party are again in power, under the name of "Justice" Party and under a new moderate leader, Suleyman Demirel. This new party, by its skillful middle-of-the-road policy, has every chance to bring a national synthesis to Turkey, so that the state can keep the positive achievement of the Reform without losing its traditional soul.

After World War I, Turkey temporarily made peace with its archenemy, Russia. It tried, as a "Middle Power," to participate again in the politics of the Balkans, and even of Europe in general. It did so very cautiously and with the clear intention to keep out of any new conflict among the Powers of Europe. Turkey remained neutral in World War II, but was driven by Stalin's threats against its domination of the Straits and its territorial integrity, to ally itself completely with the Western allies and later with NATO.

Turkey lacks the capacity, but retains the political tradition of a major Power. It will always, as far as its security requirements will permit, prefer to be a center of a political system itself, rather than simply a member of a big and even anomalous alliance. NATO will, without doubt, remain the basis of Turkish foreign policy in the economic and even political fields. It will lean more and more toward Western Europe. At the same time, Turkey will try to establish a system of good neighborly relations with the Soviet Union and with the Arab states as well. The present leaders of Turkey think that conditions today are more favorable for such a balanced political orientation than they were in the past, and they have decidedly progressed on this new road in the last five years. On the other hand, Turkey has no intention any more of getting involved in the political conflicts of the Balkan area, in spite of the importance of the Balkans as a trade and communications link with Western Europe. By its cool and detached approach to questions of foreign policy, Turkey can certainly contribute much to create an atmosphere of détente in Southeastern Europe, which will also help to improve the political maneuverability for the other states of the area.

CONCLUSIONS

There is no point in entering into a discussion at this point on whether the Soviet Union is part of Europe or not. First, it is a fact that the Soviet Union is a Superpower, and therefore the states of Western Europe cannot engage in a dialogue with the Russians on equal terms. Second, Russia has by tradition a different outlook and a different set of values than the states of Europe. In contrast, the states of Southeastern Europe have always been part of the greater cultural and political world of Europe and at the same time they are comparable to the size and the strength of their counterparts in the Western part of the continent.

The Balkans and Eastern Mediterranean is a subregion where nationalism has been the dominant political force and is re-emerging nowadays from the artificial cover of the double Communist and Soviet suppression. In Western Europe nationalism might be considered as a negative element or as a predicament for the process of Western European unification. In Eastern Europe, however, nationalism is still a very active and positive force with a well-defined historic task to be fulfilled. It was nationalism that brought these peoples into existence as states, that gave them culture, civilization, economic development and even, if we take the former subjects of the Turkish Empire, personal freedom. Today it helps these states to hold out against their new oppressors, and to hope for a better future. The nationalism of the states in Southeastern Europe might also have some negative traits, but at least it was never anti-Western or anti-European as, for instance, was Russian Slavofilism.

All the attempts at European bridge-building cannot alienate the states on the Eastern side from reasonable links with the Soviet

Union, as the Western European states, on their part, have also manifested their intention to maintain ties with the United States. However, it should be possible to establish a normal, fruitful, and positive relationship between the two divided parts of the European continent, even while respecting their respective adherences to one or the other alliance system. If the Soviet Union does not show understanding for this all-European necessity, the Balkans and Eastern Mediterranean area of Europe will soon be transformed into a dangerous cockpit of political crisis, not only for Europe, but for the whole world.

The interest and the sympathy which the Western European states are showing for the deep-rooted aspirations of their neighbors on the other side of the Iron Curtain should, on the other hand, not detract from enlarging the European orbit economically, culturally, and even politically, in directions where possibilities do exist. Again, the subregion of the Balkans and the Eastern Mediterranean offers, at least today, perhaps the best opportunities for such an enlargement of the European consciousness. Europe will sooner or later benefit from the reciprocal endeavors made to close the century-old gap between Western Europe and the nationalities of the former Byzantine or Ottoman heritage. Already now, relations with Iran are getting closer and if nationalities like Georgia or Armenia could freely decide their political destinies, they would certainly at once enter into a very close relation with Europe. On the other hand, Israel is considered by many as a European "stronghold" in the midst of the Orient. But at the same time, it is fair to say that also some Arab states, for instance Lebanon, show many aspects of European-type life. The Turkish diplomatic tradition might one day prove extremely useful in providing a link between the Europe dominated by Christianity and the Moslem world.

PART IV

Can Europe Be United?
Variations on the
Continental Pattern

In general, the best kind of political and military
"Europe" from an American standpoint would be . . .
a "Europe" including Britain which is insufficiently
united to reach for nuclear autonomy but still
united enough to go some way toward meeting the
European desire for political identity and independence, while at the same time restricting German
and French freedom of action considerably.

—*Harold van B. Cleveland*

INTRODUCTION

Post-World War II Europe has been divided two ways—first, between the East and the West, and then between the "inner Six" and "outer Seven." This has cast the peripheral areas of the British Isles and the Baltic subregion into ambiguous roles. Britain, as we know, at first was reluctant to relinquish its historic role as a "balancer" in European politics, and also wanted to retain its world outlook both in terms of the Commonwealth and Empire, and in terms of the Anglo-American "special relationship." To some extent, these two aspects of Britain's globalism were based on similar premises. The United States, after all, was an overseas Anglo-Saxon transplantation that had "made good" and was now playing a role of extending its interests over the shrinking interests of the Mother Country. The same can be said for the so-called "White Dominions" of the Empire-cum-Commonwealth. As to the non-European British overseas territories, the influence of Britain culturally and economically has persisted beyond the re-arrangement of political ties that decolonization had brought on.

After World War II, Britain only reluctantly had agreed to commit troops on the continent in advance of hostilities, and even more reluctantly has negotiated for entry into the Common Market. Some of the problems which arose for Britain on both counts are discussed below and in the Epilogue.

As to the Baltic subregion, the experience of Norway and Denmark in World War II has played as much a part in the security thinking of these states as has the post-war political cleavage of Europe. Neither state has been willing, for example, to have German troops stationed on its soil, even under NATO auspices. Furthermore, as they incline toward strengthened Baltic subregional arrangements, they have had to consider not taking positions or policies which would compromise Sweden's neutralism or Finland's political necessities vis-à-vis the Soviet Union.

Although Britain is unequivocally in the "Western camp" in terms of Soviet-American rivalries, such is not necessarily the case for the Baltic area. None of the Baltic states wish to have any greater Russian influence there than already exists, but they also are not necessarily compliant with America's interests either toward the subregion or toward the Soviet Union's anti-American moves in the subregion. The situation is becoming increasingly flexible.

Finally, as regards Western European integration, which the United States favors and the Soviet Union opposes (but not integration for Eastern Europe), the Baltic states are divided in their outlooks. Denmark appears determined to follow the British lead into the Common Market, as also appears to be the case with Norway, but certainly not with Finland. Sweden is the most difficult state to predict on this matter. If the Baltic states eventually do pull more toward each other politically, militarily, and economically than toward Europe to their south, then the nature of the inteoration movement in Europe, and also the nature of future trans-Atlantic ties, would be affected. What would NATO be like, for instance, without the Baltic states of Norway and Denmark as members? What will happen to the European Free Trade Association if the European Economic Community becomes either on the one hand more tightly integrated, with more formalized political and military dimensions, or on the other hand becomes a looser federation? Or, seen in even broader terms, what opportunities are there for the Scandinavian states to help bring about some form of all-European security settlement? Finland, for example, in the early fall of 1969 took an unprecedented initiative in raising the possibility of setting in motion moves which could bring about a general European security conference and thus lead to such a settlement. Also, the first round of the Strategic Arms Limitation Talks took place in Helsinki. In summary, the Baltic subregion, along with Britain, can play a very important part in the definition of Europe in the 1970's.

IAN C. TAYLOR

7 The Dilemma of Great Britain

BRITAIN AND THE
EUROPEAN ECONOMIC COMMUNITY

With a peculiar irony of history, the third British attempt to join the European Economic Community is under the supervision of Edward Heath, now Prime Minister, but in 1961–63 the chief British negotiator in Brussels during the initial application. Rebuffed then, he must hope this time for greater success. General de Gaulle cannot have been surprised by the turn of events, as he is reported to have commented in 1963: "After a disastrous Labor experiment, there will be a Tory government under Heath, and that one will join the Common Market."[1]

On January 29, 1963, Mr. Heath addressed the Council of Ministers of the EEC after the French veto was known. He declared:

> Although this is a sad moment for European unity, I should like to say one thing . . . We in Britain are not going to turn our backs on the countries of the Community. We are a part of Europe: by geography, tradition, history, culture and civilization. We shall continue to work with all our friends in Europe for the true unity and strength of this continent.

So Mr. Heath is now taking up the business where it was broken off seven years before. For once, there can be no doubt about the commitment of the Prime Minister to the Community deal.

Circumstances surrounding the application have altered during the last few years. Heath's statement in 1963 shocked many people

[1] Alexander Werth, *De Gaulle* (London: Penguin, 1965), p. 331.

170

in Britain who were not at all sure that they were European. Now, it would be accepted by most people—except for a need to qualify the meaning of the word "unity." This we shall discuss later. Also, General de Gaulle has abdicated, thus removing an enormous barrier to British entry into the Community. President Georges Pompidou takes a more pragmatic approach, seeing circumstances in which British membership could now be a useful counterweight to the influence of West Germany which has significantly increased in the last few years. There was in 1970 at least the chance of success, where there was little in 1962, and none in 1967.

The application has lain on the table since 1967, while discussions continued with leaders of the Western European Powers individually and through the Western European Union (WEU). The use of the latter has at times annoyed France, but it has been a valuable body for keeping Britain in touch with sympathetic member-states of the Community since the 1963 rejection. As the leadership of the Labor, Conservative, and Liberal parties in Britain are all committed to Britain's membership in the EEC (compared with the disunity surrounding the 1961 application), and the other five EEC states all desire British participation, the pressure on France has been fairly constant.

In a sense, this conflict between Britain and France is not surprising. Whatever the direction Europe had taken after 1945, it would have been likely that these two states would have been at odds from time to time. After the war, Britain had refused the French offer to be involved in rebuilding Europe, preferring to concentrate on the world role it still envisaged itself playing. Also, there was some dislike of linking with France. At a lunch in 1949 with Averell Harriman, the principal administrator of Marshall Aid, Sir Stafford Cripps, then Chancellor of the Exchequer, had retaliated to Harriman's continuous prodding to "go into Europe" by asking his American host how he would feel if Britain asked the United States to go to bed with Brazil. Harriman indicated that he would object. "Well," said Sir Stafford, "that is how we feel about France."[2]

France also has some justification for feeling that Britain is not yet ready for the European role which it seeks. This was more ap-

[2] On the French side, General de Gaulle told Duff Cooper in 1945 that he was sorry he could not declare war on Britain.

parent in 1961 than now, but it is still true that there are still considerable doubts in Britain about the "European Ideal" which motivates many persons involved in the Common Market. In this sense, somewhat ironically when de Gaulle took a stand against the federal concept for Europe, he had many supporters in Britain. We shall discuss this more fully later, but it could be said that the very failure of the Common Market to advance its superstructure as fast as the originators hoped has made British attitudes more favorable to entry than they otherwise might have been.

Stating the official position, Britain does accept the treaties establishing the Communities, including the Treaty of Rome. This is the basis of the application for membership. Parallel applications have been submitted for membership in the European Coal and Steel Community (ECSC) and the European Atomic Energy Community (EURATOM). The approach is that given certain modifications now one can accept initally the basic structure of the Communities and solving the detailed problems involved during a transitional period after membership has been granted, rather than the arduous a posteriori approach of the 1961 negotiations. The reason lies partly in the realization that has developed in the last few years, that membership in the EEC does not mean in practice British subjection to a supranational body; and partly because the areas of British concern have diminished. Instead of a large portfolio of Commonwealth interests to protect, all that remains is to ensure a reasonable arrangement for the position of New Zealand, whose trade is still very closely linked to Britain, and provision for the Commonwealth sugar producers. The other matters for prior negotiation will be over the controversial Common Agricultural Policy which by 1970 the EEC had hammered out, and the question of capital movements, and the role of sterling.

The comment of *The Times* of London in May 1967 was also true for 1970:

> The mood in which Britain makes its second approach to Europe is therefore more sober but also more realistic and committed than it was the first time. The hopes are more measured but the fears are fewer. . . . Out of all the quibbles over figures, and the disagreements over terms and details, there came no effective challenge to the view that British entry into the Common Market on reasonable terms will make infinitely more sense for Britain,

for Europe, for EFTA, for the Commonwealth, and indeed for the world than any conceivable alternative.[3]

Such a statement is equally applicable today and displays the vast change in the British attitude toward Europe—a change which has been accepted with reluctance, and with a lingering tendency to refuse to recognize the reality of Britain's position in the post-war world. As pointed out in Part II, for France, the idealism of Jean Monnet in the late 1940's became allied to the desire to limit the sovereignty of West Germany by building common institutions. Such developments failed to attract serious British interest. Building the new Europe was perhaps a good exercise for those states on "the continent." But Britain was a World Power, so it was argued, and had to have a global attitude corresponding with its responsibilities. Britain was not just a European Power, nor a state which needed to acknowledge the superiority of the United States and the Soviet Union. The persistence of this delusion of grandeur had prevented any realistic assessment of where Britain's true role lay in the world, causing British foreign policy to be based less on new initiatives, and instead more on hurried responses to conditions which the British could not control. Even the Suez crisis of 1956 failed to drive home the reality of the situation completely. It is not intended here to chart the decline of British world power, but just to point out why it was that only recently has Britain opened a major national dialogue about where to go in defense and foreign policy.

POST-WAR CHANGES IN BRITAIN'S WORLD ROLE

Britain opted out of the early growth of the "new" Europe because it mistook the prestige deriving from past power for power itself. The decision to apply again to the European Economic Community showed that the harsh realities of the British position were at last influencing foreign policymakers. Britain needed to encourage and participate in the greater unity of Western Europe for both

[3] The *Times* (London) 12 May 1967.

economic and political reasons. During the last few years the discrepancy between the economic growth and reorganization within the Common Market and in Britain has become more pronounced, despite the problems the Community has faced.

Britain has suffered from periodic economic crises over the last fifteen years which gradually brought a realization that both the pattern of trade and the structure of industry needed a radical reappraisal. Britain has to become part of a much larger, integrated economic unit if its position relative to the major Powers is not to continue to decline. The Commonwealth failed to provide the basis for economic prosperity, and indeed, the value of Commonwealth trade for Britain has been steadily declining since World War II. The reduction in the importance of the system of Commonwealth trade preference was partly caused by the negotiations centering around the General Agreement on Tariffs and Trade (GATT) and also by the trade diversion policies of the Commonwealth members themselves. There are very few people who would argue today—as members of the Labor party, for example, were arguing even up to 1965—that the Commonwealth provides any true basis for British economic prosperity.

ALTERNATIVES TO THE COMMON MARKET

In Europe it is accepted that the European Free Trade Association (EFTA) is not a long-term solution. Even a market of 100 million people is insufficient for the growth of a modern technological economy. EFTA was born in 1950 when Britain was reluctant to join the negotiations for a European customs union which would lead to a common market. At that time, Britain still had its eyes on a world role, and did not want to participate in a small grouping of continental states intending to correlate, in pre-established stages, economic policies behind a common external tariff and with the prospect of supranational institutions. Britain had, however, been urging a free trade area involving the states that had participated in the Marshall Plan (called the Organization for European Economic Cooperation—OEEC) but had failed to convince the six states involved in the Messina discussions which led to the Treaty of Rome that this approach was preferable to forming the

EEC. EFTA, therefore, was formed by the remaining OEEC members outside the EEC because they were fearful of the prospect of tariff discrimination against them when the tariff and quota provisions of the Rome Treaty would become operative at the beginning of 1959. It has never been regarded as a permanent body, but as an expedient while attempts were continued to form a wider European trade area.

Nonetheless, within its terms of reference—the Stockholm Convention—EFTA has been extremely successful. It has already had a much longer life than anyone thought possible in 1960. Yet Britain has never put so much emphasis on its possibilities as other members. As Britain is by far the most dominant member, this is hardly surprising. Moreover, almost immediately, the British realized that the Common Market was more likely to provide solutions to British economic difficulties. Ironically, the British joined EFTA because they chose not to take a full part in the preliminaries to the Treaty of Rome, but have since found that EFTA membership complicated their application to join the organization they had chosen formerly to ignore. For example, adequate safeguards would be needed for Britain's EFTA partners in the event of British membership of EEC, as only Norway, Denmark and Sweden are likely to apply.

Economically, therefore, EFTA does not provide an alternative to the Common Market. Neither does the Commonwealth. Indeed, it is significant that through a combination of natural tendencies and of the warning given by the first application in 1961, the Commonwealth provides only minor complications to British negotiators in Brussels today. The pattern of trade alone confirmed this trend. By the second half of the 1960's, the Commonwealth took less than a quarter of British exports, while Europe took more than a third. The most important single market in Europe was the Common Market.

The purely economic benefits of membership of the EEC, however, are in the balance. The Confederation of British Industry examined the problem both in 1967 and 1970, and come down firmly for membership. The main disadvantages, which were seen as "pressures on internal costs, particularly as a result of the common agricultural policy, at a time when external competition from within the enlarged Community and without is likely to increase sharply," and "some potential danger to our remaining Commonwealth trade"

were considered to be outweighed by the beneficial effects resulting
from "the speedy ending of tariff discrimination against us in the
EEC and consequent unimpeded access to a wider market; the
long-term economies of scale that this may offer," and the "disadvantages of isolation from the Community." No attempt will be
made here to discuss in detail the possible effects on the British
economy and balance of payments of entry into the EEC.[4] Suffice
it to say that the main emphasis of pro-Marketeers is on the long-
term benefits, and on the disastrous effect that permanent exclusion
would have. The favorable upswing in the British balance of payments in 1969–1970 brought on not so much a hardening of British
sentiment against membership, as more national self-confidence
in the negotiations. It had been evident all along that the negotiations would be neither quick nor easy.

Former Prime Minister Harold Wilson remarked about entry
into the EEC in May 1967: "I believe on balance it will be right
economically, but the political argument is stronger." He believed
at that time that Europe was on the verge of a great move forward
in political unity and that Britain must play a part in it. It is worth
quoting at length from an address Wilson made to his back-benchers
for the Parliamentary Labor Party in April 1967:

> When something is at stake of this degree of importance for Eu-
> rope and the World, the role of Britain is on the field, and not on
> the touchline casting praise, blame or even bottles at those who
> are doing a job in which we should be involved as full partici-
> pants. . . . Our purpose is to make a reality of the unity of Western
> Europe. But we know that this will be an empty achievement
> unless it leads first to an easing of tension and then to an honour-
> able and lasting settlement of the outstanding problems that still

[4] The Government published in February 1970 a White Paper:
"Britain and the European Communities: An Economic Assessment".
This document caused more to deepen public doubt and spread public
confusion about the EEC than any other. It estimated the impact on
current balance of payments per year of between minus £100m and
minus £1,100m. The London *Economist* weekly dismissed it as slip-
shod and absurd, giving its own estimate as a less daunting minus
£175m. But the ammunition was already in the hands of the anti-
marketeers, and the housewife for one was alerted to potentially "vast"
price rises.

divide Europe. This indeed is something that I have striven for for many years; and I am convinced that if Britain is a member of a united European Community our chances of achieving this will be immeasurably greater. . . . We in Britain are the loyal allies of one of the two great world powers, the United States; and we seek the closest and most friendly relationship, economic, commercial, cultural, with the other great world power, the Soviet Union. But, because we seek this friendly relationship with both the great powers, we do not accept the notion that all great issues should be left for settlement direct between those powers because we in Europe are not sufficiently powerful economically—and therefore politically—to make our voices heard. That is why we believe in the need to make effective our enormous potential industrial strength by giving that strength a chance to operate on a European and not a national scale—or a series of national scales. It is only if we do this that we can exercise everything that goes with industrial strength and independence in terms of Europe's influence in world affairs.

LABOR PARTY AND CONSERVATIVE PARTY ATTITUDES TOWARD THE EEC

This, in a grandiose way, signifies the full conversion of the leadership of the Labor Party to the idea of a strong, politically-important Europe. In February 1962 Wilson had said that whatever the terms, Britain should not enter a rich man's club if it meant turning its back on the rest of the world. It is interesting to follow this switch in attitude by the leaders of the Labor Party to the realization that Britain's world position needs to be related to, and based on, Europe. During the early years of the Common Market, the Labor view was one of suspicion of the "capitalists" based in Brussels, and Laborites felt much more at home with the Protestant socialists of states like Sweden. They feared linkage with France and West Germany under Charles de Gaulle and Konrad Adenauer; they were states with no welfare systems like that in Britain, with weaker trade unions and with dubious political systems. The essence of the argument of the majority of the Labor party was that Britain was set on a different path from the rest of Europe, a path of greater promise for socialists, and a promise that could not be bartered away for what was pre-eminently a capitalist association. (Yet, ironically, a large number of the "back-room boys" in Brussels were European socialists, a point which escaped the Labor party.)

The reasons for the application by the Conservative Prime Minister were also regarded as being disingenuous. Prime Minister Harold Macmillan was searching for a policy after the failure of the Paris Summit Conference of 1960; however, he dressed up the wide political implications of entry behind claims that it was essential for British industry and also essential in order to get the country out of its continual cycle of "Stop-Go" domestic economic cycles. He thought that entry would act like a bucket of cold water. The Labor party leader at that time, Hugh Gaitskell, was more concerned with the overall vision. The prospect of Western European federalism, he claimed, would "mean the end of Britain as an independent European state. . . . It means the end of a thousand years of history." In the same speech to the Labor Party Conference of 1962, he asserted his view of Britain's off-shore position:

> Let us not confuse the question of whether we think it is good or bad for the Europeans to get together in Western Europe and form their federation with the question whether we should join it. The first question is their affair and it may well be the answer to their problem. It is not necessarily the answer to ours. For we are not just a part of Europe—at least not yet. We have a different history.

Looming large in Gaitskell's "different history" was the prospect of a multi-racial Commonwealth, a vision not to be destroyed by signing the Treaty of Rome which Labor Defense Minister Denis Healey described as "a great big book, with four pages of principles and 400 pages of exceptions."

During the 1964 General Election, the issue of Europe was, in Sir Alec Douglas-Home's phrase, a dead duck. With Harold Wilson elected Prime Minister, it did not look like it would be revived. Wilson, a supporter of the Commonwealth, declared that Britain's frontiers extended to the Himalayas and that its role lay in keeping an interest east of Suez. His early acts were certainly not aimed at encouraging pro-British feeling in Europe—the Concorde Affair, the imports surchage, the handling of EFTA. Yet the continuing economic crisis caused a reassessment. America was giving financial help, but could not always be expected to do so, and it was essential to attempt to find a milieu in which long-term British economic and political power, as its relationship with the United States declined, was preserved.

The "special relationship" with the United States has been a popular myth in London until very recently. Although there may indeed be some close cultural affinity, there can be little political importance placed upon it, certainly since the days of the Macmillan-Kennedy friendship. (This friendship was more personal than national, and its greatest effect was to convince de Gaulle that Britain was too Anglo-Saxon for entry into the EEC—this was not the effect that Macmillan was seeking.) With the vast economic and military superiority of the United States, it was becoming increasingly obvious that Britain could exert little political weight—despite its long-standing ties with the United States—in the American President's decisions. The Wilson government began to search for means of promoting a counter-balance to American power. United States interests have not always been those of Britain, and vice versa, especially in Europe at a time when bilateral Soviet-American negotiations were going on. If Britain cannot speak with a loud enough voice, so the reasoning went, then it should join a multinational grouping which can. There has been little doubt that the EEC member states have had more impact on world affairs than has Britain.

For Wilson, the prospect of the Commonwealth being the basis of British power was finally seen to be a hollow one; moreover, the Common Market was proving both more successful and less dangerous to socialist ideals than had been anticipated. The failure of the government's National Plan made Labor politicians less suspicious of potential interference in socialist planning from Brussels, while it was also recognized that Labor's welfare policies could not be continued unless the economy was put in order. With the decision in July 1967 to switch defense concentration away from the Gulf and the Far East, the conversion of the Labor government was complete. It was left only for Wilson to give the switch the gloss of long-term policy carefully conceived, and relate it to his 1964 pledge to create the "White-Hot heat of the Technological Revolution."

Accordingly, he stressed the contribution to Europe that British technology could make, knowing that there had been considerable concern in Europe about the dominance of American industry in key fields. Modern technology is possible only in larger economic blocs with a fundamental degree of economic coordination. The problem identified in the book by J. J. Servan-Schreiber, *The American Challenge,* was called by Wilson "industrial helotry." As a ploy to enter the Common Market it was not overly successful. But it did fit in with his policy of not defining "alliance" as meaning "subservience."

Mr. Wilson duly applied for membership, but there was never much hope of success. Mr. Edward Heath has remarked that the second attempt to enter the EEC will probably come to be regarded as a minor curiosity of European diplomatic history. But with the advent of the new French President in 1969, the way was open for a more serious approach. In December 1969, France agreed with its five partners that negotiations should begin as soon as possible, which turned out to be at the end of June 1970. This was only a few days after the defeat of Labor by the Conservative Party in Britain.

The Conservative Prime Minister, Edward Heath has always been more clearly "European" than Harold Wilson, and has made it plain that he believes that Britain should be a member of the EEC as long as certain safeguards can be made. He is also prepared to accept that the EEC has a deeper character, and that recognition of this is a precondition to British entry.

> This organisation is much more than a Market. It is a Community. Its members live and work together as such . . . No negotiation can begin until the Community as a whole is unequivocably accepted. Then and only then will the interests of the would-be new members be considered.[5]

There has, however, been very little public debate on the wider issues and implications of "going into Europe," partly because neither Macmillan nor Wilson nor Heath had been over-keen to encourage one. Today, discussion has been even more limited than in 1961, with Gaitskell's earlier concern for history being overlooked. This is a reflection of a general apathy which came over Britain in the 1960's—a view that nothing could be done to arrest decline— and the cynicism about big issues which goes with it. In 1961 the question of loss of sovereignty through entry into the EEC was an important one; now it is rarely heard. This may be because so much *real* power has left Britain through economic crises that people now

[5] Edward Heath, "Old World, New Horizons," 1967 Godkin Lectures (Cambridge: Harvard University Press, 1970), p. 30.

realize that Britain may gain a stronger voice in the world through a united Western Europe. It is also because of the failure of the EEC to advance very far into the realms of supranationality. Yet the Treaty of Rome does envisage a political federation. The dilemma remains. Does Britain want to be part of a close-knit European union with common institutions to direct economic, social and foreign relations? Or is something looser envisaged, with national identities preserved intact? It is to this problem that we turn now.

THE PROBLEMS AND OPPORTUNITIES POSED BY A BRITISH COMMITMENT TO EUROPE

Despite the desire to enter the Common Market, there has been a lack of any clear official vision as to how that Community should develop in the 1970's. What is certain is that little hope is held out for a significant change in the context within which Europe's future will be decided. There is unlikely to be much of a shift in the European balance of power, particularly if the United States and the Soviet Union come to an arms limitation agreement. In the same way, military power will still be largely in the hands of the Superpowers. Neither of the two European nuclear Powers, Britain and France, is going to be able to withstand the high expense of undertaking the next phase of nuclear weapons development without American help, or without the creation of some multinational European defense arrangements.

Thus the present nuclear disparity between Western Europe and the Superpowers will continue unless there is a determined political act to create another military community with supranational powers, the possibility of which will be discussed below. Furthermore, the pattern of defense for Eastern Europe will remain that of the Warsaw Pact, with the Soviet Union not prepared to withdraw troops from Central Europe in the foreseeable future. Finally, because of domestic pressure and the development of long-range intercontinental troop transporters, the United States will probably withdraw substantial numbers of troops from Western Europe in the 1970's, although maintaining NATO.

Given these prognostications, and as pointed out in Chapter 4, Britain seeks to provide a strong enough Western Europe for a voice in the Atlantic Alliance, yet not one that turns its back on Eastern

Europe, nor for that matter, on the world. However, it is extremely difficult to envisage how Western Europe can be organized in order to achieve these objectives. The more likely outcome is that either relations with the United States are improved at the expense of those with the Soviet Union, or vice versa, or that Europe so fails in mutual cooperation that it is incapable of influencing any solution to the divisions of Europe. For example, a Western Europe closely linked to the United States having forgotten all ideas of a more independent Europe, in return for security and prosperity, would weaken the states of Europe and solidify the East-West division, including the division of Germany. This probably is unacceptable. Another concept, that of an independent Federal Europe, would risk the lack of security provided by the United States in an attempt to arrive at a solution to the division of Europe.[6] In reality, the Soviet Union would be unlikely to make many concessions to this new power, unless it would take on a pro-Soviet gravitation, which would be unacceptable to the United States.

Neither of these extremes is in any way completely attractive, or fully realistic. The more likely direction involves strengthening and widening the present Common Market to a point where cooperation between member states enables a cohesive economic bloc to develop. This bloc would provide a more realistic counterweight to the present vast economic strength of the United States, and would avoid any tendencies toward economic subservience. At the same time, it would enable Western Europe to play a greater part in the Atlantic Alliance, thus relieving the United States of some of the burdens which are proving increasingly irksome, yet avoiding the possibility that Western Europe can be ignored in policy calculations in Washington.[7] Through political cooperation and greater integrated economic growth, a more substantial Western European contribution could be made to NATO.

Furthermore, Western Europe needs to make a greater nuclear contribution to ensure a significant influence on Atlantic policy and to avoid the possibility of being used as a hostage in the event of open Soviet-American conflict. This idea of an establishment of a

[6]See, for example, Alastair Buchan, ed., *Europe's Futures, Europe's Choices* (London: Chatto and Windus—for the Institute for Strategic Studies, 1969).

[7] On the last point, see Heath's Godkin Lectures, p. 67.

Western European identity within the Atlantic Alliance has become particularly important since the possibilities of Soviet-American negotiations have grown. War which breaks out between Powers whose strengths are determined by nuclear parity agreements could not be influenced by legal (i.e., treaty) restraints or commitments. This explains the growing feeling that the Nixon Administration favors a stronger Western European contribution, as much as a Western European belief in the need for it.

The Czechoslovakian crisis increased Western European awareness of the need for a greater say in military affairs in the Atlantic Alliance. The invasion produced a stronger reaction in Europe than it did in the United States, where it only briefly halted the growing reluctance of Washington to bear such a heavy burden of responsibility for the defense of its European allies. It is felt in Britain that the United States would welcome a greater European contribution, while such contribution would help protect Western European interests by making it less dependent on the United States, and through this sense of security, more able to negotiate with Eastern Europe.

The actual means of organizing a stronger Western European identity within the Alliance have not been made clear. There is the possibility of French and British cooperation, hinted at by the French government of Georges Pompidou. This notion is likely to interest Prime Minister Edward Heath more than it did the Labor Government, as Heath, while in opposition, had put forward the idea that combined Anglo-French nuclear forces should be held in trust for Europe.[8] However, there are problems. Such pooling could only occur within a framework such as the Common Market, and also within NATO, which means that France would have to participate in the NATO Nuclear Planning Group. Moreover, it could only be done in cooperation with the United States because of the dependence of British nuclear weapons on American technology, and this might be unacceptable to France. The position of West Germany is also a delicate one, and both France and Britain are keen to avoid West German control of nuclear arms, with which Bonn agrees. Thus at present there seems little hope of more than the setting-up of a series of Western European committees to discuss such matters

[8] *Ibid* p. 73.

as weapons procurement, manpower coordination, research and development, within a regional context. These committees could be within NATO, but again their success would depend on the French attitude to NATO policy and especially nuclear weapons targeting criteria.

Any development in nuclear cooperation will need a closer form of Western European coordination than at present exists. The Treaty of Rome assumed that federation would result from economic unity. Yet a true Western European political union with new institutions and new supranational obligations is not part of British policy. What seems to be envisaged is a mixed system, partly intergovernmental, partly supranational. Progressive agreements could be made on all aspects of Western European problems as they arose, whether monetary, technological, etc., yet with no state losing its identity in an all-embracing structure. Mr. Heath has explained the position as follows:

> We have never committed this country to a Federal Organisation in Europe, and I have said right from the beginning, I do not believe that Europe—a group of old Nation States—is going to develop in this way. . . . There will never be a blueprint for Europe. What will happen is that as we work together we shall create the sort of institutions we want in order to deal with our common problems and reach common solutions (24th September 1969).

Is this standpoint at variance with the one laid down by the EEC? The Treaty of Rome envisages an elected European Parliament, supranational decision making, and frequent references have been made in European debates about the need for a common foreign policy.

It is difficult to feel that there is not an element of political platitude in this. The role of the European Parliament has not been defined, nor how it would effectively control the Communities Commission. And a common foreign policy would probably be so limited as to be ineffective. It is true that some democracy must be introduced into the EEC bureaucracy; it is likely, though, to be well short of a federal system. Western Europe is probably going to develop in a piecemeal, functional pattern, much more to the liking of the British and also one suspects, of the French. This is not necessarily a pessimistic view. Great advances can be made on all sides toward political cooperation; but there is no proof that political unity follows inexorably on from economic unity.

The advantages of a less-than-federal system are considerable. It should be acceptable to the United States, although not meeting the ideals of the "partnership" concept put forward by President Kennedy, and now rapidly losing favor. Even in a federal form, Western Europe would be the junior partner in such a concept, while losing much freedom of maneuver. The developments outlined above would not preclude further improvements in the prospects for an East-West European détente, because no solidification would be made of the division of Germany.

BRITISH ATTITUDES TOWARD
DÉTENTE IN EUROPE

This brings us to a discussion of the wider prospects of increased cooperation in Europe. Is it possible to envisage a détente, and subsequently an entente?

Attitudes to the possibilities for a European détente have altered since the Soviet invasion of Czechoslovakia. The previous tendencies which had seemed all to point toward a lessening of tension have to be re-examined. The Soviet Union is not prepared to relax its rigid control over the Central and Eastern European states, even at a time when relations with the United States over European questions were improving. It is apparent that the Soviet Union is especially on guard when diplomatic approaches by Western European Powers are increasing. Much of the Soviet concern for the position of Czechoslovakia has been noticed to have started about the time that West Germany began to seek closer relations with Eastern Europe. Thus the development of East-West cooperation has been placed on an extremely unstable basis. Although the invasion did not necessarily herald a deliberate attempt to create an East-West crisis, the chances of an unintended crisis may have increased considerably.

Nevertheless, it is essential that attempts are made to ensure that relations improve within Europe. The German problem is fundamental in this respect. No solution can be envisaged in the near future, but from the base of its sense of security engendered by its position in the Community, certain initiatives from Bonn are now possible, such as the talks with Moscow, Warsaw and Pankow which help defuse the Central European tension and could assist some cooperation between the two parts of Germany. The value of not forming a federal Western Europe, but a looser functional one, is that the division of Germany is not confirmed, and therefore some negotiating flexibility is retained. A wide détente could be sought also on an institutional basis.

For example, the British government favors the prospect of a dialogue between NATO and the Warsaw Pact aimed at lowering the cost of security in Europe and creating a climate of mutual confidence in which it is easier to tackle the outstanding political problems created by World War II. However, no such dialogue is likely to succeed unless the Western allies remain united and keep up their military guard. Thus Britain would welcome the Soviet-inspired European security conference as long as the circumstances were created in which the conference would have a good chance of success, and as long as the United States and Canada would participate. But on the other hand, the British have rejected the Communist suggestion of liquidating the alliances, which would lead to the fragmentation of Western Europe but not Eastern Europe, since the Soviet Union has bilateral agreements with all its Warsaw Pact allies which would presumably not disappear along with the dismantlement of the security superstructure. Britain has proposed mutual force reductions by the two alliances, not in order to alter the overall balance of forces, but so as to improve the political atmosphere in Europe. Thus, perhaps, positive steps could be taken toward cooperation in the military field, and also in the areas of trade, technology, and cultural relations.

However, détente is a long-term objective and developments in Western Europe cannot wait for the decision of the Soviet Union to relax its grip on the Eastern bloc. As has been said already, Western Europe should develop in such a way so that the possibility of a solution to the German problem and to the division of Europe, even if not solved, is at least not precluded. The concept of European development described above would seem to fit these criteria, leaving Europe several options for the future. However, it is often argued that any steps toward the growth of a strong and integrated Western European community would likely prevent the achievement of a détente. In reality, the opposite may be true. One of the most dangerous positions for Europe to be in would be that of Western states making uncoordinated initiatives, each state speaking separately to Moscow and each being suspicious of each other. The Soviet Union would be unlikely to move toward major concessions regarding East Germany in such an unstable atmosphere, and any agreement it reached would in any case be with the United States over the heads of (and possibly at the expense of) the Western European states. If harmony with Eastern Europe is to be achieved, Western Europe's own policies must be coherent and effective. Some optimum, but limited, degree of cohesion and cooperation for Western Europe is essential, with some linking of the defense arrangements with the United States, if there is to be progress toward a détente with the Soviet Union and better relations with the Eastern bloc.

Hence the pattern of developments in Europe most suitable for Britain can be seen as a widened Common Market, with extended agreements to cover monetary and technological factors and other such areas where action seems both necessary and logical. Schemes for the development of a European federal state such as the plan put forward by Walter Hallstein are really exercises in political theory rather than working documents. It is unlikely that Western Europe is in a position to adopt such a federal form; one cannot realistically propose that states give up their identities unless the external pressure becomes overwhelming. As this is not a likely development in the foreseeable future, the development of the community system is more probably going to be piecemeal. The Institute for Strategic Studies has made the following realistic forecast:

> The watchword and the motive of this mixed European system, partly inter-governmental, partly supranational, would be "efficiency": how to extract the maximum benefits at the minimum cost in a world of increasing diversity and technical complexity. . . . Unlike a federal system which is, by definition, closed and exclusive, such a functional system would be flexible and open. It could absorb changes in membership and extend itself into new fields, without a publicized confrontation with high national policies and without offending the pride of national sovereignty. Governments would be enticed by the carrot of cost-benefits and technical efficiency into participating in new supranational experiments, where the task is clearly limited and any loss of sovereignty circum-

scribed. It would be a modest form of federalism a la carte, where each move forward would be seen to satisfy a specific need.[9]

Given entry into such a Europe, Britain would be anxious to ensure that it played an active yet identifiable role within the Atlantic Alliance, preferably with France more closely involved in NATO planning decisions and within the world at large. Certainly the Conservative Government sees that British responsibilities east of Suez will not entirely be given up, but might gradually be taken on by the Common Market states together. The Conservatives are prepared to reverse the policy of the previous Labor government and retain a limited presence in the Far East and the Gulf, with the hope that other states in Western Europe will play their part in assisting. One of the concerns in Britain at the moment is that the Common Market is failing to play an adequate role in world or extra-European affairs. Whether this attempt by the Conservative Government to encourage such awareness will be popular or successful remains to be seen; it would seem to be a doubtful starter.

It has been suggested that approaches to Eastern Europe could be made on the basis of economic links through the EEC. It is unlikely that any great prospects, however, can be held out for EEC-COMECON cooperation. COMECON seems increasingly unlikely to become the Eastern European bloc's economic super-structure, its role being rather to implement the economic coordination measures of its members without acting as their common planning organ. However, as long as Western European cooperation remains functional, not federal, there is a chance of providing special provisions for the participation of Eastern bloc states in the EEC. This, however, is likely to be the result, rather than the cause, of a general lessening of tension in Europe as a whole. At present very little hope can be held out for a real détente, and certainly not an entente, which is the condition that would have to be reached before practical cooperation became a reality.

A European détente is very different from a Soviet-American détente. The latter is likely to go forward whatever the situation in Europe, as was shown after the Czechoslovakian crisis of August 1968. It is partly for this reason that Western European states are

[9] Buchan *op. cit.* p. 163.

seeking greater influence within the Atlantic Alliance so as to guard against Soviet-American decisions which would not conform to their interests. At present, the Third World instability and the growing influence of Communist China have yet to indicate what sort of long-term effect they will have on the division of Europe. Prospects for wider European unity have to be considered in the widest possible context because of this, and consequently make it even more difficult to predict the future.

PROSPECTS FOR THE FUTURE

Most of the above analysis has been made on the assumption that Britain will enter the Common Market. It is true to say, however, that it seems that there will be considerable delay before entry is actually, if ever, achieved. Much depends on the behavior of France and West Germany. Yet the assumption seems a reasonable one to make. The cynics have argued that as soon as membership becomes a real possibility, British opinion on the EEC will become less enthusiastic. Although there is a grain of truth in this, there can be no doubt that the leaders of the three main British political parties are committed to gaining entry if the terms are acceptable. The problems are largely of a technical nature, and although they certainly are not going to be easily solved, they cannot prevent entry if the determination to enlarge the Community exists. The future French position looks as if it will be more flexible on this issue of expanded membership, although giving no indication of wishing to see a rapid expansion. It is likely to be some time before serious negotiations are concluded. Such a continued delay has the effect of causing disillusionment in British public opinion about the EEC, particularly as the burden on the balance of payments would be considerable, and as the adverse effect on the cost of living index is of concern to both the economist and the housewife.

The second failure to gain entry soured British opinion toward the EEC, and the internal problems of the Community itself have hardly helped. In March 1970, after the publication of the government White Paper, an Opinion Poll reported that only 22 percent of its sample electorate approved of joining the EEC, with 64 percent disapproving, and 14 percent don't knows. This means that the terms of entry will have to be visibly favorable for any British government to be able to persuade the electorate of the correctness of entry. It was significant that the EEC was hardly mentioned in the 1970 General Election campaign, except when both Party leaders were assuring voters of the favorable terms they would demand from Brussels as a precondition to membership. The final decision will be taken by Parliament, where there is a pro-EEC majority. But no Member of Parliament can afford to ignore totally the feelings of his electors.

But there remains the fact that there is no real alternative to entry. The progressive success of GATT and the Kennedy Round has not removed the need for a large coordinated market as the basis for economic expansion. Free trade area proposals which would include the United States—such as the North Atlantic Free Trade Area (NAFTA)—would clearly lead to unacceptable economic subordination to the United States in the long run, apart from the increasing concern British opinion has shown about internal and external American policy developments. If entry is delayed for much longer, proposals for extending the scope of EFTA are quite possibly going to receive more attention, although these could in no way provide a long-term solution.

Basically, the question of the possibilities of uniting Europe is a complex one. If unity implies unification, then very few people in Britain would be enthusiastic. Neither would the chances of success be very high. What is envisaged is the sort of progressive and deeper cooperation among the Western European states described above. The accusation that Britain is not "truly European" is a specious one, especially when it was leveled by Charles de Gaulle. The important point is that the post-war British reluctance to participate in cooperative developments in Europe has now given way to a concern to take part in future advances. Memories of Britain's imperial past, the sense of frustration at seeing the fruits of victory in World War II being plucked away from it, the barriers of language, religion, and race all have combined to slow the process down. As already mentioned, it was not until 1962 when the public clash over the joining of the Common Market was in full swing that the British people began to face realities and the tide of opinion began to change.[10] Now the problem is of a different nature, less one of adapting Commonwealth links to the Community, but more one of how Britain differs from its potential partners on how the Community should develop, and how great the short-term sacrifices on both sides are to be if British membership is to be achieved. The very debate has become European-oriented.

The Conservative Government, unlike in 1961, is now much more anxious to discuss such matters as the political structure of Europe in the long term, the future of NATO and the possible European deterrent, and the role of sterling, and not just Commonwealth sugar and New Zealand butter. This will inevitably cause problems, as France and Britain still differ on the relationship of Western Europe to the United States, and the West Germans can hardly be expected to enjoy being told that one of the purposes of British entry into the EEC is to keep them in check. There is still a degree of suspicion which has always been a part of European politics, and will be for the foreseeable future.

However, the real reason for Britain entering into a grand debate as part of the British attempt to enter the Common Market is that it is likely to be the only way of starting another "relance europeene." The Common Market has not exactly been exciting in its political evolution, and the internal problems have been highlighted by the struggle to agree on a common agricultural policy, which although politically necessary, was viewed as economically hazardous. Unless some wider perspective can be introduced, it will be difficult to create any great public enthusiasm in Britain for entry. For example it would be a tragedy if a fundamentally political question were to collapse once more into arguments about the correct price of butter. For in many ways, entry for Britain would be an act of faith, at a time when the country is cynical of such things and concerned with short-term economic problems. Thus there is no easy way out for any British government.

In the long run, Britain is as much a part of Europe as France. But the question is, as said in the Introduction to this book, "What

[10] Perhaps an exaggeration. A cover of the satirical London magazine *Private Eye* once showed three men on a beach sleeping in deckchairs with newspapers over their heads. The caption read: "The Great Common Market Debate Begins".

Is Europe?" The British view still falls fundamentally short of the visions of the Eurocrats, although it has developed considerably since 1961. The members of the EEC undoubtedly realize this, and it conditions their attitude to British membership. But basically the discussion still going on in Brussels is about how the states in Western Europe can best cooperate to increase their standard of living, to maintain some economic and political influence on world affairs, and to raise the prospect of closer cooperation with the Eastern bloc. If the British view of functional development for Western Europe is less exciting, it may nevertheless ensure a more rapid advance toward the re-establishment of Europe than the political theories of the European "idealists."

NILS ANDRÉN

8   The Special Conditions of the Baltic Subregion

DEFINITIONS AND REGIONAL CHARACTERISTICS

The term "Baltic subregion" is here, with some qualifications, used as equivalent to what is usually called the Scandinavian or the "Nordic" states. In Scandinavian usage they include the states represented on the Nordic Council, i.e., Denmark, Finland, Iceland, Norway, and Sweden. Among these five states, Iceland is geographically a mid-Atlantic state and will not be dealt with in the present context except when "Nordic cooperation" is taken up in an institutional sense and in the historical survey. Properly speaking, only Denmark, Finland, and Sweden are "Baltic" states. Norway, with a one-thousand mile border toward Sweden in the East and long historical connections with both Denmark and Sweden, has so much in common with the other states that it may well be included in the subregion.

The Baltic subregion, as defined, has a population of almost 22 million people (Denmark and Finland about 5 million each, Norway almost 4 million, and Sweden around 8 million). With the exception of Finland, they speak very similar languages which on the whole can be understood by all. The Finnish language, spoken by the majority of the Finnish people, is totally different, but there is a considerable Swedish-speaking minority in Finland and Swedish is, along with Finnish, an official language in the country. Culturally, the subregion is an area of considerable homogeneity. Economically, the region is rich, but with considerable differences between the states. Sweden is very rich, even in a trans-Atlantic comparison, while the others reach a good Western European level of prosperity.

It is only natural that this area, looked upon from the outside, is usually regarded as a unit. The Nordic peoples themselves, however, are far more conscious of the many little ways in which they differ from one another. From time to time this consciousness has completely dominated their mutual relationship. However, during the last decades the gradual progress of Nordic cooperation and the general development of Nordic interrelationships have actively contributed toward the awareness of common interests and ties among the states of the region. In general, the centripetal tendencies have increased in the subregion, at least when looked upon in a short perspective. In the political field, however, there has, as yet, not been a definite breakthrough. The Nordic states are subjected to the influence of competing loyalties and different interests, not least in the field of security. Thus, in spite of the increasing significance of centripetal forces, the centrifugal surge is still very strong.

A HISTORICAL PERSPECTIVE

In this respect the historical traditions of the Nordic states reflect influences in both directions. Even if it seems possible to notice a continuing change in the balance, these traditions have on the whole rather facilitated a centrifugal trend than otherwise. Periodic attempts have been made to unite the Nordic states into a single national unit, but success has been both limited and temporary. Toward the end of the Middle Ages all the Nordic peoples were joined together for some time in an actual Baltic and North Sea empire under Danish leadership. This was the "Kalmar Union"; its first two or three decades were tolerably happy but they were followed by a century-long death struggle with intermittent wars between union supporters and Swedish separatists. A permanent result of the union was, however, a close association between the Danes and the Norwegians. The union between the two peoples was soon completely dominated by the Danes, and from the middle of the sixteenth century Norway was in actual fact a Danish province. Finland assumed a somewhat similar position in relation to Sweden during the six hundred years that it formed part of the Swedish Kingdom.

When the Kalmar Union was virtually dissolved by the establishment of the modern Swedish Kingdom in 1523, a pattern had hence emerged, according to which the Baltic subregion was divided into two political entities, Denmark-Norway and Sweden-Finland. This pattern remained for about three hundred years, but during the Napoleonic Wars a new phase of disintegration took place. Sweden was forced to give up its sovereignty over Finland after an unsuccessful war with Russia (1808-1809). Finland became a Russian province with the status of a separate Grand Duchy under the Russian Czar.

A few years later Sweden sought compensation for this loss in the East by forcing Denmark to give up Norway. Norway became united with Sweden, no longer a subordinate province as was its relation to Denmark, but a self-governing state joined in a union under the same monarch. The leadership in foreign affairs, however, remained in Swedish hands, and the monarch was thought of as principally representing Swedish interests. It was an increasingly unhappy political marriage. The union was peacefully dissolved in 1905, and Norway gained full sovereignty.

Finland took advantage of the Russian Revolution in 1917 to establish itself as an independent state. A few words may here also be allowed for Iceland. Iceland had enjoyed a few centuries of independence during and after the heroic Saga Age. After growing internal disorder it came first under Norwegian and subsequently under Danish rule. In 1944 it cut off the last ties with Denmark and became an independent republic. Furthermore, during the post-war period Denmark has from time to time encountered difficulties from increasing nationalism on the Faroe Islands. Thus disintegration and not unity has in actual fact been the predominant tendency in the political development both of the Nordic area as a whole and of the Baltic subregion.

Since the days of the Kalmar Union, no attempts have thus far been successful in persuading the Nordic states to surrender part of their national sovereignty in favor of some kind of common Nordic superstructure. While the nationalistic movements of the nineteenth century contributed toward the unification of both Germany and Italy, the only positive effect of "Scandinavianism" (the "Pan-Scandinavian movement") was to accelerate the dissolution of old traditional prejudices among the Nordic states, making it in the terms of Professor Karl Deutsch into a "security community," within which the recourse to armed force for settling internal conflicts is regarded as impossible. Only recently have the forces of disintegration within the Nordic area been gradually counterbalanced by conscious efforts to establish a more effective rapprochement. These attempts, however, have not in any formal sense touched upon the sovereignty of the states involved. In fact, sovereignty may have become an obsolete concept, even if in law it is still totally unscathed. Thus it would not seem incorrect to conclude that the Nordic states have been more and more separated from each other by their long common history.

This brief perspective should serve the purpose of underlining what may be called the centrifugal conditions for the centripetal forces in the Baltic subregion which have been created by its traditional experiences and attitudes. They have provided one basic axiom for the relations between the states of the subregion: whatever cooperation takes place between them must not affect their position as completely sovereign states. This axiom is also reflected in the institutional framework which has emerged for the post-war cooperation between these states.

GROWTH AND INSTITUTIONALIZATION
OF NORDIC COOPERATION

From what has been said it should be clear that Nordic cooperation, as we know it, is of comparatively recent origin. In its present form it has on the whole been created after 1945. The main innovation in the field of Nordic cooperation during the post-war years is primarily that the governments have in fact accepted such cooperation as one of their duties. This new departure could draw inspiration from several sources, such as: pre-war developments, however inconclusive, which also included the feeling of cultural identity and common interests stimulated by participation in international organizations; also the deep frustration created by the enforced wartime alignments, partly with different mutually hostile camps.

Cooperation in the subregion has thus moved from the area of voluntary effort to that of public policy. The most important expression of this acceptance is—apart from numerous declarations by responsible political leaders—the creation of permanent political and administrative institutions for cooperation on different tasks connected with governments, parliaments, and public administration is general. Another expression of the same phenomenon is regular consultations among the governments and among ministers representing the same area of activity in the states concerned.

Nordic cooperation within the public sector is, of course, best illustrated by a description of the various institutions through which it operates. The most important institution is the Nordic Council which was established in 1952 and which has been operating since 1953. The Council is primarily an instrument for cooperation between the Nordic parliaments. It consists of elected representatives from the parliaments, sixteen members each from Denmark, Finland, Norway, and Sweden, and five from Iceland. In the deliberations of the Nordic Council representatives of the governments also participate. By this device conflicts between parliamentarians and responsible government leaders have by and large been avoided. In a sense, however, the government representatives hold a subordinate position. They are not entitled to take part in the decisions of the Council.

The Statute of the Council does not include any rules limiting its competence only to matters that are specified. The basic rule is that the Council is an organ for joint consultation in matters on which joint measures by the five states or by any among them may take place. The fact that the Council lacks committees for foreign affairs, security and defense indicates, nevertheless, that there are practical limitations for the work of such a council. One such limitation is obvious. The five states represent at least three different positions in respect to national security.

It is often, and rightly, emphasized that the Nordic Council is exactly what its name implies. It is a council, not a parliament. This character is marked in the first place by the fact that its decisions, except for its internal administration and organization, can only take the form of recommendations to the governments of the states represented. This means that the states have not given up any of their national sovereignty to the Council. It is not a supranational organ but only an international, subregional organization for joint consultation.

The role of the Council as an instrument for consultation between the parliaments—and, to some extent, between the governments and the parliaments—of the Nordic states gives it both educational and integrating functions and an important coordinating task. By its mere existence the Council serves as a reminder that there may be a possible approach to many problems which is Nordic, not national, and which many times can offer valuable solutions to questions which seem to be difficult to solve if isolated on a national level. So far the joint Danish-Norwegian-Swedish enterprise, the Scandinavian Airlines System (SAS), established long before the Council (1946), has served as the most successful instance of a wider-than-national approach in the Baltic subregion. Nevertheless, it is true that the Council has not always been successful in its attempts to realize the hopes which—on more or less over-optimistic grounds—have been fostered around its activities. Even so it is evident that the Council is filling an essential practical function in the manner just referred to.

As already indicated there are regular meetings between ministers and they are not limited to such non-controversial fields as social policy, cultural policy, legislative harmonization, and communications. They deal also with matters of foreign policy and defense. In actual fact hardly any category of ministers meets as regularly and as often as the foreign ministers. This is in itself both interesting and significant. It shows that irrespective of the various security policies represented in the Balic subregion there is a number of matters on which a common Nordic attitude seems to be both natural and necessary. One large block of such questions is represented by the items on the agenda of international organizations of which the states are members. The United Nations and EFTA provide two important instances. And even if cold war issues related to the power blocs in Europe may be excluded from the formal agenda, it is unlikely that they are totally banned from the less formal parts of the meetings.

PRINCIPLES AND IDEOLOGIES
OF NORDIC COOPERATION

The Nordic Council was formed, on Danish initiative, in order to provide a counterbalance to the centrifugal forces represented by the different security policies of the Nordic states. On the whole, the position assigned to the Council reflected faithfully the limits to which the participant states were willing to go in the field of political coordination and harmonization. But certainly, those who promoted the formation of the Council also entertained hopes that the existence of a permanent agency for consultation on the official level should also in itself serve as a potent integrative force in the Baltic subregion. Even if the Council has not lived up to the expectations of its most eager supporters, it has nevertheless been the single most important stimulus in this direction. Gradually, during its development, a more clear ideology of Nordic cooperation has evolved. Its most authoritative expression so far was the Nordic Agreement on Cooperation, concluded in 1962 (the so-called Helsinki Treaty). In this Agreement the manner in which the aims of the cooperation should be fulfilled is specified, along with the tasks which are regarded to be of primary interest.

The Nordic governments expressed their wish to further the close connection existing between their states in regard to cultural, juridical, and social problems. Furthermore they wanted to establish uniform rules in the Nordic states in as many respects as possible; and, finally, to achieve an appropriate division of labor in all fields where the necessary prerequisites exist.

What was obviously lacking in this Agreement was a definition of long-range goals. The common Nordic fields of joint activities specifically embrace, according to the agreement, questions of law, culture, social affairs, and communications. Foreign policy was not specially mentioned. Nor was it formally excluded. Certain areas of foreign policy in a more restricted sense were nevertheless mentioned. The Agreement aimed in the economic field not only to break down trade barriers between the Nordic states, but also to deal with international trade questions, in order to promote Nordic interests both individually and jointly. For this purpose the states should consult each other. Joint consultations were also prescribed whenever possible for questions of mutual interest which are dealt with by international organizations and at international conferences. Another item was expressed in an undertaking to coordinate their activities for aid to and cooperation with developing countries whenever it would be possible and expedient.

The Agreement on Cooperation of 1962 was viewed as a summary of the cooperation that was in fact already taking place and as a codification in terms acceptable in international law. Not on any single point could the Agreement be regarded as pioneering new fields for Nordic cooperation. The conditional nature of all the undertakings is another characteristic feature—both of the agreement and of Nordic cooperation as it virtually exists. These undertakings have no binding form. They may be characterized as "gentlemen's agreements" between sovereign states, declaring their wish and intent to act according to certain principles but with their formal liberty of action preserved.

Even if this agreement has been, generally speaking, a codification of the direction of Nordic cooperation so far, it may nevertheless serve as an expression both of the possibilities for further developments and of the unique character of Nordic cooperation. It has aimed at reaching common solutions, on a voluntary basis, of questions which normally could be solved only after the creation of a common institutional basis in the form of a rather stable, common state, normally a federation.

From what has been said so far we could draw the conclusion that Nordic cooperation is marked by both vague and cautious aims and diffuse ideology. Rather, Nordic integration has taken place within various functional areas. We can speak of integration in the fields of social welfare policies, legislation, communication, education, research, and many other fields, mainly on a rather low level of integration with very limited spill-over effects. Further, it must be admitted that the problems involved have as yet not been subjected to much systematic investigation. Nevertheless, some hypotheses or tentative answers—based on practical experiences by numerous practitioners in the field of Nordic cooperation (including the author) rather than on theoretical and empirical investigations—may be suggested.

Even if fixed and declared goals are lacking to a large extent, it seems that there exists a kind of "cooperation ideology" containing both idealistic-emotional and utilitarian-pragmatic elements. The attitude of the "idealist" may be summarized in the following way: the Nordic peoples are related to one another in many different respects. Hence, it is natural, indeed a duty, for them to cooperate and to carry on cooperation in such a manner that the consciousness of this relationship is reinforced. Efforts based on these ideas may be said to express a kind of Nordic "nationalism" or, with a term connecting the present Nordic movement with that of the nineteenth

century, a modern "Pan-Scandinavianism." Others, probably a majority, look upon Nordic cooperation in a less ideological, more
pragmatic manner: considering that the Nordic states together constitute a linguistic, cultural, economic, social, and political-ideologi-
cal area of considerable homogeneity, possibilities should exist for
taking practical advantage of the benefit to all parties concerned of
the existence of such a large common milieu. Problems which cannot be effectively solved in each single state separately may be given
a common solution which can often yield substantial material advantages to all the participating states.

These two attitudes have been represented here in a more pure
form than they usually possess in reality. As a matter of fact, the
pragmatic Nordist is not often quite unaffected by the ideas of the
ideological "Nordism"; nor is the ideological Nordist completely
alien to pure utilitarian arguments. The distinction can nevertheless serve to clarify the conditions of Nordic cooperation. With a
terminology that is current in the field of Western European integration, the idealists may be called conscious functionalists—in
their short perspective aims and their techniques—who would rather
prefer to be federalists—in the ultimate aims of their efforts.

STRATEGY, DYNAMICS, AND LIMITATIONS OF NORDIC COOPERATION

We have noted that the concrete and long-range goals which
the theorists of integration usually demand as a basic prerequisite
for an integration process are hardly possible to trace in the practical politics of Nordic cooperation. On the other hand, there are,
no doubt, varying individual and special goals. Some people would
like to go very far; others are prepared to take one step at a time as
long as this can be defended on practical grounds. All have decided
to merge their differences in a kind of common Nordic utilitarian-
ism. The knowledge of the differences in goals leads to great caution
in respect to statements of principle.

As far as a "strategy" of integration in concerned, this is certainly
a very cautious method. In this pragmatic approach without fixed
long-range goals, there is nothing of the audacity which allows far-
reaching principles to lead to bold decisions followed by investiga-

tions and executive measures necessary for their implementation.
The Nordic strategy of action is definitely more "Fabian." It starts
with investigation, it proceeds to decision and execution only if the
matter under consideration is not one for which national interests
or external pressures draw distinct borders which have not been possible to overcome; indeed only if the investigation has led to complete political agreement concerning the desirable steps and measures. This technique will subsequently be illustrated by the efforts
toward Scandinavian unity in the field of security and the Nordic
efforts to establish closer economic cooperation. As they both
represent failures, total or partial, of Nordic cooperation, and as
both outcomes were influenced by external factors related to the
bipolar situation, they rather belong to the analysis of centrifugal
than of centripetal characteristics. The failures may also be taken
as instances of the weaknesses of the procedures adopted, of their
propensity of emphasizing rather than moderating political disagreement.

In spite of the obvious institutional weakness of Nordic cooperation, with practically no power for the common Nordic institutions
to make and enforce binding decisions on the member states, it is
obvious that the whole post-war development has been characterized by increasing interdependence between the states involved.
Following the process on a day-to-day or even year-to-year basis
this progress may appear as almost imperceptible. If one chooses,
however, to compare the situation in 1945 or in 1953, when the
Nordic Council started its work, with the present situation the trend
is very clear indeed. A few areas in which significant achievements
have been made could be mentioned: legal coordination and harmonization, social welfare, industrial production and labor mobility,
scientific research, cultural matters, education.

It is, hence, proper to ask the question: Which are the dynamic
factors behind this development? The answer is partly implied in
what has already been said about the institutional framework and
its conditions of operation. The existence of permanent institutions,
however limited in their authority, is one such factor. They have
facilitated regular contacts and developed a firm habit of joint
consultation. The pragmatic approach is both a weakness and a
strength. When successful it has clear spill-over effects. An immense
quantity of small interdependencies have been created, a virtual

"cobweb" in which most threads are very thin but which together form a fine-meshed net of considerable strength and with a steady tendency of growing even more fine-meshed. The best promise for future further growth may, however, be a growing impatience in many quarters with the slow progress and with the institutional weakness—in coordinated leadership, administrative and research capacity, and independent decision-making authority—of the whole Nordic organizational set-up.

Even so, it would be unrealistic and incomplete not to emphasize that the states have hardly as yet succeeded in taking full advantage of the machinery for closer cooperation and consultation that has been created. Understanding of the immense advantages which can be derived from closer cooperation still seems to be somewhat obscured by traditional attitudes of national isolation and jealousies, and by a conspicuous lack of vision of long-range goals. These shortcomings are, among other things, reflected both in the reluctance of the politicians to take up major questions for serious and persistent consideration and in the rather uninspired way in which many national administrative authorities are dealing with Nordic matters submitted to them for appropriate action. In addition, it is still—after so many years—an open issue whether Nordic "integration" will ever be able to develop according to its inherent potentialities and attain maturity and permanence, or whether it will be overtaken by international developments involving wider schemes of cooperation with greater appeal and strength. The "United States of Norden" seems to be an unrealistic dream. But a Nordic Commonwealth kept together by a growing, invisible network of obligations and traditions is emerging already and may, if given the support of favorable external conditions, become a vital political reality. The proposed Nordic customs union, "NORDEK," was intended by its authors to be a significant part of such a network. However, so far it has proved to be another instance of Nordic failure due to the overwhelming strength of centrifugal forces. While Denmark and Norway, after the fall of de Gaulle, looked upon the proposed NORDEK as a step towards the EEC, this very attitude made NORDEK objectionable to the Soviet Union and hence politically impossible for Finland. Nevertheless, it is likely that some of the ideas included in the NORDEK Treaty will be pursued in less spectacular forms than those originally suggested.

This brings us to the question of the relationship of the centripetal forces in the Baltic subregion to the Superpowers. In one respect the existence of competing, even mutually hostile, Superpowers has definitely had a positive effect on the centripetal forces. The cold war forced a divisive security pattern upon the Nordic states. The formation of the Nordic Council was a reaction against this development. Its purpose was to a large extent to establish a counter-balance to the negative effects for the Nordic regional community created by the different security roles forced upon the Nordic states by the cold war.

Of the Superpowers, the Soviet Union was definitely suspicious of the Nordic integration movement. This was especially obvious in regard to the formation of the Nordic Council. Moscow expressed fears, indeed definite accusations, that the Council, combining NATO countries and neutrals (Sweden in the first instance), aimed at an expansion of NATO influence in the Baltic subregion. After a few years Moscow accepted the Nordic Council at its face value. Its fears were removed and as a result, in 1955, Finland, which had not been a "charter member," also joined the Nordic Council.

Another aspect of the relationship between Nordic cooperation and the Superpowers deals with efficiency and competitive strength. Very often, Nordic cooperative enterprises have been recommended and supported in order to reach a combined subregional strength which would yield a total efficiency, unavailable for each of the states separately. A pooling of efforts could make them competitive also in relation to the immense scientific, technological, and industrial strength not only of the Superpowers but also of other leading industrial states such as West Germany, Great Britain, and Japan.

PERSPECTIVES ON SECURITY

The centrifugal characteristics of the Baltic subregion, related to the Superpowers, are most obvious in the field of security, although they are also discernible in the approaches among the states of the region to institutionalized, international economic communities. In both cases, as already mentioned, there has been a clear struggle between centripetal and centrifugal forces. In spite of some determined efforts to reach solutions of an exclusively subregional nature, the centrifugal trends have so far been prevailing. This is especially clear in the case of security. Just as for the discussion of the conditions for Nordic cooperation and integration, it is now necessary to have a look back in history in order to understand the conditions for the security policies of the Nordic states.

A quick glance at the map shows Denmark as a peninsula—with surrounding islands on the Baltic side—connected with West Germany by its only land frontier. Finland has two land frontiers —a long borderline in the East with the Soviet Union and a shorter border in the West with Sweden. Norway's long mountainous "back" is chiefly turned to Sweden, but a short part of it in the north faces the Soviet Union. Sweden alone in the Baltic subregion has no frontier contact with any present or past Great Power.

These geographical, indeed strategical, conditions have to a great extent influenced the security problems of the states concerned. Ever since the fratricidal wars between Sweden and Denmark ended—their last outbreak occurred during the Napoleonic Wars—Germany has constituted the chief external security problem for Denmark. The rise of German nationalism during the nineteenth century made the problem an acute one. Danish national and dynastic ambitions clashed with the rising Bismarckian empire. The Danish efforts to balance the German threat with a Scandinavian orientation was of no avail. In a war in the 1860's Denmark had to face the combined aggression of Prussia and Austria alone, without any outside help either from Sweden-Norway or from the sea Powers. It led to heavy territorial losses, portions of which were restored to Denmark only after World War I, during which Denmark along with Sweden and Norway had been able to remain neutral. Except for the limitations imposed by membership in the League of Nations, Denmark based its foreign policy between the wars on neutrality. This policy was not supported by resolute efforts to maintain a strong defense. In part, this was due to unrealistic hopes for peaceful international development, and in part to a realistic appreciation of the difficulties of conducting an effective defensive war against an aggressor.

When Hitler, on the eve of World War II, offered nonaggression treaties with the Scandinavian states, Denmark alone felt unable to reject the offer. In April 1940, when Germany invaded Denmark and Norway, the treaty proved of no value. World War II did not bring about a re-evaluation of the basic doctrines of Danish foreign policy. When the war ended Denmark wanted to resume a neutral position, with only such limitations as were imposed by membership in the United Nations. Christmas Møller, Foreign Minister in the first Danish post-war government, had declared that Denmark should act with the United Nations and that it would not participate in such special arrangements as a Western regional pact. At the time of this declaration, Soviet troops still remained on the small Danish island of Børnholm. At the same time, however, there were also strong currents in favor of a stronger Scandinavian orientation.

Finland's foreign policy after independence was marked by efforts to reach security in relation to its Eastern neighbor, from which it had extricated itself during the Russian Revolution. Imperial Germany had effectively assisted in this liberation, but after the German collapse Finland oriented itself toward the Western Powers. Subsequently some abortive efforts had been made to provide for better security in combination with the other new border states emerging after the downfall of Czarist Russia. Eventually Finland embarked in the mid-1930's on a suspicious neutrality, seeking with little success support from the other Nordic states in the region. Sweden seemed in the late 1930's prepared to embark on a joint Swedish-Finnish scheme to protect the Aland Islands (demilitarized under Finnish sovereignty but with a purely Swedish population). However, Sweden withdrew from the scheme when it faced stubborn Soviet opposition.

Finnish neutrality was supported by a strong defense. Neither proved sufficient to keep the country out of war when the Soviet Union took advantage of the opportunities created by the Molotov-Ribbentrop Pact (between the Soviet Union and Germany) in 1939 to embark on a policy of restoring the old borders of Russia. Finnish resistance in the famous Winter War of 1939–1940 was, however, sufficiently successful to ensure survival as an independent state. Subsequently Finland rejected the idea of returning to neutrality with Swedish support, and found it necessary to seek German help in order to resist continued Soviet pressure. As a result, Finland again became involved in World War II when the German-Soviet understanding was broken by the German invasion in 1941. Finland was however able to extricate itself from the German alliance before the collapse of Hitler's Reich. The armistice in 1944 was followed by a formal peace treaty only in 1947.

Norway adopted neutrality as the official basis for its foreign policy when, after the separation from Sweden in 1905, it assumed complete responsibility for its own relations with other states. As a state facing the Atlantic and with large seafaring interests—reflected by its enormous mercantile marine—it was from the beginning dependent on the goodwill of the maritime states—for a long time chiefly Great Britain. Even if Norway kept out of World War I, it was hardly able to retain a strict neutrality. It was too dependent on overseas supplies to be able—or even willing—to resist the pressure to adjust its resources toward the needs of the Entente war efforts. It became the "Allied Neutral." After the war, however, Norway returned to neutrality as the basis for its foreign policy. Membership in the League of Nations meant more a formal than a real infringement on this principle. Like its Scandinavian neighbors it contracted out of the obligations of League sanctions when the storm clouds again gathered over Europe in the 1930's. In contrast to Finland—and Sweden—but like Denmark, Norway did not support its neutrality with adequate military preparations, in spite of the fact that the country, through its geographical structure, was on the whole not difficult to defend. This negligence, for which the Norwegians were to pay a heavy price during World War II, was both due to a lack of political realism and political ideology and to too large a reliance on the protection offered by its maritime position in relation to the Great Powers.

When Germany occupied the country in 1940, its responsible government moved to London and continued the war as an Allied Power with support of the vast Norwegian shipping resources operating outside the area controlled by the Germans. Already during the war, the Norwegian government had made up its mind that in the future Norway had to revise its traditional policy of isolated neutrality. A Scandinavian defense alliance offered no realistic alternative; the future of Norwegian security lay in close cooperation with the Atlantic naval Powers, Great Britain and the United States.

The events of the war had increased the significance of the Soviet Union vis-à-vis Norway; Soviet troops played a major part in the liberation of North Norway, and Finnish territorial losses made the Soviet Union an immediate neighbor. This did not, however, create any acute problems, in view of the fact that the Atlantic Powers, Norway's natural allies, and the Soviet Union were wartime partners. When frictions between the victors became serious, Nor-

way's official position was that of offering to moderate the differences ("bridge-building"). Even if the policy of neutrality had been
abandoned, the policy, thus, had led in fact to a new neutrality-like
policy—between the new conflicting forces, both in European and
in world affairs. The initial success of Norway's position was reflected in the selection of Trygve Lie as the first holder of the office
of Secretary-General of the United Nations. In one of the first declarations of Halvard Lange, Lie's successor as Norwegian Foreign
Minister, it was emphasized that "Norway should cooperate with
everybody, without participating in any bloc formations."

Turning now to Sweden, we should note that it was not until
World War I that neutrality emerged as the basic doctrine of Swedish foreign policy. This transformation derived from a number of
causes. Sweden had been involved in numerous wars right from the
beginning of its emergence as an international actor. In the seventeenth century and the early eighteenth century Sweden had actively
participated in the formation of Europe's affairs as a major Power
(e.g. under Gustavus Adolphus and Charles XII). However, from
the end of the Napoleonic Wars and onwards the international
balance of power had undermined the basis for Swedish power
politics. At the same time the relative power balance in the Baltic
area contributed to offering Sweden a position of relative security.

Sweden has now clearly the most favorable strategic position in
the Baltic subregion. This situation is illustrated by the fact that
Sweden has not participated in a war for more than 150 years. During the earlier part of this era of peace, foreign policy was not marked
by a conscious desire for neutrality. Sweden attempted to safeguard
its national security by orienting itself in turn to different Great
Powers. During the Crimean War this policy almost brought Sweden
to the brink of war—against Russia. Under the influence of pan-
Scandinavianism, Sweden made attempts to help Denmark in the
dispute over Schleswig-Holstein. Although Swedish troops were
held in preparedness on Danish territory in 1848, they were not
called upon to intervene actively. In 1864 Sweden was restrained
only by its own weakness from helping Denmark against Prussia
and Austria.

The years between the World Wars were of great importance for
Sweden's foreign policy outlook and view of international affairs.

Swedish thinking on foreign affairs may be said to have moved along a continuum on which the one extreme was represented by nationalistic, largely isolationist and suspicious views of the outside world. This view has been traditionally conservative, supporting the idea of a strong defense. The other extreme has been more idealistic, marked by an optimistic belief in international cooperation and organization as a means to achieve a lasting peace. Traditionally this is a "leftish" view, often with pacifist undertones. During the interwar years the two conflicting attitudes were especially demonstrated on two occasions: when Sweden was to enter the League of Nations, and when the government decided in 1925 to reduce the defense establishment.

The tension between the two attitudes was greatly reduced by the developments after the mid-1930's. At first the conservative, "realist" school of thought appeared to have gained ascendancy. Sweden began to rearm in 1936 in response to the rapidly deteriorating international situation. The impotence of the League of Nations, underlined by Italy's attack on Ethiopia, made Sweden participate with its Scandinavian neighbors and other small European Powers in a declaration that Sweden did not regard itself to be bound by the League's sanction rules.

The new, positive view on the need for defense was dictated by external circumstances. It had, however, been foreshadowed by economic and social developments at home. The socialist idea that armed forces were primarily an instrument in the interest of the privileged classes had by and large vanished. Further, the Molotov-Ribbentrop Pact, followed by the Soviet attack on Finland, undermined the traditional socialist view that armed force and warfare were the political instruments of capitalism. Hence there was general national agreement on quick rearmament during World War II to support a policy of neutrality that could keep Sweden out of the conflict.

The war imposed great strains on the Swedish political leadership in foreign affairs. From time to time major departures from the demands of strict neutrality according to the concepts of international law were made. Germany's initial successes led to the complete encirclement of Sweden. Several concessions had to be given, especially on transit rights for German troops and materials over

Swedish soil. Toward the end of the war concessions had also to be made to the wartime "United Nations"—with much less reluctance, however.

By the end of the war little was left of the old dichotomy of attitudes on foreign policy. The foundations had been laid for the remarkable national unity that has marked Sweden's activity in the international field during the post-war years. This unity has rested on certain guiding principles: neutrality in relation to Great Power blocs; a strong defense; active participation in international organizations and in international cooperation in general; and greater cooperation, if possible even integration, with the other Nordic states. Sweden's emphasis on both neutrality and Nordic cooperation was clearly illustrated by its reactions to the first critical phase in the cold war, in 1948.

THE COLD WAR AND NORDIC SECURITY

Two conclusions of the previous survey of the traditions and experiences of the states of the subregion are of special importance in this context. The first is that all the states on the eve of World War II had developed a policy of isolated neutrality. All the states were not aligned with any other Power. Nor were there any bonds of mutual security between the states. The second is that World War II had taught the states different lessons. Denmark, Norway, and Finland had all, in different ways, found that they had not been able to obtain security in "splendid isolation" from the external political environment. After the war Finland had to accept the necessity of establishing a relationship which involved both confidence and a certain dependence in its relationship to the Soviet Union. For Denmark and Norway the lesson of the war was that their exposed position made it difficult or impossible for them to reach security by remaining isolated from other states. For Sweden alone neutrality, supported by a strong defense, remained a practical political possibility. But for Sweden also, the awareness of the importance of the international environment was an obvious lesson of the war. This had been emphasized by the fact that the concern for maintaining a strong defense has on the whole remained unbroken during the whole post-war period.

The conclusions of these experiences were drawn by the four states involved when the cold war revealed the new pattern of Super-power confrontation. The first phase of significance for the Baltic subregion was the Marshall Plan, the largest economic aid program so far in history. This plan divided in fact the Nordic states into two groups.

Finland could not, in view of its relations to the Soviet Union, participate in this program. For Denmark and Norway it created no problems. Sweden could also participate in spite of its neutrality and in spite of the fact that the Soviet Union officially interpreted the Marshall aid program as an American attempt to interfere in Swedish internal affairs. Sweden's participation could be justified with the argument that the Marshall Plan meant uniting in tasks of reconstruction, not of political bloc formation directed against any non-participating states. This was of course at most only half the truth of the situation. The Swedish government had already in 1945 declared that, if contrary to expectation, a tendency would appear within the United Nations of a subdivision of the Great Powers into two camps, the policy of Sweden must be "not to let us be forced into such a group or bloc formation." Hence, the view of Sweden was that the Marshall Plan did not constitute a "bloc formation." This attitude bore much similarity to the declaration during the same period by Norwegian Foreign Minister Lange, quoted above.

The full effect of the differences in experiences and attitudes in the Baltic subregion were not to appear until the emergence of a Western European and subsequently an Atlantic security system. The first step was the establishment, on British initiative, of the de-fense alliance between Great Britain, France, and the Benelux states. This was met with "interest and sympathy" by Norway, as a contribu-tion to "the work towards a stabilization of the conditions in our part of the world." Sweden, on the other hand, emphatically rejected the idea of being connected with these efforts. It was declared to be in conflict with Swedish wishes and interests to choose sides by joining any Great Power bloc, "either by an explicit treaty of alliance or by tacit understanding on joint military action in case of a conflict." If the United Nations Organization was to be under-mined by political bloc formations or if it was otherwise paralyzed in its power of action, Sweden must have the liberty to choose the road of neutrality. Certainly, it was admitted that success for such a neutral policy did not depend on Sweden alone. But the wish was stressed not "to deprive ourselves of the possibility of keeping out of a new war" by any advance commitments.

Denmark represented on the whole an intermediate position between Norway and Sweden. While emphasizing loyalty to the United Nations and to the idea of Nordic cooperation, Norway expressed some understanding of the need for a Western defense arrangement of the states involved. But at the same time Norway also stressed that participation in the Marshall Plan must not be interpreted as an act of taking sides on the political issues between the Superpowers.

A SCANDINAVIAN DEFENSE ALLIANCE

Before a further division of the security pattern in the Baltic subregion became an established fact, a dramatic effort was made to avoid a split by finding an alternative solution. The Norwegian Foreign Minister had on the one hand stressed the desirability of a joint Nordic policy in the new situation. On the other hand he also warned that the military problems and security issues were not identical for Norway, Denmark, and Sweden. Hence it might be difficult to find a common solution to the problems. The initiative for such a solution came from Sweden.

The significance of the new situation can be summarized as follows. It was obvious that the subregion was in the process of being incorporated in the orbit of Superpower interests. Finland's position was clear. It was further confirmed in 1948 when Finland felt compelled to conclude a Treaty of Friendship and Mutual Assistance with the Soviet Union. Obviously Norway was attracted by the now emerging Atlantic security project. Denmark, on the other hand, was, in view of its geo-strategical situation, not in a position to affect the development. The two chief Scandinavian actors in the new security game thus were Norway and Sweden. For Sweden the prospects of the new situation appeared as definitely disquieting. Any constellation inside the Nordic area which would put Sweden between blocs, dominated by rival Superpowers, without any buffer, was seen as undesirable. From a Nordic point of view, affiliation of Norway within an Atlantic security pact, in combination with Finland's relations with the Soviet Union, would mean increased disintegration in Scandinavia and also a menace to the initial efforts toward Nordic cooperation which already at this time had been developed in more ambitious forms than ever before in modern times.

Even though the problem was clear, the solution was difficult. Participation in an Atlantic bloc was out of the question, but isolated neutrality could impose great strains on Sweden if its neighbors were all committed. In this situation the Swedes decided to explore a third solution—a Scandinavian defense alliance. Its basic principle was an arrangement according to which all the three states should together conduct a foreign policy according to the Swedish model. Scandinavia should be made into a credible neutral zone. This emerged clearly from Swedish declarations and from the three leading principles of the treaty that Sweden offered to its neighbors by the end of 1948. The first was a joint pledge that an attack against one of the three states should be regarded as an attack against all. The second was a pledge of neutrality. All parties of the treaty should declare that they would endeavor to keep out of possible future wars. Further, the parties should undertake not to conclude military treaties with any third Power. Thirdly, the joint Scandinavian neutrality should be an armed neutrality. Plans for joint defense should be worked out and the armaments of all the states should, within a reasonable time, be brought to a level corresponding to the actual need but with due regard for economic capabilities.

The plan failed to materialize. It did not meet the Norwegians' ideas of their security requirements. These included a demand, unacceptable for Sweden, that a Scandinavian solution must be supplemented with advance arrangements for outside help, if necessary. Other difficulties concerned the costs for rearmament. Norway was practically defenseless and had at that time expensive reconstruction projects in progress in the war-devastated areas in the north. The United States was the obvious source for cheap or free weapons, but these were reserved for members of the future NATO and other states to which the Americans had special commitments.

Finally, there were also psychological undercurrents. A certain bitterness against the eastern neighbor, Sweden, lingered from the experience of the Union, then dissolved for more than forty years, and from World War II. Certainly these were not decisive factors but they may have contributed to the Norwegian decision. The orientation toward the West of Norwegian trade was another factor.

Finally, to accept the Swedish view that a small Power or combination of Powers, if well-armed, could stand a reasonable chance of keeping out of war would, in a way, have constituted a strong or even devastating judgment of the defense policy conducted by Norway before April 1940.

During the defense negotiations Denmark was on the whole reduced to a rather passive role. Its first option was along the lines of the Swedish proposal. When the Norwegians had made up their mind, the Danes investigated the possibility of a bilateral Swedish-Danish defense arrangement patterned on the original Swedish offer. Sweden did not, however, regard this as a politically and strategically viable solution. In this situation, Denmark had no choice except to follow the Norwegian example of accepting membership in the emerging NATO. There is now clear evidence that this decision was met with Swedish understanding—and even with discreet approval.

THE NORDIC SECURITY SYSTEM

In retrospect it is obvious that the Swedish fears that led to the offer of a Scandinavian defense alliance have not materialized —at least not so far. The pattern of the security orientation of the Nordic states has in fact created a situation in which direct border confrontations between East and West in the Baltic subregion have been reduced to a minimum; namely, the Norwegian-Soviet border on the "Northern Cap" of Scandinavia.

In principle, however, the different security policies of the Nordic states seem to represent a fundamental and unbridgeable political separation. In practice, this view is modified in several respects. Denmark and Norway made their choice from necessity rather than inclination. Both states, especially Denmark, have retained a certain nostalgia for the position chosen by Sweden. The split in the political "personality" of the two states is illustrated by the fact that Denmark and Norway have both succeeded in acquiring NATO membership and protection on "minimum conditions." Politically this means that they have sought maximum protection with minimum provocation of the Soviet Union. Practically, it means that they both have refused to receive Alliance troops on their territory on a permanent basis, and do not want nuclear arms unless they regard themselves exposed to an immediate threat. Since Sweden has in fact refrained from using its technological capability to procure nuclear weapons, this means that the Baltic subregion is virtually a nuclear-free zone. Finland, although clearly within the Soviet security orbit, is not a member of the Warsaw Pact; it has gradually succeeded in acquiring recognition as a neutral state, and its political system has a Western structure. Finnish neutrality remains, however, qualified by the conditions of the 1948 Treaty of Friendship and Mutual Assistance with the Soviet Union, which under current arrangements will remain in force until 1975.

Since the failure of the plan for a Scandinavian defense alliance, it has been clearly recognized that—given the present European situation, which does not appear to have changed in any fundamental respect since 1948—closer cooperation between the Nordic states in the field of national security is neither in the interests of the individual states nor likely to improve the general position of the Baltic subregion as a whole in relation to the Superpowers. It is, nevertheless, possible that the increasing cooperation and "harmonization"—in some respects even integration—among the Nordic states may provide a favorable point of departure for closer relations in the field of security, should the external situation favor such a development. So far there is little evidence that such a situation is likely to materialize in the foreseeable future, and the general question of Danish and Norwegian membership in the EEC will continue to keep the question open.

The approach of the crucial year of 1969 for the NATO Alliance caused considerable restlessness and speculation about NATO within the Scandinavian states, and especially in Denmark and Norway, where the diversity of feelings about the NATO affiliation has never been completely subdued by the necessities of national security. The feeling that the cold war had receded encouraged both criticism against the NATO engagement and speculation about other possibilities for the future. The growing uneasiness over the Vietnam engagement of their chief ally and protector also had been a potent factor behind the criticism of the Atlantic security solution of the two states. However, on the level of practical politics this restlessness did not produce any tangible alternatives to the existing policies. On a more "academic" level it served as a stimulus for a discussion of various other options and the external conditions—recognized to be different from those then prevailing—which would be necessary for their realization. Even before the Czechoslovakian crisis of 1968, these analyses generally concluded that the existing pattern was better than any conceivable alternatives. Since then, both Denmark and Norway have unambiguously confirmed their intention to retain NATO membership.

For Finland the situation has always remained absolutely clear and without alternatives. It has had no choice—indeed no wish —except to find the best possible modus vivendi in relation to its "big neighbor." In Sweden the doctrines of non-alignment and neutrality are now so firmly entrenched that it would take a profound change to effect a reappraisal. In principle, the extension of the neutrality area along the lines of the 1948 plan is not entirely ruled out. But it is clear that a new initiative for such an extension of Sweden's security commitments will not come from the Swedes. It will have to come from its neighbors. Except for the most ardent Scandinavians, committed ideologically to Nordic unity, there appears to be very little enthusiasm for such a development.

SECURITY PROSPECTS FOR THE FUTURE

The conclusion is, then, that in the short perspective the states of the Baltic subregion still feel that the conditions which have been responsible for their present security policies are by and large still operative. In a longer perspective, however, it is reasonable to assume that the forces at work regionally and globally in the international system may change the security environment of the subregion. In order to appreciate to what extent such changes may affect the present Nordic security system it is necessary to define the major factors affecting the security of the four states involved.

The present security arrangement is largely a product of the bipolar situation characterizing the era of the cold war. The major hazards of this situation may be identified as the proximity of the overwhelming power of the Soviet Union—whose long-range goals are by no means as clear as its immediate security requirements— and the danger of confrontation between the two blocs centered on the Superpowers. Behind this danger lie the risks connected with the still unsettled state of Europe after World War II, particularly the German problem which has not only not been solved but remains the target of different, irreconcilable ambitions.

The German problem is of paramount importance to the future of all the Nordic states. Even if Germany was eclipsed by World War II and remains divided, West Germany is the single most important economic factor in Western Europe and could occupy the same position in a military sense. The German problem concerns Denmark especially. The German strategic evaluation of the position of Denmark has an almost ominous ring: "The Sound, the Belt, the Danish islands and Jutland with the bordering Schleswig-Holstein have become the No. 1 strategic position in Northern Europe." Obviously, there is no Western solution to the Danish security problem in a non-German context. Hence, it should be equally clear that Denmark, in order not to be overwhelmed economically, politically, or strategically, or even culturally, by its southern neighbor, must always be interested in a security system which includes an effective counterweight to actual or potential German domination. Among theoretically possible solutions only the United States is sufficiently strong and friendly (and conveniently distant) to be able to fulfil the role of containing possible West German ambitions in a manner consistent with Danish interests.

What has been said of Denmark is to some extent relevant for Sweden in its capacity as master of the eastern shore of the Sound separating Sweden and Denmark. From a purely strategic point of view, it is in the Swedish interest that possible West German ambitions be tempered by the global efforts to preserve the international power balance represented by the chief NATO Power. This fact cannot be affected by the temporary low tide of American popularity in Sweden caused by the Vietnam conflict. For Finland, whose obligations under its treaty with the Soviet Union are conditioned by the German "danger," the interest in containing possible West German ambitions must obviously be even greater.

Norway is in a different position in relation to the German question. Its strategic position is definitely Atlantic. Norway's concern for the Cap area leads to an America-oriented security policy rather than to a Europe-oriented one, as the Cap is thought to be more significant for Atlantic than for European strategic requirements. To some extent this concern for the Northern Cap is shared both by Finland and by Sweden whose territories may offer some logistic possibilities for controlling and supplying installations in the area via Finland from the east.

Judging the future security problems of the Baltic subregion, it is hence necessary to keep in mind that the four states have somewhat different primary threat perceptions. Both Denmark and Norway have, for different reasons, a direct and vital interest in a continuing American engagement in European and North Atlantic security. For Sweden and Finland the same interest exists but in a less direct way. Sweden's central position in the area is underlined by the fact that the chief security problem of both Denmark and Norway is Sweden's concern also. If the Öresund (the Sound) and the Cap were the only considerations for Sweden, another security solution might have been sought in 1948 than non-alignment and neutrality. Sweden is, however, in a strategic sense predominantly a Baltic Power, whose security policy must be conditioned by the Baltic situation as a whole.

ECONOMIC COOPERATION—
A HISTORICAL PERSPECTIVE

Security has been the first, and most constant, area in which post-war efforts have been attempted toward closer cooperation in the Baltic subregion. With some reservations, which will be further elaborated, economic cooperation constitutes the second area of major failure.

Historians of Nordic cooperation can point to the fact that proposals for closer cooperation in the economic field were raised as early as the middle of the nineteenth century. The first tangible result was the establishment of a monetary union in the 1870's. It foundered on the strains caused by World War I, lacking the support of a common policy in relation to foreign exchange and trade. For two decades toward the end of the nineteenth century Swedish-Norwegian trade was unhampered by tariffs. The mutual economic interdependence of the Scandinavian states increased during World War I, when German submarine warfare reduced the normal flow of overseas imports to these states. The exchange of goods between them was then more than doubled. After the war it receded back to "normalcy" (then around 12%).

New efforts in a somewhat wider context were made during the Great Depression when the Nordic states, now including Finland, together with Belgium and the Netherlands, agreed that none of the states would raise their tariffs without giving the other partners to the treaty an opportunity to express their views on the proposed increases. In the more limited Nordic arena, special committees were established in the mid-1930's in order to investigate the possibilities for closer Nordic cooperation in the economic field. World War II interrupted these efforts, when all the states, Sweden only excepted, were dragged into the maelstrom.

After the war the work to promote economic cooperation was gradually resumed. The need for small states to combine efforts in order to survive and thrive in a world dominated by industrial and economic giants was gradually recognized. There was a growing recognition of the many signs indicating that the significance of the small state would be much smaller than in the past. Closer cooperation might even be a necessary condition in order to enable the Nordic countries to play a role in international cooperation at all. For these countries Nordic cooperation could hence be a natural step toward, not an obstacle to, international cooperation.

A NORDIC COMMON MARKET?

However, basic truths of this kind are more easily open to theoretical recognition than to translation into practical policies. This truth may be illustrated by the official treatment during the past two decades of Nordic economic cooperation. A new joint Nordic Committee for Economic Cooperation was formed in 1948. For political reasons Finland was unable to participate at this juncture. The Finns joined in the work of the Committee only seven years later, after entering the Nordic Council. The purpose of the Committee was primarily to investigate the possibilities for a common Nordic tariff and for reduced tariffs, for limitation of other trade restrictions and expansion of cooperation in the field of trade policies. A preliminary report in 1950 raised expectations in many quarters by recommending in principle the establishment of a customs union to be gradually implemented over a period of ten years.

The report was not politically acceptable. It was the work of experts, not of politicians. The ensuing discussion revealed the tension between long-range visions and short-range interests. The chief stumbling block was Norway's fears that its weak, warworn, and strongly protected industry would not be able to survive the keen competition of Swedish and Danish industries in a "Common Nordic Market." Hence, a new and more limited goal was set for the experts; namely, to investigate the possibilities for tariff reductions on limited groups of products. This phase of preparation for Nordic economic cooperation was however disturbed by Western European developments, leading eventually to the Rome Treaty in 1957 and the inauguration of the Common Market in 1959.

A new formula then had to be provided. It was agreed that the Nordic investigation should be carried out with special consideration for the wider Western European schemes. The new situation served to emphasize that the effects of the integrating forces in the Baltic subregion always have to be judged and measured in relation to the competition existing between these forces and integration movements on a wider regional basis, affecting all the Nordic states or the majority among them. The issue of Nordic economic cooperation, both in the 1950's and subsequently, has clearly demonstrated that the integration movement has had to face two very real obstacles, which so far have combined to produce a very effective resistance. The movement has had competition not only with the growing internationalism stretching far beyond the borders of the Baltic subregion, but also with the persevering nationalistic interests and emotions of the states involved.

In spite of the ingeniousness of the Committee for Economic Cooperation, its proposals did not lead to political decisions. The very procedure which was followed tended to maximize differences and hence to reduce the possibilities for success. The Committee could not base its work on a firm political decision but was charged to do the research which would help the political decision-makers establish if there was a basis of common interests necessary for a political decision. There is little doubt that this "Fabian" strategy contributed to the failure to create a Common Nordic Market in the 1950's. The defeat was a recognized fact in 1958. However, due to other, simultaneous events it became a defeat more in form than in fact. Even if the Nordic scheme was buried, many of its goals were soon realized in a wider Western European regional context.

FACING A EUROPEAN COMMON MARKET

This brings us to the subject of the role of the Baltic sub-region in the movement for European unity. We have already noted that all the states except Finland joined the Marshall Plan and, consequently, also the OEEC (Organization for European Economic Cooperation). With the same exception they also became members of the Council of Europe. After the Messina conference in 1955, paving the way for the Rome Treaty two years later, negotiations were opened between the OEEC states on the establishment of a European free trade area, as discussed briefly in the preceding chapter and in the Epilogue. The aim, shared by the Nordic states involved, was not to prevent the Community as planned by the six Powers composing it. It was rather to seek a way of avoiding the split in Western Europe into different economic blocs, which might be the result if the six states insisted on a scheme in which the remaining states of OEEC were unable or unwilling to participate. Great Britain was reluctant at that time to give up its system of Commonwealth preferences, and Scandinavians had adopted, for different reasons, the same attitude. All the three states (Denmark, Norway, and Sweden) depended considerably on their trade with Britain. For Sweden a close integration with six NATO states, many of whom confessed ultimate political aims for their economic cooperation, could also raise problems of serious consequences for its chosen security policy.

The end of this phase in the European unity movement was the split of Western Europe in two trade "blocs," the EEC and EFTA (European Free Trade Association), the former consisting of the "inner Six" of the Coal and Steel Community, the latter of the "outer Seven" states, later to be joined by Finland through a special association treaty. From a purely Nordic point of view, however, this development meant that some of the goals for a Nordic Market were realized in the wider framework of EFTA. A closer look at the trade statistics since the formation of EFTA indicates not only that there was a substantial general increase in inter-EFTA trade at the expense of the trade with the EEC states, but also that inter-Nordic trade increased more rapidly than the trade of the Nordic states with EFTA as a whole. The free trade conditions for industrial products, together with other special measures in the Baltic subregion—e.g., the creation of a Common Nordic Labor Market —have also facilitated a growing integration in the economic field. In general, the EFTA period has been one of rapidly raising productivity and prosperity in the Baltic subregion.

To what extent was the development related to the Superpowers? One such relationship is clear: the cautious and slow Finnish approach to the Free Trade Association and the special trading favors which the Finns had to grant to the Soviet Union in order to get approval for their participation as an associate of EFTA. Further developments made this Superpower relationship even more clearly discernible.

The American attitude was of considerable significance. Ever since the establishment of EFTA the United States view has been that the creation of European trade blocs tended to favor inter-European trade at the expense of American exports (an effect which has since been heavily offset by enormous United States industrial investments in several Western European states). This "discrimination" could be tolerated insofar as EEC was concerned, because EEC aimed at promoting one of the recognized goals of American policy: political unity in Europe. Hence it could contribute to the strength of NATO. For EFTA, no similar excuse could be found. For these reasons a further expansion of EEC was in the interests of the United States.

This attitude, together with a growing British reappraisal of the relative significance of the Commonwealth and Europe for its future political and economic development, was an important factor in the 1961 initiative of the European unity movement. In actual fact, a rapprochement between the inner Six and the outer Seven was one of the recognized, original goals of EFTA. The EFTA states were anxious to keep in step with the Common Market in reducing tariffs in order to facilitate a future amalgamation in some form of the two trade blocs. During the first years of EFTA this desire to bridge the gulf to EEC played a predominant part. An agreement in 1961 that the member states, in future negotiations with EEC, should remain united and keep their organization intact at least until all the member states had seen their legitimate interests provided for, reflected this aim.

This declaration of mutual solidarity soon assumed special significance when, also in 1961, Britain announced its intention to open negotiations with the Common Market concerning membership. The British example was immediately followed by Denmark. In Norway and Sweden there was more hesitation. Eventually, Norway followed Britain and Denmark and applied for membership. The reaction of Sweden, however, was another illustration of the significance of the Superpower relationships. Sweden's attitude to EEC had already previously been conditioned by its choice of security policy. Now, Sweden officially declared that only association, not full membership, could be reconciled with non-alignment and neutrality and with other Swedish interests.

In a widely-broadcast declaration Prime Minister Tage Erlander declared that in order to enable Sweden to provide for its own interests in foreign affairs it was necessary to safeguard "a certain degree of freedom of action both in practice and as laid down by formal agreements." Sweden's non-aligned policy played an important part toward safeguarding this freedom of action, but it had to be supplemented by consistent efforts toward avoiding commitments outside the military realm which might make it difficult or impossible to choose a neutral course when confronted with a conflict and which could make the outside world lose confidence in the genuineness of Sweden's desire to select such a political course.

The danger involved in affiliation with EEC was hence not that the policy of non-alignment would be impossible but rather that it would be inefficient as an instrument for Swedish foreign policy. In order to keep this policy efficient in wartime, Sweden had to avoid incorporation in the economic system of states who were members of Superpower blocs. In other words, in order to function at all, the non-aligned policy had to be credible. If this was not so, Sweden might run the danger of an attack from states that might believe that Sweden had in actual fact committed itself to the other side. Further, if the non-aligned position ceased to be credible, the possibilities for Sweden to play a useful international role could be weakened.

General de Gaulle's veto of the application of Britain for membership in EEC in 1963, ended this phase of the attempts of the EFTA states to join the Common Market. Within the field of European trade politics the Scandinavian states had to fall back on EFTA now in order to make the Free Trade Association function as a viable and competitive economic organization, and not only to create a basis for negotiations for amalgamation with the EEC.

The stalemate in EFTA-EEC relations raised fresh interest in further cooperation within the Baltic subregion itself. In 1966 the Swedish government presented a package of proposals for tariff harmonization, better conditions for agriculture and fisheries, harmonization of legislation concerning their economies, closer co-operation in external trade, etc. Although the term was not directly used, it amounted to a significant step toward a Nordic Customs Union. Prime Minister Erlander said:

> The situation being what it is, we believe, that it is important for the Nordic countries to keep even more closely together—it is important for ourselves, for the advancement of our own economies and our own prosperity; and it strengthens EFTA if this substantial market of ours keeps together. Also when some time in the future, it may be a question of trying to come into negotiating contact with EEC—which all of us hope for in a relatively near future despite of our many failures—we think if all the Nordic countries present a joint front it will give all the countries who are members of the Nordic Council a much better chance to obtain conditions that we can all accept.[1]

The proposal did not lead to the expression hoped for of "a political determination which will make it possible for us to tackle rather more energetically the problems we must indeed try to solve in some way or another." The Danes especially were very hesitant about its usefulness. As usual there was the permanent Danish preoccupation with the conditions for the export of agricultural exports. Also, the Danes feared that, in view of the Swedish neutral position, the possibilities might be reduced for a joint future Nordic entry into the Common Market. In fact, the Danes even seemed prepared to take such a step before the British had again decided to renew their efforts to be admitted to EEC.

When Prime Minister Harold Wilson in 1966 announced that Britain should make a new attempt to approach the Common Market, the reaction of the Nordic states followed very closely the pattern of 1961. Denmark immediately declared its readiness to follow the British example. Norway slowly followed suit, also applying for

---

[1] *Documents on Swedish Foreign Policy 1966* (Stockholm: Royal Ministry for Foreign Affairs, 1967), p. 69.

full membership. This time Sweden was not as sure as before about the possible form of affiliation. Economic interests weighed heavily in favor of membership and the changes in the Common Market brought about by de Gaulle's European antifederalism, had clearly made EEC less objectionable to Sweden. However, hesitation was great, and the Swedish government, with general political support, decided to ask for negotiations on affiliation, leaving the form in which this should be accomplished an open issue. The formula covered the dissensions still existing on the kind of affiliation that would be reconcilable with the demands of Swedish non-alignment and neutrality. It was, however, obvious that the government still regarded association as the only safe form. In spite of support from the majority of EEC member states for expanding the organization, as described in the preceding chapter, de Gaulle again succeeded in barring the entry of the hopeful applicants. Britain was still not "worthy" and the question was for the second time brought to a standstill.

And again the lack of success for a broadly based definition of European economic integration gradually turned the attention of the Nordic states to the possibilities for strengthening the economic bonds within their own subregion. In 1968 a change of government took place in Denmark. It was followed by a new official attitude toward Nordic economic cooperation. The Danes seemed to have come round to accepting the idea that the Nordic states ought to strengthen their mutual economic ties in order to establish a position of greater strength in their negotiations with the Common Market.

A new period of negotiations by experts followed. It led to a report based on the following principles: cooperation should have as a goal the capability of the states to participate in or to cooperate with a larger European community; it should be carried out with due consideration for the duties of the Nordic states in relation to EFTA; the security and foreign policies of the states should not be affected by Nordic economic cooperation; finally, cooperation should ensure a balance between advantages and disadvantages for all the participating states.

In spite of a promising opening, the outcome soon appeared to be uncertain. The new hopes for Britain and EFTA raised by the disappearance of General de Gaulle as a major actor on the French and

European scene threw EFTA and NORDEK into some confusion. There has been far from full agreement as to the possibilities of realizing the Nordic goals without violating the principles accepted as basic conditions for the enlarged economic cooperation. This seems to be the case especially in relation to the security condition and to the principle of equal advantages and disadvantages. In 1970, however, agreement seemed to be reached between Denmark, Finland, Norway, and Sweden on the establishment of the NORDEK customs union. For reasons already referred to, Finland subsequently felt unable to ratify the NORDEK treaty.

SUMMARY AND CONCLUSIONS

The purpose of the preceding pages has been to present some major aspects of the centripetal and centrifugal forces at work in the Baltic subregion of Europe and to illustrate the significance of the Superpower relationships on their effects. The aspects chosen have dealt with the growth and institutionalization of Nordic cooperation, with security and with economic integration, both Nordic and Western European. Other aspects have intentionally been neglected as they seem to have very little to add to the general picture emerging from the three "heavy" subjects chosen for analysis.

One further instance only will be added in support of this assertion. Centrifugal and centripetal forces are reflected also in the behavior of the Nordic states in international organizations on which both these states and the Superpowers are represented. A number of studies have been made of this subject. The findings are hardly surprising. Over the ten-year period 1956–1965 the Nordic states voted in the United Nations General Assembly more often with the United States than with the Soviet Union. This tendency was, quite naturally, strongest among the NATO member states and weakest for Finland, while Sweden held an intermediate position. As a whole, this investigation confirms the conclusions that can be drawn from an analysis of the behavior of the Nordic states on the issues covered in this survey. This behavior can be summarized in the following propositions:

1) There is a clear tendency toward Nordic cooperation and

toward seeking joint Nordic solutions to an increasing number of problems.

2) This tendency is especially evident when a) the security interests, evolving from the different positions chosen in the international system by the states are unaffected by the issues; b) when strong economic interests, such as export trade, the development of weak or new domestic industries, etc., are not involved; c) to this could be added, although the matter has not been explicitly dealt with in this chapter, when no over-riding interests of domestic party politics have pressed for an isolated, non-Nordic approach.

As shown in various contexts, the Superpower relationship is especially strong in security matters but it has also had effects—both direct and indirect—in economic matters. In general the centrifugal effects have dominated in matters of security while in the economic sphere the effects have clearly worked in both directions. If we look upon the EEC—stretching the use of the term—as an economic Superpower, the effects of actual or expected Superpower relationships assume obviously larger proportions than if the term is used in a conventional sense only.

One final question: What has been the part performed by the Baltic subregion and its component parts in the work of Western European unity and what may in this respect be expected in the future? The answers are, by and large, contained in the previous survey. Clearly, the situation is not the same everywhere. Three factors seem to be of special importance: the need for security and the solutions chosen to meet this need; the demands of the economies; and the attraction of Nordic cooperation. The calculations based on these three factors do not yield the same result in all the four states. Denmark is traditionally the most vociferous protagonist of Nordic cooperation. Its security and economic interests, as presently understood, make it nevertheless the most decisive Nordic applicant for full membership in EEC. Denmark's security needs present no obstacles for its European ambitions. Norway is basically in a similar position. For Sweden, the security requirements present, as we have noted, a definite difficulty for the realization of a whole-hearted Western European policy. Finland's position is even more restricted. Its freedom of maneuver toward Western Europe is strictly limited. Hence Nordic cooperation assumes for Finland special significance both as an externally acceptable opening to the West and probably also as a valuable goal in itself.

For the Baltic subregion as a whole, the goals and methods of Nordic cooperation indicate that Nordic subregionalism is not looked upon as a substitute for a wider Western European regionalism. The conflicting priorities of security and economic interests make, however, the subregion a rather hesitant actor on the European scene. This situation seems likely to last as long as the present security interests and restrictions remain.

. . . what men think is
more important in history
than the objective facts.

—*A. J. P. Taylor*

NOTE TO THE EPILOGUE

This book is more than an overview of the personal views
of Europeans toward Europe in the mid-twentieth century. Each of
the essays reaches out for some larger perspective which should be
of value for students of international politics. One of the pitfalls
of studying human affairs from the position of the political scien-
tist is that it is easy to see events as either dominated by short-run
factors, or else as subject to certain "mechanistic" predilections
which the new discipline has developed.

The affairs of Europe resist both attributions, not only because
they are of themselves complex but nonetheless increasingly important as we near the twenty-first century, but also because Europe,
taken from the long view, has been so overwhelmingly the shaper
of the international system in which all of the world now lives and
operates. In a very real sense, most of the political groupings of the
world are, in terms of international politics, heirs of the European
tradition.

In the Introduction, we examined some of the ways that Europe
might be defined, without coming to any conclusions. After looking
at Europe in the intervening chapters, it is pretty apparent why no
categorical definition has been attempted. In this Epilogue, some
further observations about the nature of European international
politics—as evolved from post-wartime European attempts at integration—are offered in the hope that they can provide an added

dimension to the general subject of this book. "Europe and the Superpowers" means just as much an intermingling of traditions, values, and hopes, as a melange of nationalistic sentiments and aspirations, and conflicting interests. The "European Movement," if it is to have continuing life, must consist of both.

**HAROLD K. JACOBSON and
ROBERT S. JORDAN**

EPILOGUE

Economic and Political Integration:
From the Schuman Plan
to the European Communities

One of the most significant developments in the West since the end of World War II has been the growth of European integration. Since the days of Charlemagne there have been numerous plans and various attempts (some by force) to unify Europe, but prior to 1945 none of these succeeded. In fact, trends seemed to be running in the opposite direction; national boundaries were becoming more and more pronounced. Nationalism had reached new heights of exclusiveness in Nazi Germany, and throughout Europe the growth of the welfare state had brought with it unprecedented barriers to intercourse between states. It took World War II, with its tremendous devastation and misery and the events which occurred in its aftermath—especially the Cold War and the process of decolonization—to limit and reverse these trends and to make European integration a practical issue. The increased pace of technological change in the postwar world also was important. Under the pressures which resulted from this combination of circumstances, events moved rapidly. Within less than 15 years after the close of World War II, it was evident that the competitive nation-state system was changing in Europe and that forms of economic and political integration were emerging.

Extract from: Andrew Gyorgy, Hubert S. Gibbs, with Robert S. Jordan, eds., *Problems in International Relations*, 3rd ed. (Englewood Cliffs, N.J.: Prentice-Hall, Inc., 1970), pp. 174–192.

Prior to 1945, the case of European integration had generally been phrased in fairly simple political terms, and most of the advocates of this goal had envisaged a rather straightforward progress toward political amalgamation. The postwar scene, however, was far more complex. Although the simple case for integration remained and had gained considerable strength, a variety of new political and economic arguments were added, not all of which implied identical courses. Some argued that integration would be a means of buttressing the West against Soviet pressures. Others saw a united Europe as a third force in the Cold War. Still others thought that integration would be a way of gaining otherwise unobtainable national goals or of compensating for national weaknesses. Many proclaimed that modern economic conditions demanded a mass market, free of internal barriers to commerce. Almost every one of several arguments had its detractors, and there were disagreements on priorities. The appeal of the individual arguments varied from state to state and within each country. Moreover, some saw action in the economic field as a means of working toward political goals, while for others the converse was true. Perhaps as a consequence, the movement toward European integration produced a bewildering array of institutions, with varying and overlapping memberships and differential powers. And although the movement toward European integration had the effect of relieving many problems, it also created others. The record of the process is a fascinating series of interactions between various pressures, national policies, and international and supranational institutions. Individuals, too, played an important role.

EARLY STEPS TOWARD UNIFICATION

The voluntary integration which has occurred in Europe has taken place only west of the Iron Curtain line marking the limits of Communist Party control. Efforts were made, however, to secure all-European cooperation. At one time, many in the West believed that such cooperation held the only true solution to Europe's problems, and steps were taken in this direction during World War II, in the United Nations Relief and Rehabilitation Administration and later in the United Nations Economic Commission for Europe

(ECE). Unfortunately, these efforts failed. Although ECE still exists, and all of the states in Europe, plus the United States, are members, it has only nominal functions. Basically, even though other factors were also involved, the U.S.S.R. was responsible for the absence of all-European cooperation. The Soviet Union would not in any way relinquish its freedom of action and it insisted that the Eastern European states which fell under its control during World War II establish Communist, pro-Soviet regimes, reorient their economies toward the Soviet Union, and follow Soviet leadership exclusively in international affairs. Indeed, the very vigor with which the U.S.S.R. pursued its goals in Eastern Europe provided the principal impetus toward integration in the West. Those in the West who were interested in integration had the choice of either working within the framework of the non-Communist states or abandoning their ambitions.

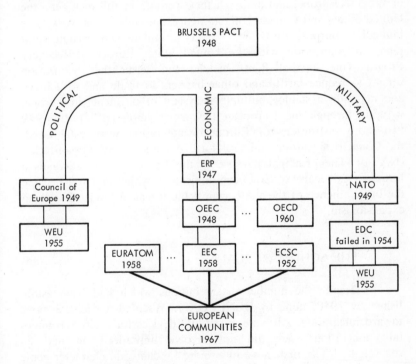

FIGURE 1. Movement toward Western European Integration

The first modest step toward integration in Western Europe occurred in September 1944, when the governments in exile of Belgium, Luxembourg, and the Netherlands agreed that after the conclusion of the war they would form an economic union (BENELUX) (see Figure 1). In 1948 the three governments established a common external tariff and began to eliminate obstacles to internal trade. That same year, in response to aggressive Soviet tactics made glaringly evident in the Czechoslovakian coup, the United Kingdom, France and the BENELUX powers formed a military alliance known as the Brussels Pact. A high degree of multinational cooperation was established in the logistical activities of the Western Union Defense Organization (WUDO), established under the Brussels Treaty.

Later in 1948 the Organization for European Economic Cooperation (OEEC) was formed. This body included most of the states of Western Europe, and although they were never full members, the United States and Canada collaborated extensively in its work. The immediate purpose of OEEC was to formulate and execute joint plans in connection with the United States European Recovery Program (the Marshall Plan). In long-range terms, the organization sought to reduce tariffs and other barriers to trade and to achieve and maintain a stable, multilateral system of payments in Europe, working through the European Payments Union (EPU). In 1949 two more institutions of European integration were established: the Council of Europe and the North Atlantic Treaty Organization (NATO). The principal purpose of the former was to serve as a forum for advocates of Eruopean unification, while the latter became the basic alliance of the West against the threat of Soviet European expansionism.

THE SCHUMAN PLAN

Despite the number of institutions which had been established by 1950, none by BENELUX represented a decisive move toward integration. All were essentially devices for intergovernmental cooperation; they did not involve limitations on national sovereignty.[1] The first move of a more fundamental character came

[1] The Brussels Treaty provided for an automatic response by all its

in May 1950, when Robert Schuman, then French Foreign Minister, proposed that France and West Germany place their coal and steel producing industries "under a common higher authority, within the framework of an organization open to the participation of the other countries of Europe." The European Coal and Steel Community (ECSC) grew out of this suggestion. The treaty which instituted ECSC was signed in April 1951 and went into effect in July of the following year. It committed the signatory states—Belgium, France, the German Federal Republic, Italy, Luxembourg, and the Netherlands—to create a common market in coal and steel and to establish supranational institutions to implement this.

Although the economic reasons for merging the coal and steel industries of the six states were strong and no doubt played a significant part in the decision to establish ECSC, political motivations were even more important. Because of the geographical distribution in Europe of the resources which are involved in the manufacture of steel, there was a sound economic rationale for the plan. The basic reason for Schuman's proposal, however, was a desire to gain security against Germany. The French Foreign Minister indicated this clearly when, in introducing his proposal, he said: "The solidarity in production thus established will make it plain that any war between France and Germany becomes not merely unthinkable, but materially impossible."

The French had viewed the remarkable resurgence of the German economy with concern, since by comparison the French economy lagged. Moreover, it was apparent by 1950 that the Allied controls on Germany's steel production could not be maintained indefinitely. In effect, Schuman proposed to give up control of the French coal and steel industries in return for creating international control over those industries in West Germany. For the Germans, an international control system in which they would participate was preferable to Allied control. Furthermore, the ECSC could provide a useful vehicle for bringing Germany back into the community of nations. Both France and West Germany saw the Schuman Plan as a way of easing the troublesome Saar problem. Long-range political motivations

---

signatories if any one or more of them were the objects of aggression, but the signing of NATO diminished its importance.

were also involved. Some supported Schuman's proposal because they regarded the integration of one segment of national life at a time as the most feasible method of uniting Europe. These persons were known as "functionalists."

The institution established by the ECSC treaty which most clearly illustrates its supranational character was the High Authority, the Community's executive body. It was composed of nine individuals, eight of whom were chosen by the member states and one by co-option. No more than two members of the High Authority could be of any one nationality. All held office for six years, and reappointment was possible. According to the Treaty, the members of the High Authority must "exercise their functions in complete independence, in the general interest of the Community." They could neither solicit nor accept instructions from national governments. Decisions were taken by a simple majority vote. The High Authority could deal directly with the coal and steel industries in the six member states without going through the national governments. It could raise money by imposing levies on the industries, it could direct the industries by means of decisions which must be carried out, and it could fine individual industries.

The ECSC treaty provided for three institutional checks on the High Authority: the Council of Ministers, the Court of Justice, and the Common Assembly. The Council of Ministers was composed of representatives of the member states—usually the ministers for economic affairs for industry and commerce. Its principal function was to "harmonize the action of the High Authority and that of the governments which are responsible for the general economic policy of their countries." The High Authority had to obtain the consent of the Council of Ministers to take certain actions, and the Council by unanimous vote could reverse some decisions of the High Authority. In addition, the Council had limited powers of initiative, in that it could request that the High Authority examine and consider proposals. Where unanimity was not required, decisions were taken by weighted majority vote. In practice, the consent of either France or West Germany was necessary for any decision. In the over-all structure of ECSC, national views have been accorded greatest representation in the Council.

The Court of Justice was the only judicial body which was competent to review the decisions of the High Authority; no national court has had this jurisdiction. It also has had sole competence with respect to resolutions of the Council of Ministers and the Common Assembly, but in view of the nature of the powers of these organs, this has been somewhat less important. The Court has consisted of seven judges who were appointed by the governments for six-year terms. The Court could annul decisions of the High Authority "on grounds of lack of legal competence, major violations of procedure, violations of the treaty or of any rule of law relating to its application, or abuse of power." It could not go beyond these legal issues to question the High Authority's judgment on economic questions. Access to the Court was open to the Council of Ministers, member governments, enterprises or their associations, and individuals. Judgments of the Court have had the force of law within the six member states.

The ECSC treaty assigned ultimate political responsibility to the Common Assembly. This body, which consisted of 78 delegates from the parliaments of the six states (France, West Germany, and Italy each had 18 representatives; Belgium and the Netherlands, 10; and Luxembourg, 4), could force the collective resignations of the members of the High Authority by passing a vote of censure by a two-thirds majority of those members present and voting, providing that this equaled at least a simple majority of the total membership. The Common Assembly's principal task was to meet annually to receive and consider the general report of the High Authority. It could also meet in extraordinary session to debate special questions.

THE SET-BACK OF EDC

Proponents of European unity saw in the Schuman Plan a perfect vehicle for the achievement of their ambitions, and the progress of the ECSC amply fulfilled their hopes. Even before the ECSC treaty was completed, it became a model for further efforts toward integration. Immediately after the outbreak of the Korean War, the West almost frantically sought to increase its military capabilities, under strong American prodding. One alternative was to rearm West Germany. Aware that this course might be chosen, René Pleven, the French Premier, suggested, in October 1950, that the six states which were involved in the ECSC should also pool their armed forces in Europe and place them under joint control, thereby creating a European Defense Community (EDC). The obvious purpose of the Pleven Plan was to permit German rearmament, but only under controlled conditions. Again, fear of Germany was the dominant motive for France. For Germany, EDC could be another step on the road to full acceptance in the community of nations.

After arduous and complicated negotiations which lasted almost two years, the EDC treaty was finally completed and was signed on May 27, 1952. It provided for the merger of the armed forces of the six states in Europe. The combined forces were to be placed under the control of institutions which were similar to those of ECSC, although the executive body, the Board of Commissioners, did not have as extensive powers as the High Authority. As a temporary measure, the Common Assembly of the Coal and Steel Community was to serve as the parliamentary body for EDC, but the treaty envisaged the ultimate creation of an assembly which would be chosen by direct election and which would serve both communities. On the basis of this provision, in 1952 and 1953 plans were drafted for the creation of a European Political Community (EPC). The six states seemed to be moving rapidly and decisively toward federation.

But first the EDC treaty would have to be ratified. This proved to be a difficult process, particularly in France. Successive French governments, unsure of their political strength and preoccupied with other problems, refused to submit the treaty to the National Assembly. Meanwhile, important changes occurred on the international scene. Soviet policy became less bellicose. Partly, this appears to have been the result of Stalin's death in 1953 and the consequent changes in the U.S.S.R.'s ruling hierarchy. It was apparent, though, as early as the Nineteenth Congress of the Communist Party of the Soviet Union, in October 1952, that the U.S.S.R. might adopt more moderate tactics. The hard line had only provoked a firm Western response, and Stalin himself called for policy changes at that gathering. In 1953 and 1954, the Korean and Indo-Chinese conflicts were settled and a general atmosphere of détente prevailed in East-West relations. In Europe, West Germany continued its economic resurgence, while France, embroiled in a series of costly colonial wars and caught in a web of contradictory forces internally, languished. When Premier Pierre Mendes-France half-heartedly submitted the EDC treaty to the French National Assembly in August 1954, the atmosphere and many of the treaty proposals were sharply different from what they had been when the Pleven Plan was introduced. Even though the other five governments had ratified the treaty, the French Assembly rejected it by a vote of 319 to 264.

The immediate problem which this action raised was that of finding a way to rearm West Germany. By now this had come to be regarded as essential for the defense of the West. At two hurried conferences in London and Paris in September and October 1954, a much more traditional scheme was adopted. The Brussels treaty was renamed Western European Union (WEU), and the German Federal Republic and Italy were invited to join. WEU, through its Armaments Committee, would exercise some control over West German rearmament, especially over the so-called ABC weapons (atomic, bacteriological, and chemical), but would not be involved in the merger of military forces. It was also decided that West Germany should be admitted to NATO, and, as a measure of reassurance, the United Kingdom agreed to maintain specified military forces on the European continent. The problem of West German rearmament was solved, but the London and Paris decisions did little to advance European unity.

As a consequence of the refusal of the French Assembly to ratify the EDC treaty, the entire integration movement was brought into question. The plans for a European political community were set back with EDC. The idea of a political community however, was revived briefly in the early 1960's. There were also some doubts about the future of the Coal and Steel Community as a result of the demise of EDC.

RENEWED INTEGRATION EFFORTS

That further steps were taken must be credited in large part to a number of individuals who were dedicated to the ideal of European unity and who decided that a concerted effort must be made to re-ignite the integration movement, or, in their words, to "re-launch Europe." Jean Monnet, who had played an important role in the creation of ECSC and who had been chosen as the first President of the High Authority, resigned from his position so that he

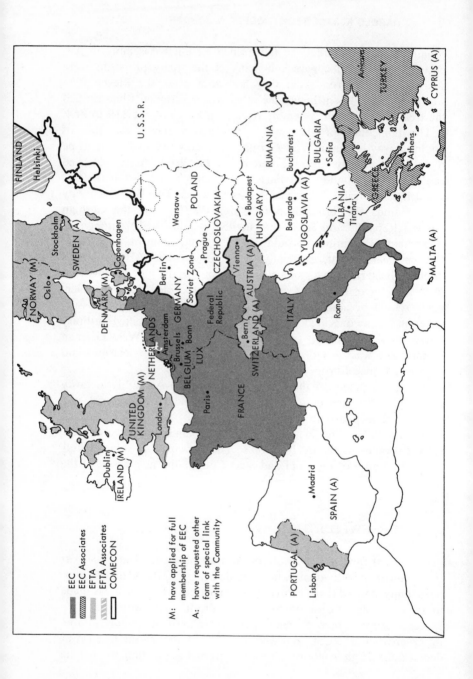

EEC

EEC Associates

EFTA

EFTA Associates

COMECON

M: have applied for full membership of EEC

A: have requested other form of special link with the Community

FINLAND
Helsinki

U.S.S.R.

NORWAY (M)
Oslo

SWEDEN (A)
Stockholm

DENMARK (M)
Copenhagen

Berlin
GERMANY
Soviet Zone
Federal Republic

POLAND
Warsaw

CZECHOSLOVAKIA
Prague

RUMANIA
Bucharest

BULGARIA
Sofia

HUNGARY
Budapest

AUSTRIA (A)
Vienna

YUGOSLAVIA (A)
Belgrade

ALBANIA
Tirana

GREECE
Athens

TURKEY
Ankara

CYPRUS (A)

UNITED KINGDOM (M)
London

IRELAND (M)
Dublin

NETHERLANDS
Amsterdam

BELGIUM
Brussels
Bonn
LUX

SWITZERLAND (A)
Bern

FRANCE
Paris

ITALY
Rome

MALTA (A)

SPAIN (A)
Madrid

PORTUGAL (A)
Lisbon

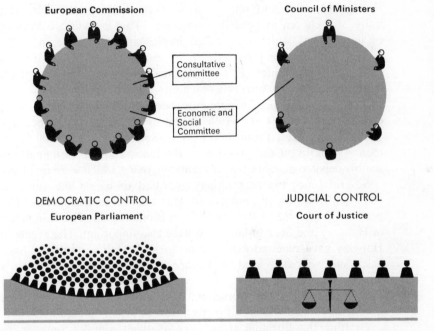

FIGURE 3. Organization of European executive action, democratic control, and judicial control. Source: By courtesy of the European Communities Information Service, Washington, D.C.

could form an Action Committee for a United Europe. Shortly thereafter, the Common Assembly of ECSC endorsed the idea of expanding the competence of the Community, and later this same body requested that the foreign ministers of the six member countries meet and consider further steps toward integration. The foreign ministers met at Messina in June 1955. They decided, on the basis of a suggestion put forward by the BENELUX powers, to appoint a committee to study the creation of a general common market and an atomic energy pool. Paul-Henri Spaak, the Belgian Foreign Minister and one of those most dedicated to European unity, was chosen to head the committee. This inaugurated a series of negotiations which culminated in the signing, in March 1957, of two treaties: one provided for the establishment of a European Economic Community (EEC or Common Market); and the other, a European Atomic Energy Community (EAEC, or Euratom).

The Coal and Steel Community was actively involved in these discussions. The ECSC High Authority provided assistance for Spaak's committee. From time to time, Spaak reported to the Common Assembly on the progress of the talks, and the Common Assembly debated many of the substantive issues which were involved.

Several times the negotiations appeared to be on the verge of collapse. That they did not can be attributed to several factors. The pertinacity of some of the participants is one reason. The twin crises of Hungary and Suez in late 1956 were also important. The events in Hungary gave renewed evidence of Soviet brutality, while the Suez fiasco engendered a kind of European nationalism and created a sense of urgency concerning the need to expand Europe's traditional sources of energy. The worsening Algerian crisis had an important impact in France which indirectly favored further integration.

Drafting the Euratom treaty was relatively simple. Since it involved a new field, few vested interests were affected. Moreover, at that time Europe still seemed to face a continuing energy shortage.

Most of the difficulties which arose during the negotiations concerned the Common Market treaty and were mainly the result of the French position. From the outset the French insisted that the participating governments should have greater control over the Common Market than they had over the ECSC. Initially, France even argued that the structure of EEC should be completely separate from that of ECSC. Although this position was not accepted, the

EEC treaty is considerably less supranational than the ECSC treaty. France adamantly maintained that the Common Market Treaty should include provisions concerning the harmonization of social policies, special arrangements for agricultural products, and the association of colonies and former colonies with the community. The French argued that because of their extensive social welfare programs they would be at a competitive disadvantage unless the other member states also moved to put such programs into effect. With regard to agriculture, France wanted an arrangement by which there would be guaranteed minimum prices. The French wanted to insure that the Common Market would not separate them from their overseas territories: they even hoped that it might serve as a means of strengthening their ties with these areas. Substantial concessions were made to the French position on all of these issues. Everyone realized that the acceptance of the treaties by France was crucial and no one desired to repeat the EDC debacle.

The two treaties were signed at Rome on March 25, 1957. This time the other five states were unwilling to ratify the treaties until France had done so. In July, the French Assembly acted. It ratified the two treaties by large majorities, but in the words of *The Manchester Guardian,* "in an atmosphere of resignation rather than enthusiasm." The other parliaments swiftly followed suit, and the Common Market and Euratom came into effect on January 1, 1958.

THE COMMON MARKET AND EURATOM

One purpose of Euratom was to establish a common market among the six states in atomic energy by eliminating barriers to trade in nuclear materials and equipment, allowing the free movement of capital for investment in nuclear endeavors, and allowing freedom of employment for nuclear specialists. In addition, Euratom has had functions which are analogous to those of the United States Atomic Energy Commission (AEC). Its tasks include developing research and insuring the dissemination of technical knowledge, establishing safety standards, encouraging investments in nuclear activities, and providing a regular supply of nuclear ores and fuels to users within the Community. A significant difference between the AEC and Euratom is that the latter is not concerned with the use of atomic energy for military purposes. In fact, Euratom is supposed to guarantee, by appropriate control measures, that nuclear materials are not diverted for improper uses, and in this connection the Treaty confers upon the Community property rights to all special fissionable materials.

The provisions of the EEC treaty are much more extensive. The purpose of the treaty is ultimately to establish a common market for all goods within the six states. During a 12- to 15-year transition period all obstacles to trade between the six states are to be progressively eliminated, and gradually the six states are to establish a single tariff schedule which will apply to trade with other states. The timing of the establishment of the European Common Market was divided into three stages of 4 years each, and all other action under the Treaty has been geared to these three stages. Although the Common Market was initially to deal with industrial goods, it also was to be extended to cover agricultural products. Special exceptions have been made which reflect a strong distrust of market forces in agriculture. The EEC treaty contains provisions concerning some of the less formal obstacles to trade, such as cartels, but they are not as strong as those of ECSC. The EEC treaty contains several provisions concerning the harmonization of social policy. The provisions on overseas territories apply to the non-European states and territories which have a special relationship with Belgium, France, Italy, and the Netherlands. According to the Treaty, the Common Market is open to these territories. Most of the former French African colonies became associate members, and also Somalia and the Congo (Brazzaville). A special relationship was negotiated for Nigeria, and also for Kenya, Uganda, and Tanzania, which are forming themselves into the East African Common Market. Through its Development Fund and in other ways, the Community has channeled investments to these new states. The EEC treaty also contains a provisions, in Article 238, which allows third states to become associated with the Community (see Figure 2).

The institutions of the European Atomic Energy Community and the European Economic Community were patterned on those of the Coal and Steel Community. As counterparts to the High Authority, there was a separate Commission for each of the new Communities. The EEC Commission consisted of nine persons who were chosen by common agreement among the participating governments for four-year terms. Their appointments were renewable. As Professor Walter Hallstein, the first President of the European Communities Commission, put it:

> The Commission's task is to safeguard the Community interest. It is the mainspring of the Community, for it alone can initiate legislation. It mediates between the Community and the particularist interests of the member states—and not only in the final phase of the decision-making process in the Council. . . .

The Euratom Commission consisted of five members chosen in a similar fashion. Neither body has had as extensive powers as the High Authority, though, of the two, the Euratom Commission has had the greater latitude for independent action, probably because of the relatively technical nature of the issues with which it is concerned. In practice, however, the differences between the two Commissions and the High Authority may be less significant than a comparison of the treaties would indicate: the High Authority has backed away from using its full powers. The basic power of the EEC Commission has been to formulate proposals for decision by the Council of Ministers. The Euratom Commission could also do this and, in addition, was empowered to control the supply of nuclear materials, to authorize inspections and to impose penalties for infringements of the control system.

On February 25, 1964, the EEC Council of Ministers agreed in principle that the executives of the three Communities should be merged by the end of 1964, and the Communities themselves by the end of 1966. During the summer of 1964, the Council explored further the merger of the executives, and also the extension of the authority of the European Parliament. On July 1, 1967, the merger took place. The three executives were merged into one Commission, which was increased from nine members to fourteen as a transitional measure. The membership will drop back to nine in 1970, if all the transitional arrangements are fulfilled (see Fugure 3).

The most important policy-making body in the Common Market has been the Council of Ministers, which has broad powers of decision. Composed of representatives of the governments of the participating states, it has taken decisions under a variety of procedures. During the three stages of the Common Market's transitional period, most of the decisions must be by unanimous vote; after that, various majorities would be required, depending on the issue and the way in which it is presented. Usually France, the German Federal Republic, and Italy have four votes each, Belgium and the Netherlands two, and Luxembourg one. In most cases a majority of twelve is required. Generally, therefore, the three largest states must approve any action. The competence, composition and procedures of the Council of Ministers for Euratom were similar.

At one point during the drafting of the Rome treaties, the creation of a separate parliamentary body for the Common Market and Euratom was envisaged, but partially because of complaints by the three existing assemblies in Europe (the Common Assembly of ECSC, the Consultative Assembly of the Council of Europe, and the Assembly of WEU), this plan was abandoned. It was decided to create a new body, the European Parliamentary Assembly (EPA) which would serve ECSC, EEC, and Euratom. Basically, the European Parliament is a modified version of the Common Assembly of the Coal and Steel Community. The total membership was enlarged and the relative strength of France, West Germany, and Italy was increased. The representation of these three states was set at 36, doubling the previous figure. That of Belgium and the Netherlands was raised from 10 to 14, and that of Luxembourg from 4 to 6. At present the representatives are chosen by their respective parliaments.

There has been considerable discussion about expanding the powers of the European Parliament, and in 1969 the Council of Ministers officially took note of some proposals. This meeting was partly in response to student demands for a "federal Europe." One indication of the general unrest over this question was an item contained in the April 1969 issue of *European Community,* which reported:

> The European Parliament may take the Council of Ministers to the European Communities Court of Justice if the Council fails to take action on the Parliament's resolution of March 12. The resolution called on the Council to introduce direct universal suffrage for the election of members of the European Parliament, as laid down in the Rome Treaty.

Generally, national delegations reflect the composition of their parliaments except that Communists are excluded. The European

Parliament has appeared to have had less control over the former separate Commissions of the Common Market and Euratom than it had over the High Authority of the ECSC. It can, however, compel the collective resignation of the executive body by a vote of censure.

The EEC and Euratom treaties provided that the Court of Justice of ECSC should also serve for the two newer Communities. The jurisdiction and competence of the Court is roughly similar under all three treaties.

Although the Rome treaties are generally less supranational than the one which established ECSC, there can be no question that they go considerably beyond traditional forms of interstate cooperation. It is clear that they were based on a broad conception of European integration, one which looked forward to further collaboration and ultimately a possible federation. As Miriam Camps put it:

> The Community is today a mixed system, a construction that is *sui generis,* which cannot be equated with either a federal state or an international organization in the conventional sense, although it has some of the attributes of each. It promises to remain a mixed system for a long time, with the members acting collectively for some purposes, individually for others, with the amount of coordination of policy and of common action depending on the extent to which the interests of the member countries coincide and with the advantages to be gained from common action.[2]

The EEC and Euratom treaties came into effect on January 1, 1958. Since then, despite the demise of the French Fourth Republic and the accession to power of General Charles de Gaulle and other less sweeping changes in other member states, the two Communities became firmly established. The reduction of obstacles to trade with the Common Market began in 1959 and actually proceeded faster than was required by the treaty. Intracommunity trade expanded substantially: in 1960 it was almost 50 per cent greater than it had been in 1958. By July 1, 1968, the Community completed forming the customs union, a year and a half ahead of the Rome treaty timetable. The partial integration of the six states which were bound

[2] Miriam Camps, *European Unification in the Sixties* (New York: McGraw-Hill Book Company, 1966), p. 20.

together in ECSC, EEC, and Euratom has become an established fact in international politics. The major question for the future is if the customs union can proceed to become a true economic union. The Commission listed six essential tasks for the Communities for 1969. They were: to coordinate economic policies and monetary cooperation; to establish a common commercial policy towards nonmember countries; to decide on final arrangements for financing the common agricultural policy; to choose the means of reforming the structure of agriculture; to decide on the means of reforming the European Social Fund so that workers can be retrained before serious labor imbalances arise; to adopt a long-range program for the Atomic Energy Community and put into effect the Council's resolution of October 1967 assigning priority to seven key areas.

REACTIONS OF OTHER STATES

Other states inevitably were affected by the progress of the six states toward integration, and they reacted in various ways. The Soviet Union was the most outspoken and critical. It opposed all of the steps toward unity in Western Europe and especially objected to the tight integration involved in ECSC, EEC, and Euratom. Under Stalin, the Soviet attack on the ECSC was blunt. Similarly aggressive tactics were used with regard to EEC and Euratom after Stalin's death. Just before the Rome treaties were signed, the Soviet Foreign Ministry issued a statement which charged that only monopolists and militarists would benefit from the creation of the Common Market and Euratom, and that their establishment would be a hostile move which would lead to increased tensions. Subtler tactics were also employed. In April 1956, during the drafting of the two treaties, the Soviet Union proposed, in the United Nations Economic Commission for Europe, that an all-European economic agreement be formulated in that body and an agency created to deal with the peaceful application of atomic energy. The proposals were obviously designed as alternatives to the Common Market and Euratom. Even though the potentialities for meaningful cooperation between Eastern and Western Europe at that time were extremely slight, and despite the vagueness of the proposals, they put the West in the difficult position of seeming to prefer an exclusive rather than all-European framework for cooperative activities. Soviet opposition to European integration was based on a fear of successful Western economic development.

Although their reaction was considerably different, the British were also concerned about the integration of the six continental states. The United Kingdom had close ties with the European continent, and the process of integration was bound to affect these. The alternative of joining the Six was always open, but such a step would have had very serious repercussions on Britain's role in the Commonwealth and on her Atlantic relationships. There was also the British tradition of insularity. It was one thing, however, for the British to stand aloof from the limited common market which ECSC established in coal and steel, and quite another for it to stand outside of the general common market which was involved in EEC. While the economic consequences for the United Kingdom of abstention from the Schuman Plan were not too extensive, the effects of the Common Market have been much more far-reaching. For example, its competitive position within the EEC states has been affected by the establishment of the Common Market.

Other non-member European states were relatively even more dependent on trade with the EEC area. Consequently, in July 1956 the Organization for European Economic Cooperation began exploring the possibilities of associating the remainder of the OEEC member states with the Common Market. Early in the negotiations the British proposed the creation of a free-trade area which would include the Common Market states and all other OEEC countries. There would be no tariffs against any of the members of the free-trade area, but the individual countries would be free to control their external tariffs. The British proposal did not apply to agricultural products; therefore, the United Kingdom would be able to maintain its system of Commonwealth preferences. Several countries objected to this feature. They were only willing to allow British manufactures to enter their country duty-free if their agricultural products would have the same privileges in the United Kingdom. Some of the potential members of the EEC took the position that they were involved in much more than a mere economic agreement and argued that if other states were to share in the economic benefits of the Common Market, they should also accept the supranational control which was involved. Austria, Sweden, and Switzerland felt that because of their neutral status they could not consider such a step. Nor were the British willing to move in this direction, because they felt that it would cut them off from the Commonwealth and the United States. Despite compromises by all parties, it was impossible to find a mutually acceptable solution and the OEEC talks collapsed in late 1958.

Even before the breakdown of these negotiations, there had been some discussion of the possibility of Austria, Denmark, Norway, Sweden, Switzerland, and the United Kingdom forming a trade agreement. The purpose would be to attempt to offset the exclusionary effects of the establishment of the Common Market by increased trade among themselves. Formal negotiations began among these countries in 1959, and Portugal also joined the discussions. In November 1959, meeting in Stockholm, the seven states signed a convention which created a European Free Trade Association (EFTA). Ratifications were completed quickly and EFTA came into effect in May 1960. The member states of EFTA are committed to eliminate almost all obstacles to trade among themselves over a ten-year period. Although the EFTA Convention does not extend to trade in agricultural products and fish, it does pledge the member states to attempt a liberalization of trading conditions for these commodities. Beyond that, membership in EFTA carries few obligations. The Convention did not provide for the establishment of supranational institutions. Important decisions require the unanimous consent of the participating states. Nevertheless, with the creation of EFTA, Europe seemed to be divided into two rival trading groups: the Six and the Seven.

Whether or not in the long run the Free Trade Association would prove adequate for the needs of the European states which were not members of the Common Market, was far from certain. Rather than joining EFTA, in the spring of 1961 Greece signed an agreement with the Common Market under the terms of Article 238. This agreement provided for the establishment of a customs union over a period not to exceed 22 years. Turkey and other states were considering similar action. Even the United Kingdom began to explore the possibilities of a closer relationship with EEC. Indeed, the tight integration of the Six seemed to have a magnetic force.

In January 1963, and again in November 1967, French President de Gaulle announced that France could not accept the conditions under which negotiations for British entry into the EEC had been taking place. Although a part of this was the General's personal convictions about such matters as Britain's relationship with the United States, even with the passing of de Gaulle from the leadership of France, neither French nor British political leaders have expressed optimism that a resumption of negotiations for British entry would be easy or quick. The difficulties are formidable if the tightness of the Community is to be maintained. The alternative, a loosened Community that would not press for stronger economic—and later on, political—unification, probably would suit both French and British political interests but might not suit the other negotiating states.

Throughout the postwar period the United States favored the various moves toward European integration, especially those which involved the six continental states. In some instances, for example with regard to EDC, American support was so strong that it was politically embarrassing for the participants. The United States had both economic and political motivations for its position. It wanted Europe to become a strong element in the world economy and to prevent the outbreak of another war between France and Germany. It was also anxious to create a bastion against Soviet expansionism. European integration seemed to be the best way to achieve these goals. American support was constant, therefore, although at times European integration involved economic disadvantages for the United States. It continued even after the United States began to suffer deficits in its balance of payments.

Since the United States was concerned about the development of the split between the Six and the Seven, it attempted to facilitate a solution. One such effort was the suggestion, made and adopted in 1960, that the functions of OEEC be expanded and that the body be reconstituted as the Organization for Economic Cooperation and Development (OECD). Both the United States and Canada became full members of OECD. The United States hoped that OECD might serve as a vehicle for mitigating the effects of the division in Europe. The General Agreement on Tariffs and Trade (GATT) provided another forum for attempts to ease the differences. The Kennedy Round of negotiations helped to keep the respective U.S.-EEC tariff alignments in approximate parity. But the United States made it clear that it would not favor any solution which would dilute the integration of the Six, and its achievement, it felt, should be encouraged, not discouraged.

THE ROAD AHEAD

The record of the European integration movement illustrates how complex and difficult a task it is to break down national barriers even in as small and homogeneous an area as Europe. Where the movement for European integration will lead is not clear. Conceivably, the present situation, with a clutter of institutions, and with sovereignty severely restricted in some areas but quite unfettered in others, could be a long-lasting one. The combined Communities of ECSC, EEC and Euratom could turn out to be the *apex* of supranationalism, rather than mere milestones. There was ample evidence early in the 1960's to support such a forecast. Under General de Gaulle, France became more nationalistic and less interested in integration. West Germany, because of the strength of its economic ties with states that were not members of the Common Market (especially Britain) became reluctant to go further toward integration within the framework only of the Six.

At the same time, once it was under way, there has been a certain compelling force to the integration movement. Habits have begun to change. Delegates in the Common Assembly and then the European Parliament have organized themselves and operated on a party rather than on a national basis. Progress in economic integration has served as a stimulus to further moves in the same direction, producing a spill-over effect which has pointed toward political community.[3] While it is true that the Rome treaties were less supranational than the Schuman Plan, their combined effect has been much more far-reaching. The full impact of the European integration movement remains unmeasured, yet within a relatively short time-span it has already produced certain revolutionary changes.

[3] See Ernst B. Haas, *The Uniting of Europe: Political, Social, and Economic Forces, 1950–1957* (Stanford, California: Stanford University Press, 1958); Kenneth Lindsay, *European Assemblies: The Experimental Period, 1949–1950* (New York: Frederick A. Praeger, Inc., 1960); and Camps, *ibid.*

CHRONOLOGY

Chronology of Major European Political Developments

1815

Congress of Vienna. The Congress of Vienna convenes to construct post-Napoleonic Europe. The Quadruple Alliance, Britain, Russia, Prussia, and Austria, provide the components of the European balance of power. The balance is jeopardized when the conservative powers (Russia, Prussia, and Austria) seek in the face of British opposition to institute a status quo based on preservation of monarchical regimes. The conservative powers form the Holy Alliance as a body to protect their status quo concept.

1818

September–November:
Conference of Aix-la-Chapelle convenes as the first of the post-war conferences following the Congress of Vienna. Ideological differences begin to appear between Britain and the conservative powers of the continent as Britain indicates that British actions against Napoleon were due to the special exigencies of the time and would not charactorize British policy in times of peace.

1819

August:
Conference at Carlsbad. The second post-Vienna conference is convened by Metternich to force representatives of the nine German states to promulgate his measures aimed at repressing rising Ger-

man liberalism and reasserting Austrian predominance among the German states.

1820

October:
Conference of Troppau at which Britain refuses to agree to Metternich's protocol that states succumbing to revolution are no longer members of the Holy Alliance and therefore subject to intervention by the members of the Holy Alliance in order to restore stability.

The revolutions of 1820, centering on the Iberian Peninsula and concerning differences between the monarchy and the military, flare up, presenting the concert of Europe with a challenge to the status quo envisioned at the Congress of Vienna.

1821

January:
The Conference at Laibach provides the final breach between Great Britain and the conservative powers of the concert of Europe. The immediate question involved intervention in the Italian states but the significance was to be found in the dissolution of the Quadruple Alliance and the ideological separation of the Holy Alliance (Russia, Prussia, Austria) from Britain.

1822

September:
The Conference at Verona proves the last of the conferences of the Quadruple Alliance. Canning's succession after Castlereagh's suicide quickened British disengagement from the continent. The immediate issue is French intervention in Spain, which Britain openly opposed.

1830

The Revolutions of 1830 characterized by separate uprisings in France, Belgium, and Greece (the latter actively supported by England, France, and Russia at the expense of the Ottoman Empire) disrupts the stability of the European international political order.

1848

The Revolutions of 1848 culminate a series of such socio-political outbursts begun in the 1820's. Like its predecessors of the 1820's and 1830's the liberal outbursts of 1848 are silenced, but the ideological consequences continue to affect policies throughout the latter half of the nineteenth century.

1854–1856

The Crimean War, growing out of a religious dispute between Russia and the Ottoman Empire over Christian rights in Jerusalem, turns into a general dispute about Russian encroachments into the Ottoman Empire (the sick man of Europe). It was on this latter matter that England and France were drawn into the dispute.

1856

February 25–March 30:
The Congress of Paris settles the immediate issues of the Crimean War but from that point forward Russia becomes a revisionist power unhappy with the exclusion from the Danube and Ottoman Empire that the Paris status quo imposed.

1859–1870

The unification of Piedmont, Lombardy, Venetia, Parma, Modena, Romagna, Tuscany, the Papal State, and the Kingdom of the two Sicilies into the nation-state of Italy.

1866

The Austro-Prussian War is the last hurdle successfully surmounted by Bismarck in his policy to unify the states of Germany under Prussian leadership.

1870–1871

The Franco-Prussian War, arising out of a Franco-Prussian dispute over the matter of succession to the Spanish throne, provides Bismarck with the opportunity to meet and defeat France and extend the German empire to the dimensions he envisions. The end of the Franco-Prussian War marks the final unification of Prussia, Hanover, Schleswig, Holstein, Alsace, Lorraine, Bavaria, Mecklenburg, and Bohemia, into the German nation-state.

1878

June 13–July 13:
The Congress of Berlin brings the Great Powers of Europe into the near East question that had involved Russia, Turkey, Austria, and the Balkans since 1875. Russian success at overturning the status quo following the Crimean War is overextended, at the expense of the other Powers and at Berlin they join to oppose Russian over-extension into the Balkans and Russian unilateralism in establishing a new status quo that would affect all the Powers.

1890

Bismarck is removed from the office of Chancellor by Kaiser Wilhelm.

1914

World War I begins.

1917

October:
The Bolshevik Revolution overthrows the Provisional Government which had been in power since February when the Tzar abdicated.

1918

March 3:
The Treaty of Brest-Litovsk is signed removing Russia from the war.

1919

June 28:
The Treaty of Versailles is signed.

1920

The League of Nations begins to operate.

1925

October 16:
The Locarno Pact is signed signalling acceptance of the Franco-German border by France, and the Treaty of Versailles by Germany. Germany is brought back into the fold of European Powers and the Powers are guaranteed of continued German disarmament.

1928

August 27:
The Kellogg-Briand Pact is signed renouncing war as a means of settling international disputes.

1938

September 29–30:
The Munich Agreement is signed sealing the fate of Czechoslovakia and severing the Russo-French connection.

1939

August 23:
German Soviet Non-Aggression Treaty is signed.

September 1:
Germany invades Poland; World War II begins.

September 17:
The Red Army enters Poland.

September 28–October 11:
Agreements granting the Soviet Union bases in the Baltic States signed.

December 14:
The League of Nations expels the Soviet Union.

1940

End of June:
The Soviet Union claims Bessarabia and annexes the Baltic States.

November 18:
Hitler decides to invade the Soviet Union.

1941

April 5:
The Soviet-Yugoslav nonaggression pact is signed.

June 22:
Germany invades the Soviet Union.

August 14:
The Anglo-American promulgation of the Atlantic Charter takes place.

December 5, 1941–February 4, 1942:
State Department decides not to make any wartime commitments about Russia's postwar western boundaries.

December 6:
The first Soviet counter-offensive to the German invasion begins.

December 7:
Japan attacks the United States at Pearl Harbor.

December 11:
Germany declares war on the United States.

1942

January 1:
The Declaration of the United Nations, which is a summary of the
war aims of the anti-Axis coalition, is promulgated.

November 19:
The Soviet counter-attack begins at Stalingrad, and marks a turning-
point in World War II.

1943

January:
President Franklin D. Roosevelt and Prime Minister Winston Churchill meet at Casablanca. The principle of unconditional surrender is
adopted.

April 25:
The Katyan massacre is discovered and the rupture of Soviet-Polish
relations takes place.

May 22:
The Comintern is dissolved.

August 14–24:
President Roosevelt, Prime Minister Churchill and their military aides
confer on cross-channel invasion plans, and arrangements for the
Italian surrender are discussed.

September 8:
Italy surrenders.

October 18–30:
Secretary of State Cordell Hull, Foreign Minister Vyacheslav Molotov,
and Foreign Secretary Anthony Eden confer in Moscow. The first
substantive political discussions between the three major allies
covering Eastern Europe, Germany, the Italian surrender and the
Soviet entry into the Pacific War take place.

November 22–26:
First Cairo Conference. Prime Minister Churchill and President
Roosevelt confer prior to meeting Premier Stalin at Teheran, to dis-
cuss China's role in the Far Eastern Theater. In addition, Prime
Minister Churchill and President Roosevelt meet with Generalissimo
Chiang Kai-shek.

November 28–December 2:
Premier Stalin, President Roosevelt, and Prime Minister Churchill

meet in Teheran to discuss the issues of a coordinated strategy against Germany; ideas for a post-war international organization for international security; and numerous political questions.

December:
Prime Minister Churchill, and President Roosevelt at the Second Cairo Conference, in the name of the Big Three Allies, meet with President Inonu of Turkey to convince him to enter the war.

December 4:
The Yugoslav National Committee is created.

1944

June 6:
The Anglo-American-French Allies land in Normandy.

July 21:
A pro-Soviet Polish National Committee is formed at Chelm, behind Soviet lines. The committee was mainly composed of Polish Communists and Communist sympathizers. This group is later known as the Lublin Poles, as opposed to the Polish Government-in-Exile in London (London Poles).

August 23:
The Soviet-Rumanian armistice is signed.

August 25:
The Red Army enters German territory; Paris is liberated.

August 26:
Bulgaria seeks an armistice with Britain and the United States.

September 5:
The Soviet Union declares war on Bulgaria and invades it on September 9.

September:
At the Second Quebec Conference, Prime Minister Churchill, President Roosevelt and their military aides meet to discuss plans for the final thrust into Germany and the future course of the Pacific War.

September 14:
The Western Allies enter Germany.

October 9:
Prime Minister Churchill and Premier Stalin discuss post-War spheres of influence in the Balkans.

October 20:
Belgrade is liberated by Tito and the Soviet army.

December 3:
Civil war breaks out in Greece.

December 10:
General Charles de Gaulle goes to Moscow to sign a Franco-Soviet Treaty of Alliance.

1945

January 12:
An armistice is agreed upon in the Greek civil war.

January 12:
The Soviet army enters Warsaw after watching the retreating Germans put down the "Warsaw Uprising."

January 17:
The Armistice with Hungary is signed.

January 30:
Prime Minister Churchill, President Roosevelt and their military aides meet at Malta prior to meeting Premier Stalin at Yalta. America's concern for China and Britain's concern for parts of Asia South of China displays a difference in Anglo-American and Asian interests.

February 4:
At Yalta conference, Prime Minister Churchill, President Roosevelt, and Premier Stalin meet to discuss issues in the Far East, Poland, Germany, the smaller European States, and the United Nations Organization. The prime topic of conversation was Poland and Eastern Europe.

February 13:
Budapest is occupied by the Soviet army.

March 23:
The Western Allies cross the Rhine.

April 12:
President Roosevelt dies; Harry S. Truman becomes President.

April 13:
Vienna is captured by the Soviet army.

April 23:
The Russians enter Berlin.
Truman's White House lecture to Foreign Minister Molotov on the post-war composition of the Polish government takes place.

May 8:
The Third German Reich surrenders.

June 25:
The United Nations Charter is promulgated as a result of the San Francisco Conference.

July 6:
The United States and Britain recognize the Polish government in Warsaw, composed for the most part by members of the Polish National Committee (Lublin Poles).

July 16:
The first test of the American atomic bomb is successful.

July 17:
The Potsdam Conference is held to settle all the outstanding differences of the War. This first major post-War conference evidenced a lessening of the cooperation that the War had dictated.

July 25:
The Labor Party wins the British elections, and Winston Churchill is succeeded by Clement Attlee as Prime Minister.

August 6:
The atomic bomb is exploded over Hiroshima.

August 14:
Japan surrenders unconditionally.

August 17:
The Polish and Soviet governments agree on the Oder-Neisse Line as the western boundary of Poland. The United States claims that the line must only be provisional.

September:
The Council of Foreign Ministers is deadlocked over concluding the peace treaties for the former East European Axis States.

November 18:
Soviet army occupies Iranian Azerbaijan.

November 29:
The People's Republic of Yugoslavia is proclaimed with Marshal Tito as the leader.

1946

January 20:
Charles de Gaulle gives up the leadership of the French Provisional Government.

March 5:
Winston Churchill delivers his famous "Iron Curtain" speech at Westminster College, Fulton, Missouri.

March 25:
Soviet troops leave Iran.

April 23:
The Socialist and Communist parties are merged in the Soviet occupation zone of Germany.

April 25:
The Paris Peace Conference opens to negotiate treaties for Italy, Bulgaria, Romania, Hungary, and Finland.

June 24:
The Soviet Union rejects the Baruch Plan for internationalizing the control of atomic energy.

September:
The Greek civil war begins anew.

September 6:
Secretary of State James Byrnes delivers his Stuttgart speech offering American friendship and support to the German people, in the face of growing Soviet-American hostility.

September 19:
Winston Churchill, in Zurich, proposes that a Council of Europe be created as the first step toward a "United States of Europe."

October:
Peace Treaties with Italy, Bulgaria, Hungary, Rumania, and Finland are agreed upon.

December 12:
The United Nations General Assembly calls for the diplomatic boycott of Spain.

1947

January 1:
The British and American occupation zones of Germany are merged into "Bizonia."

January 17:
Winston Churchill launches the Movement of European Unity in London.

March 4:
The Anglo-French Treaty of Dunkirk is signed to reassure France against the possibility of a renewal of German aggression.

March 10:
Big Four Foreign Minister's Conference held in Moscow.

March 12:
The Truman Doctrine is promulgated, which commits the United States to global anti-Communism.

May 5:
The French government dismisses those ministers who are members of the Communist party.

June 5:
The European Recovery Program (Marshall Plan) is launched.

June 14:
The United States signs peace treaties with Italy, Rumania, Bulgaria, and Hungary.

July 2:
The Soviet Union rejects the Marshall Plan. Eastern European States, Czechoslovakia, and Finland follow suit.

October 5:
The Cominform is created. The Saar is linked to France in an economic union.

November 21:
Communist opposition parties are dissolved in Poland and Hungary.

1948

January 22:
A plan for a Western Union in Europe is announced by Foreign Secretary Ernest Bevin.

February 25:
The Prague coup takes place, which results in a pro-Soviet Communist regime; the United States is outraged.

March 17:
The Brussels Pact is signed among Britain, France, Belgium, Luxemburg, and the Netherlands.

April 6:
The Convention for European Economic Cooperation is signed; the Organization for European Economic Cooperation (OEEC) is created.

May 8:
The First Congress of the European Movement is held in The Hague.

June 5:
The Vandenberg Resolution adopted by the United States Senate opens the way for signing of the North Atlantic Treaty.

June 18:
Currency reform in the western zones of Germany and Berlin is carried out over Soviet objections.

June 20:
The Berlin Blockade begins.

June 28:
Yugoslavia is expelled by the Cominform.

September:
Wladyslaw Gomulka is expelled from the Politburo of the Polish Workers' Party.

September 27–28:
The Defense Ministers of the Brussels Treaty Powers create the Western Union Defense Organization (WUDO).

October 25–26:
The Consultative Council of the Brussels Treaty Powers announces agreement on the principle of a defensive pact for the North Atlantic area, and the steps to be taken in that direction.

December 28:
Anglo-French-American agreement on international status of the Ruhr is signed.

1949

January 25:
The Council for Mutual Economic Assistance (COMECON) is established within the Soviet Bloc.

January 28:
The Council of Europe is created.

April 4:
The North Atlantic Treaty is signed.

May 5:
The German Federal Republic (or West Germany) is proclaimed.

May 5:
The London Ten-Power Agreement sets up the Council of Europe.

May 11:
The Berlin Blockade is lifted. The Western Allies have successfully withstood the Soviet challenge to their access rights to Berlin.

July 14:
The Soviet Union explodes its first atomic bomb.

September 12:
The German Federal Republic is constituted.

September 21:
The Allied Military Occupation of the western zones of Germany is ended.

1950

January 31:
President Harry Truman approves the proposal to build a hydrogen bomb.

February 14:
The Sino-Soviet friendship pact is signed.

May 9:
The Schuman Plan creating the European Coal and Steel Community (ECSC) is launched.

June 6:
East Germany recognizes the Oder-Neisse line.

June 25:
The Korean War begins.

August 11:
West Germany joins the Council of Europe. Sir Winston Churchill launches the idea of a European army.

September–October:
Strikes fomented by the Soviet Union in Austria collapse.

September 12:
The United States opens the question of the rearmament of West Germany.

September 26:
The North Atlantic Council agrees on the principle of a West German contribution to common defense.

October 21:
The Pleven Plan for a European army within a European Defense Community (EDC) is launched.

November 5:
The diplomatic boycott of Spain is ended.

December 19:
The North Atlantic Council appoints General Dwight D. Eisenhower as Supreme Allied Commander, Europe, and he begins the formation of a Supreme Headquarters (SHAPE).

Discussions with West Germany are authorized by the North Atlantic Council on possible German contribution to the defense of Western Europe.

December 20:
The Consultative Council of the Brussels Treaty Powers decides to merge the military organization of Western Union into NATO.

1951

Early 1951:
The Mutual Security Administration (MSA) succeeds the European Recovery Program, as American emphasis changes from European recovery to rearmament.

April:
ECSC Treaty signed in Paris.

April 4:
SHAPE is established.

October 7:
Sir Winston Churchill and the Conservative Party return to power in England.

1952

February:
The Lisbon meeting of NATO agrees on objectives of Western rearmament. Greece and Turkey are admitted to membership.

March 10:
The Soviet Union proposes the neutralization of Germany.

May:
General Eisenhower ends his tenure as Supreme Allied Commander in Europe.

May 27:
A draft treaty to create a European Defense Community (EDC) is negotiated.

July:
European Coal and Steel Community is established.

July 21:
The Egyptian monarchy falls. A military government takes over.

November 1:
The first American hydrogen bomb is successfully detonated.

November 4:
General Dwight D. Eisenhower is elected President of the United States.

1953

March 5:
Premier Stalin dies.

March 6:
Georgi Malenkov succeeds Stalin.

May 11:
Sir Winston Churchill repeals Fulton speech and calls for an end to the cold war based on guaranteeing Russia's security in Eastern Europe.

June 16:
The people of East Berlin rise up against Soviet authority.

July 4:
Imre Nagy becomes head of the Hungarian Communist Government.

July 26:
A Korean cease-fire is signed.

August 8:
Premier Malenkov announces that the USSR possesses the hydrogen bomb.

December 4–7:
A Western summit meeting is held in Bermuda, attended by President Eisenhower, Prime Minister Churchill, and French Premier Joseph Laniel to discuss the European Defense Community (EDC).

December 8:
President Eisenhower launches an "atoms for peace" plan in an attempt to solve the dilemma of nuclear inspection.

1954

January 25–February 18:
The Berlin Four-Power Conference ends with no agreement on Germany's future. The ground is laid, however, for a meeting in Geneva to discuss Far Eastern affairs.

February 25:
Colonel Gamel Abdul Nasser comes to power in Egypt.

June 18:
Pierre Mendes-France becomes French Premier. He is determined to resolve the Indochinese conflict, and to break the deadlock over EDC.

August 9:
The signing of the Greco-Turkish-Yugoslav Treaty of Alliance takes place.

August 19–22:
The Brussels conference on the European Defense Community (EDC) fails.

August 30:
The French Parliament rejects EDC. President Eisenhower signs the Atomic Energy Act.

September 28:
The London Conference, under the initiative of British Foreign Secretary Anthony Eden, is held to seek an alternative to the EDC.

October:
The Western European Union (WEU) is formed by the accession of the German Federal Republic and Italy to the Brussels Treaty.

October 3:
The London Agreements on the rearmament of West Germany are negotiated.

October 23:
The Paris Agreements on West Germany's entry into NATO are negotiated.

November 1:
The Algerian War begins.

1955

February 6:
French Premier Mendes-France falls and is replaced by Edgar Faure.

February 8:
Premier Malenkov is replaced by Nikolai Bulganin; Foreign Minister Molotov accepts in principle the neutralization of Austria.

March 9:
The Hungarian Central Committee condemns Imre Nagy.

March 27:
France concludes the ratification of the Paris Agreements.

April 5:
Sir Anthony Eden succeeds Winston Churchill as British Prime Minister.

May 5:
The Federal Republic of Germany officially becomes a member of NATO.

May 14:
The Soviet Union concludes the Warsaw Pact with its European satellites.

May 15:
The signing of the Austrian State Treaty ends the Four-Power Occupation.

June 3:
The Messina Conference results in an agreement to create a European Economic Community (EEC).

July 18:
The East-West Summit Conference in Geneva is held, at which the American "open skies" plan is proposed to the Soviet Union.

September 9:
West German Chancellor Konrad Adenauer goes to Moscow, and diplomatic relations between the USSR and the German Federal Republic are agreed upon.

September 27:
Egypt negotiates an agreement with Czechoslovakia on arms.

October:
Monnet launches Action Committee for the United States of Europe.

December 30:
The USSR signs a treaty with the German Democratic Republic (East Germany).

1956

January 29:
Guy Mollet succeeds Edgar Faure as Premier of France.

February 14–25:
At the Twentieth Congress of the Communist Party of the Soviet Union (CPSU), Nikita Khrushchev denounces the crimes of Stalin.

April 6:
Wladyslaw Gomulka of Poland is freed.

April 17:
The Cominform is dissolved.

June 28:
The workers of Poznan, in Poland, rise up in protest to Polish Stalinists.

July:
Britain proposes seventeen-nation Free Trade Area and Nuclear Energy Agency.

July 18:
Matyas Rakosi resigns from the leadership of the Hungarian Communist Party.

July 19:
The Americans withdraw their offer to Egypt to finance the Aswan High Dam.

July 26:
The Suez Canal is nationalized by Egypt.

October 22:
Gomulka becomes First Secretary of the Hungarian Communist Party.

October 23:
The Budapest uprising begins, inspired by the Polish demonstration, demanding the resignation of the Stalinist Government.

October 24:
Imre Nagy becomes Hungarian Prime Minister.

October 25:
Janos Kadar becomes First Secretary of the Hungarian Communist Party.

October 28:
A cease-fire in Budapest is arranged between the Stalinists and anti-Stalinists.

October 29:
Israel launches an offensive in the Sinai Peninsula; the French and British issue a cease-fire ultimatum to Egypt and Israel.

October 30:
The Soviet Union issues a declaration on equality of rights between Socialist countries.

November 4:
The Soviet Union intervenes militarily in Budapest.

November 5:
Franco-British landings in Port Said take place.

November 6:
A cease-fire in Egypt is forced on the British and the French by the United States and the Soviet Union.

November 20:
Imre Nagy is abducted and later assassinated.

December 24:
French and British troops in Port Said are withdrawn.

1957

January 1:
The Political integration of the Saar with the Federal Republic of Germany is set up.

January 5:
The Eisenhower Doctrine for the Middle East is announced; it was designed to neutralize the area.

January 6:
A Hungarian-Soviet-Rumanian-Czech declaration on Imre Nagy's "treason" is promulgated.

January 9:
As an aftermath of the 1956 Suez crisis, Harold Macmillan succeeds the ailing Anthony Eden as Prime Minister.

January 20:
Gomulka triumphs in Polish elections.

February 11:
The Soviet Union proposes that the Middle East be viewed, in East-West terms, as a neutral region.

March 21:
Anglo-American agreement on strategic nuclear missiles is an-

nounced, according to which the Royal Air Force operates American missiles from British bases. However, the warheads remain in U.S. custody and a dual control launch system is implemented.

March 24:
The signing of the Rome Treaty setting up the European Economic Community and EURATOM takes place.

End of June:
The uncovering of an "anti-party group" plot in the USSR is revealed.

August 26:
The first Soviet intercontinental ballistic missile is successfully fired.

October 2:
The Rapacki Plan to create a neutral zone in Central Europe is proposed.

October 4:
The first Sputnik is launched, demonstrating the Soviet Union's capability to build an intercontinental ballistic missile.

1958

January 31:
Syria and Egypt unite, forming the United Arab Republic.

February:
The first American satellite "Explorer" is launched.

March 1:
Nikita Khrushchev replaces Nikolai Bulganin as Soviet Prime Minister. He retains his post as First Secretary of the CPSU.

March 31:
The Soviet Union suspends nuclear testing.

May 3:
The United States rejects the Rapacki Plan.

May 13:
A coup in Algiers occurs, upsetting French European control.

May 29:
Charles de Gaulle returns to power.

June 17:
Imre Nagy is executed.

End of June:
Civil war breaks out in Lebanon.

July 14:
The United States intervenes in Lebanon and the British intervene in Jordan.

August 21:
The U.N. votes to end the Middle East Crisis.

August 23:
Communist China begins to shell Quemoy.

September 28:
The Fifth Republic in France is established under the leadership of Charles de Gaulle.

September:
De Gaulle proposes reorganization of NATO.

October 31:
A tripartite Conference of the United States, Great Britain, and the Soviet Union on the cessation of nuclear testing opens.

November 4:
Premier Khrushchev threatens to turn the Berlin issue over to the German Democratic Republic.

November 10:
The Conference on the prevention of surprise attacks opens at Geneva.

November 27:
The Soviet note on transforming Berlin into a free city is presented to the Western Allies.

1959

January 1:
Fidel Castro takes power in Cuba.

January 10:
The USSR proposes a German peace treaty to be concluded with the two German Republics and not with a reunited Germany.

March:
De Gaulle's tripartite directorate fails. France withdraws her Mediterranean Fleet from NATO.

May 11:
The Conference of Foreign Ministers opens in Geneva, in another attempt to settle the Berlin and German problems.

May 24:
Secretary of State John Foster Dulles dies.

May 27:
The USSR's Berlin ultimatum to sign a peace treaty with East
Germany passes with no action taken.

June:
Jean Monnet proposes "partnership" between U.S. and Europe.
Leads to creation of Organization for Economic Cooperation and
Development (OECD) with U.S. and Canada as members.

July 5:
The Saar becomes a *Land* in the German Federal Republic.

September 15:
Premier Khrushchev arrives in the United States on the first visit
of a Soviet leader, resulting in "the spirit of Camp David."

November 20:
The Stockholm Convention to establish a European Free Trade
Association (EFTA) is negotiated.

1960

February 8:
Prime Minister Harold Macmillan gives his "winds of change" speech,
ending the idea of the white man's burden, and initiating 1960 as
the prime year for decolonization in Africa.

February 13:
France explodes an atomic bomb.

March 23:
Premier Khrushchev visits Paris, in connection with the scheduled
Big Four Summit Conference.

April 16:
Communist China criticizes Khrushchev's "revisionism," without
naming him, in a "Long Live Leninism" article. This is a public
widening of the Sino-Soviet breach and a reflection of Chinese
suspicions over Khrushchev's policies toward the United States.

May 1:
Khrushchev announces that two American planes have been shot
down while engaged in spy flights over the Soviet Union.

May 16:
The abortive Paris Summit Conference opens and after the de-
nunciation of President Eisenhower by Khrushchev, ends.

August:
De Gaulle broaches plan for European Confederation in Rambouillet meeting with Chancellor Adenauer.

November 7:
John F. Kennedy is elected President of the United States.

November 11–25:
A conference of 81 Communist parties is held in Moscow to confirm a common ideological base in order to settle the Moscow-Peking dispute in favor of the Soviet Union.

December 14:
The OEEC becomes the Organization for Economic Cooperation and Development (OECD).

1961

January:
Macmillan sees De Gaulle at Rambouillet to discuss Britain's association with the Common Market.

January 3:
Diplomatic relations between Cuba and the United States are ruptured.

January 6:
Premier Khrushchev gives a speech on "Wars of National Liberation," in which he applaudes such efforts as being attacks against American imperialism.

February:
Summit meeting of the Six in Paris. Fouchet Committee to study Confederation Plan.

June 3:
President Kennedy and Premier Khrushchev meet in Vienna; no agreements are negotiated. Shortly thereafter Premier Khrushchev renews his threat to sign a separate peace treaty with East Germany.

June:
De Gaulle declares Britain should enter Common Market.

July 31:
Macmillan announces Britain's decision to apply for membership in the Common Market.

August 13:
The Berlin Wall is constructed to stem the flow of East German emigres.

August 29:
Soviet nuclear tests are resumed.

September 17:
Dag Hammarskjold dies.

September 26:
The U.S. Arms Control and Disarmament Agency is set up.

September 28:
The Syrian-Egyptian Union is dissolved.

October 17–31:
Twenty-Second Congress of CPSU is held.

December 10:
The Soviet Union breaks off relations with Albania.

1962

January:
EEC members reach agreement on a common agricultural policy.
De Gaulle repudiates French concessions in the Fouchet Committee.

February 7:
British and American nuclear testing is resumed.

March 18:
The Evian Accords ending the Algerian war are announced.

March 29:
The European Space Vehicle Launcher Development Organization
(ELDO) is established.

April 14:
Georges Pompidou replaces Michel Debre as Prime Minister of
France.

April 17:
Breakdown of negotiations on European political union.

May 4:
Secretary of Defense Robert McNamara sets forth the doctrine of
"flexible response" at the ministerial meeting of the North Atlantic
Council held in Athens.

June 14:
The European Space Research Organization (ESRO) is established.

June 16:
Secretary of Defense Robert McNamara's speech at Ann Arbor ex-
pounds the policy of "controlled response."

July 4:
President Kennedy's speech at Philadelphia endorses Atlantic partnership.

September 2:
The Soviet Union announces an increase of economic and military aid to Cuba.

September 13:
The United States warns the USSR on the installation of offensive nuclear weapons in Cuba.

October 18:
The United States Air Force reports the presence of Soviet ballistic missiles in Cuba.

October 22:
The United States establishes a "quarantine" on naval blockade around Cuba to prevent any further positioning of Soviet missiles.

October 28:
Premier Khrushchev announces the withdrawal of Soviet missiles from Cuba.

November 20:
Soviet bombers are also removed from Cuba and the American quarantine is lifted.

December 21:
The Nassau Agreement between Britain and the United States on sharing nuclear weapons is signed, as a consequence of the United States having continued development of the "Skybolt" ballistic missile, originally promised to Britain.

1963

January 14:
President de Gaulle rejects the Nassau agreement as being an indication of British dependence on the United States, and denies Great Britain entry into the Common Market.

January 22:
The Franco-German Treaty of Cooperation is signed; it provides for periodic Heads of Government meetings between the two States.

June 10:
President Kennedy gives his American University speech in which he revitalized prospects for arms talks with the Soviets.

June 20:
The "hot line" between Washington and Moscow is set up.

June 23–July 3:
President Kennedy tours Europe to restore the closeness of the German relationship and to signal the new strategy for NATO.

July 15:
British-Soviet-American negotiations on the cessation of nuclear testing are begun.

August 5:
The Nuclear Test Ban Treaty is signed in Moscow, calling for the cessation of controllable tests, with the exception of underground detonations.

October 9:
Both Prime Minister Harold Macmillan and Chancellor Konrad Adenauer resign.

October 16:
Ludwig Erhard becomes Chancellor of West Germany.

October 19:
Sir Alec Douglas-Home becomes British Prime Minister.

November 22:
John F. Kennedy is assassinated and Lyndon Johnson becomes President of the United States.

December 17:
President Johnson urges an end to the Cold War before the U.N. General Assembly.

December 31:
Premier Khrushchev proposes a general agreement on non-recourse to force in the settlement of territorial conflicts.

1964

January 7:
France recognizes Communist China.

April 20:
The Soviet-American-British agreement pledging a reduction of the production of fissionable material for military use is announced.

May 8:
Communist China refuses to participate in a world conference of Communist parties.

July 28:
Khrushchev's son-in-law, Alexei Adjubei, goes to Bonn to prepare Premier Khrushchev's visit to West Germany.

October 15:
Nikita Khrushchev is relieved of all posts, and is replaced by Leonid Brezhnev as First Secretary of the Party and Alexei Kosygin as Head of Government.

October 16:
The "Kennedy Round" of tariff negotiations opens in Geneva.

The Labor Party wins British General Elections; Harold Wilson becomes Prime Minister.

The Communist Chinese explode a nuclear bomb for the first time.

November 9:
Lyndon Johnson is elected President of the United States.

1965

January 24:
Winston Churchill dies.

February 15:
Bonn suspends all economic aid to Egypt.

May 12:
Relations between the German Federal Republic and Israel are restored.

December 19:
President de Gaulle is re-elected President of France.

March 7:
President de Gaulle announces France's withdrawal from NATO.

March 29:
The Twenty-Third Congress of the CPSU, Leonid Brezhnev as Secretary General of the Party.

April 21:
Pope Paul VI receives Andrei Gromyko on visit to Rome.

June 20:
President de Gaulle visits the Soviet Union.

June 25:
An agreement is signed between the Vatican and Yugoslavia.

July 1:
The six-month boycott of the EEC by France begins.

October 7:
President Johnson speaks on East-West détente, saying that differences over Vietnam will not prevent the United States from seeking
other opportunities for cooperation, mainly in Europe.

November 10:
Prime Minister Harold Wilson announces he is going to open consultations on Great Britain's eventually joining the Common Market.

December 1:
Alexei Kosygin visits France. Chancellor Erhard resigns and is replaced by Kurt Georg Kiesinger.

December 2:
U Thant is re-elected Secretary General of the United Nations.

December 21:
An agreement on the stationing of French troops in West Germany
is negotiated.

1966

March 9:
France announces that all NATO bases will have to be removed from
French soil.

May 9:
The Chinese hydrogen bomb is detonated.

July 1:
France withdraws its troops from the NATO military command but
does not renounce the Treaty.

Aleksandar Rankovic, number two man in the Yugoslav Regime, is
dismissed.

September 14:
The North Atlantic Council decides to move SHAPE Headquarters to
Brussels.

November 17:
The U.S. and USSR sign an agreement for direct air service between
New York and Moscow.

December 1:
The "Grand Coalition" in the Federal Republic of Germany is formed,

composed of the Christian Democrats and the Social Democrats. Kurt Georg Kiesinger becomes Chancellor and Willy Brandt becomes Foreign Minister.

1967

January 24:
Pope Paul VI receives President Nikolai Podgorny of the Soviet Union.

January 27:
A treaty on the peaceful uses of outer space is signed between the United States and the Soviet Union.

January 30:
Diplomatic relations between Rumania and the German Federal Republic are established.

April 21:
A military coup takes place in Greece.

June 5–9:
The third Israeli-Arab war begins.

June 23:
President Johnson and Prime Minister Kosygin meet at Glassboro, New Jersey; no specific agreements are announced.

September 18:
The United States decides to erect a billion-dollar "thin" antiballistic-missile system.

September 29:
President Johnson delivers his San Antonio speech.

December 13–14:
The Harmel Report is approved by the North Atlantic Council.

1968

January 3:
Dubcek replaces Novotny as First Secretary of the Czechoslovak Communist Party. "Spring" in Prague begins.

January 19:
The USSR and U.S. agree on a draft Nuclear Non-Proliferation Treaty.

March 31:
President Johnson announces he will not run for a second full term.

May–June:
Political and economic turmoil in France, caused by workers and students, shakes the Gaullist government.

July 15:
The Soviet Union and four of its partners in the Warsaw Pact warn Czechoslovakia about the nature and extent of liberalization.

August 3:
The Bratislava agreement between the Czechs and the Warsaw Pact is negotiated, ratifying the previous discussions on curbing the internal liberalization in Czechoslovakia.

August 21:
The invasion of Czechoslovakia by Soviet, East German, Polish, Bulgarian, and Hungarian troops takes place.

August 24:
The first French hydrogen bomb test takes place.

November 5:
Richard Nixon is elected President of the United States.

1969

January 1:
The federal state structure is set up in Czechoslovakia.

January 6:
The Soviet and French proposals for Four-Power intervention in the Middle East are put forth.

January 16:
The NATO Defense Minister's meeting at Brussels is held.

January 20:
Richard Nixon is inaugurated as the 37th President of the United States.

February 6–7:
At the WEU Ministerial Council meeting France threatens to walk out in opposition to the Council's taking up political questions not related strictly to WEU responsibilities.

February 10:
West German-Yugoslavia economic and technical cooperation agreement is signed.

February 17:
France boycotts the WEU Council meeting.

February 22:
The Soames affair takes place, resulting in conflicting Anglo-French interpretations of French intentions toward a renewed British application for entry into the Common Market.

February 23–March 2:
President Nixon embarks on an eight-day visit to Western Europe and addresses the North Atlantic Council to reassure the Alliance of continuing American support to the defense of Western Europe.

March 5:
The Bundestag meets in West Berlin to conduct the election of the President of West Germany, over Soviet-East German objections.

March 14:
President Nixon decides to deploy the ABM system.

March 15:
Soviet-Chinese border clashes intensify.

March 17:
The Budapest meeting of the Political Consultative Committee of Warsaw Pact is held.

April 12–13:
The First Congress of the New Communist Party of West Germany is held.

April 17:
Dubceck is replaced by Gustav Husak as First Secretary of the Czechoslovak Communist Party.

April 1–24:
The Ninth Chinese Communist Party Congress is held.

April 10–11:
The ministerial meeting of the North Atlantic Council is held in Washington, D.C.

April 28:
Charles de Gaulle resigns as President of the French Republic. Alain Poher assumes the Interim Presidency.

June 5–17:
The Moscow Conference of Communist Parties is held in Moscow.

June 15:
Georges Pompidou is elected President of the French Republic.

July 20:
The U.S. lands men on the moon.

August 10:
France devalues the franc.

August 12:
The EEC suspends the common agricultural policy for two years.

September 28:
West German elections are held—Kurt Georg Kiessinger is defeated,
Willy Brandt forms a new coalition government, and the Christian
Democratic-Christian Socialist coalition goes into opposition.

October 1:
Olaf Palme is elected by the Swedish Social Democratic Party as its
Premier.

October 3:
Special Drawing Rights (SDR) are created by the International Monetary Fund to foster stability and steady growth in international finance.

October 5:
Britain shuffles her cabinet to include the appointment of a minister
to negotiate her entry into the Common Market.

October 21:
Willy Brandt is elected the fourth chancellor of West Germany by
the Bundestag.

October 24:
Chancellor Brandt's government revalues the West German mark.

November 17:
The U.S. and the Soviet Union begin preliminary discussions for
the SALT talks at Helsinki.

November 24:
The U.S. and the Soviet Union simultaneously sign the Non-Proliferation Treaty (NPT).

November 28:
West Germany signs the NPT.

December 1:
At a Common Market Conference held at The Hague, French President Georges Pompidou warns that the Common Market might be
weakened if Britain were allowed to join.

December 3:
The Nuclear Defense Affairs Committee of NATO approves guide-
lines for the use of tactical nuclear weapons.

The Warsaw Pact states meet in Moscow to discuss the question of an all-European security conference.

December 8:
The Soviet Union and West Germany open talks on the mutual renunciation of force in the settlement of disputes between them.

December 12:
Greece withdraws from the Council of Europe in the wake of widespread criticism concerning human rights violations by the military
government.

December 15:
Greek Premier George Papadopolous rules out the possibility of
early elections in Greece.

December 16:
Western proposals for Four-Power talks on improving the Berlin
situation are presented to the Soviet government.

December 17:
The East German government proposes negotiations with West Germany concerning the division of Europe.

December 22:
The first and preliminary round of SALT talks ends in Helsinki with
agreement to begin substantive negotiations the following April in
Vienna.

1970

January 13:
The Soviet Union announces that it favors American participation in
an all-European security conference.

January 14:
European Communist parties meet in Moscow to discuss the October
1969 Warsaw Pact proposal for an all-European security conference.

January 20:
The United States and Communist China resume ambassadorial
talks in Warsaw.

January 22:
West German Chancellor Brandt sends a letter to East German
Premier Willi Stoph proposing negotiations between the two parts of
Germany.

January 23:
France and Great Britain discuss British entry into the EEC during
two days of talks in London.

January 28:
President Nixon and Prime Minister Wilson meet in Washington to discuss world problems. Nothing definite comes from these talks.

February 3:
President George Pompidou and Chancellor Brandt meet in Paris to discuss respective foreign policies in the semiannual Franco-German meetings of Heads of State and Government.

February 5–6:
West German and Polish representatives meet in Moscow for two days of talks aimed at improving relations between the two countries. The question of the Oder-Neisse boundaries, and the "lost provinces" dominates the background of the discussions.

February 10:
The Soviet Union proposes to the other three Occupying Powers that talks should take place over Berlin.

February 23:
President Pompidou visits the United States to discuss Franco-American relations with President Nixon and to tour the United States. Nothing concrete comes from this visit.

February 27:
The United States accepts the Soviet proposal for Four-Power talks on the future status of Berlin.

March 3:
Chancellor Brandt visits London to discuss world problems with Prime Minister Wilson. As a result, there is some concern in France of an emerging "London-Bonn" diplomatic axis.

March 4:
Britain announces that it will send back to West Germany the Brigade it has withdrawn from the British Army of the Rhine in 1968.

March 5:
The Nuclear Non-Proliferation Treaty goes into force.

March 19:
Chancellor Brandt and Premier Stoph meet in Erfurt, East Germany to discuss mutual political problems, and especially the division of Germany.

March 26:
Ambassadors of the four Occupying Powers meet in West Berlin to discuss the status of Berlin.

March 27:
Italian Premier Mario Rumor announces the formation of a new Center-Left coalition, thus ending Italy's longest post-war cabinet crisis.

April 10:
Chancellor Brandt meets with President Nixon in Washington to discuss European problems. West Germany seeks reassurances that the United States will maintain a strong military "presence" in Western Europe beyond mid-1971.

April 20:
The Foreign Ministers of the EEC reject the British proposal for full and early talks on Western European political union.

April 22:
The Common Agricultural Policy for EEC is agreed upon, and in return for concessions to France, it is agreed in principle to take up formally the question of British entry in the Common Market.

June 18:
The Conservative Party wins an upset victory in Britain, and Edward Heath becomes Prime Minister.

July 26:
West Germany begins formal negotiations in Moscow with the Soviet Union on the subject of a non-aggression treaty.

August 6:
Spain and the United States sign a five-year pact for American use of Spanish air and naval bases, amid talk that the agreement makes Spain a de facto beneficiary of NATO.

August 12:
West Germany and the Soviet Union sign a treaty renouncing the use of force and acknowledging the existing frontiers in Europe as inviolable.

SUGGESTIONS FOR FURTHER READING

Aron, Raymond. *The Century of Total War*. Garden City, New York: Doubleday, 1954.

Beer, Francis A. *Integration and Disintegration in NATO*. Columbus: Ohio State University Press, 1969.

Beloff, Max. *The Future of British Foreign Policy*. London: Secker and Warburg, 1969.

Beloff, Max. *The United States and the Unity of Europe*. Washington, D.C.: The Brookings Institution, 1963.

Benes, Vaclau; Gyorgy, Andrew; and Stambuk, George, eds. *Eastern European Government and Politics*. New York: Harper and Row, 1966.

Brandt, Willy. *A Peace Policy for Europe*. New York: Holt, Rinehart and Winston, 1969.

Bromberger, Merry and Serge. *Jean Monnet and the United States of Europe*. New York: Coward-McCann, Inc., 1969.

Brzezinski, Zbigniew. *Alternative to Partition*. New York: McGraw-Hill, 1965.

Buchan, Alastair, ed. *Europe's Future, Europe's Choices, Models of Western Europe in the 1970's*. London: Chatto and Windus—for the Institute for Strategic Studies, 1969.

Buchan, Alastair. *NATO in the 1960's*. London: Wiedenfeld and Nicolson, 1960.

Calleo, David. *Britain's Future*. New York: Horizon Press, 1968.

Calleo, David. *Europe's Future*. New York: Norton and Company, 1965.

Calvorcoressi, Peter. *International Politics Since 1945*. New York: Frederick A. Praeger, 1968.

Camps, Miriam. *Britain and the European Community 1955–1963*. Princeton, New Jersey: Princeton University Press, 1964.

Camps, Miriam. *European Unification in the Sixties.* New York: Mc-Graw-Hill—for the Council on Foreign Relations, 1966.

Carter, W. Horsfall. *Speaking European.* London: George Allen and Unwin Ltd., 1966.

Catlin, George E. G. *The Atlantic Commonwealth.* Baltimore: Penguin Books, 1969.

Chadwick, H. M. *The Nationalities of Europe.* London: Cambridge University Press, 1969.

Clark, W. Hartley. *The Politics of the Common Market.* Englewood Cliffs, New Jersey: Prentice-Hall, 1967.

Curtis, Michael. *Western European Integration.* New York: Harper and Row, 1965.

Davison, Roderic H. *Turkey.* Englewood Cliffs, New Jersey: Prentice-Hall, 1968.

De Carmoy, Guy. *The Foreign Policies of France 1944–1968.* (Translated by Elaine P. Halperin.) Chicago: University of Chicago Press, 1970.

Deutsch, Karl W.; Burrell, Sidney A.; Kann, Robert A.; Lee, Maurice, Jr.; Lichterman, Martin; Lindgren, Raymond E.; Loewenheim, Francis L.; and Van Wagenen, Richard W. *Political Community and the North Atlantic Area.* Princeton, New Jersey: Princeton University Press, 1957.

Deutsch, Karl W.; Edinger, Lewis J.; Macridis, Roy C.; Merritt, Richard L. *France, Germany, and the Western Alliance.* New York: Charles Scribners Sons, 1967.

Feis, Herbert. *Churchill, Roosevelt, and Stalin: The War They Waged and the Peace They Sought.* Princeton, New Jersey: Princeton University Press, 1957.

Fontaine, Andre. *History of the Cold War.* (Translated from the French by Renaud Bruce.) New York: Pantheon Books, 1969. Translation copyright.

Fox, W. T. R.; and Fox, Annette Baker. *NATO and the Range of American Choice.* New York: Columbia University Press, 1967.

Friedrich, Carl F. *Europe: An Emergent Nation?* New York: Harper & Row, 1969.

Gladwyn, Lord. *The European Idea.* London: Wiedenfeld and Nicolson, 1966.

Grosser, Alfred. *French Foreign Policy Under de Gaulle.* Boston and Toronto: Little, Brown and Company, 1965.

Grosser, Alfred. *The Federal Republic of Germany: A Concise History.* New York: Frederick A. Praeger, 1964.

Gustavson, Carl. *Europe in the World Community since 1939.* Boston: Allyn and Bacon, 1971.

Halle, Louis J. *The Cold War as History.* New York: Harper and Row, 1967.

Hartmann, Frederick H. *Germany Between East and West: The Reunification Problem.* Englewood Cliffs, New Jersey: Prentice-Hall, 1965.

Henderson, W. O. *The Genesis of the Common Market.* Chicago: Quadrangle Books, 1962.

Hoffman, Stanley. *Gulliver's Troubles or the Setting of American Foreign Policy.* New York: McGraw-Hill, 1967.

Hugo, Grant. *Britain in Tomorrow's World.* New York: Columbia University Press, 1969.

Jordan, Robert S. *The NATO International Staff / Secretariat, 1952–1957: A Study in International Administration.* London and New York: Oxford University Press, 1967.

Kissinger, Henry A. *The Troubled Partnership.* New York: McGraw-Hill—for the Council on Foreign Relations, 1965.

Kleiman, Robert. *Atlantic Crisis: American Diplomacy Confronts a Resurgent Europe.* New York: W. W. Norton and Company, Inc., 1965.

Krause, Laurence B., ed. *The Common Market: Progress and Controversy.* Englewood Cliffs, New Jersey: Prentice-Hall, 1966.

Lefeber, Walter. *America, Russia, and the Cold War, 1945–1966.* New York: John Wiley and Sons, Inc., 1967.

Lerche, Charles O. *The Cold War: . . . And After.* Englewood Cliffs, New Jersey: Prentice-Hall, 1965.

London, Kurt, ed. *Eastern Europe in Transition.* Baltimore: Johns Hopkins Press, 1966.

Lyons, F. S. L. *Internationalism in Europe 1815–1914.* Leyden: A. W. Sythoff, 1963.

Majonica, Ernst. *East-West Relations: A German View.* New York: Frederick A. Praeger, 1969.

Moore, Barrington, Jr. *Social Origins of Dictatorship and Democracy.* Boston: Beacon Press, 1966.

Morgenthau, Hans J. *A New Foreign Policy for the United States*. New York: Frederick A. Praeger—for the Council on Foreign Relations, 1969.

Mulley, F. W. *The Politics of Western Defense*. New York: Frederick A. Praeger, 1962.

Neuman, William L. *After Victory: Churchill, Roosevelt, and Stalin, and the Making of the Peace*. New York: Harper and Row, 1967.

Osgood, Robert E. *Alliances and American Foreign Policy*. Baltimore: Johns Hopkins Press, 1968.

Osgood, Robert E. *NATO the Entangling Alliance*. Chicago: University of Chicago Press, 1962.

Rothman, Stanley. *European Society and Politics*. New York: Bobbs-Merrill, 1970.

Sapin, Burton M. *The Making of United States Foreign Policy*. Washington, D.C.: The Brookings Institution, 1966.

Scott, Andrew. *The Revolution in Statecraft*. New York: Random House, 1965.

Serfaty, Simon. *France, de Gaulle, and Europe*. Baltimore: Johns Hopkins Press, 1968.

Stanley, Timothy W. *NATO in Transition, The Future of the Atlantic Alliance*. New York: Frederick A. Praeger—for the Council on Foreign Relations, 1965.

Steel, Ronald. *Pax Americana, The Cold-War Empire—How it Grew and What It Means*. New York: The Viking Press, 1967.

Steel, Ronald. *The End of Alliance: America and the Future of Europe*. New York: The Viking Press, 1962.

Strauss, Franz-Josef. *Challenge and Response: A Program for Europe*. New York: Atheneum, 1970.

Taylor, A. J. P. *The Struggle for Mastery in Europe 1848–1918*. Oxford: The Clarendon Press, 1954.

van B. Cleveland, Harold. *The Atlantic Idea and Its Rivals*. New York: McGraw-Hill, 1966.

Willis, F. Roy. *France, Germany, and the New Europe, 1945–1967*. New York: Oxford University Press, 1968.

Zaring, J. *Decision for Europe: The Necessity of Britain's Engagement*. Baltimore: Johns Hopkins Press, 1969.

INDEX

Acheson, Dean, 4, 106
Adenauer, Konrad, 63, 106, 136ff, 177
Albania, 55, 75ff, 99, 159
Alexander of Battenberg, Prince, 158
America (see United States)
Armenia, 166
Ataturk, Kemal, 163
Atlantic Alliance (see NATO)
Atlantic Community, 16, 108ff
Atlantic Studies, Committee on, 10
Austria, 35, 53, 95, 134, 248–49
Austria-Hungary (see Austro-Hungarian Empire)
Austro-Hungarian Empire, 6, 47, 72, 149, 154

Bakaric, Vladimir, 156
Balance of power, 6, 8, 14, 22, 47–48, 81, 168
Balkan Federation, 151
Balkan League of 1934, 151
Balkan Pact, 133
Balkans, 4, 83, 133, 140–41, 149ff
Baltic subregion, 4, 43, 142, 168–69, 193ff, 205
Barraclough, Geoffrey, 134n
Bayar, Celal, 163
Belgium (see BENELUX and NATO)
Beloff, Max, 5n
BENELUX, 30, 34, 113, 143, 234
Beria, Laurenti, 57
Berl, M., 5
Berlin, 15, 17, 52, 60–61, 62, 65, 67, 78, 139
  blockade of, 52, 92, 105
  Congress of 1878, 158
  Wall, 60, 65, 136
Besson, Waldemar, 73
Bismarck, Otto von, 134–35, 147
Bolle, Thomas Geoffrey, 10
Brandt, Willy, 87, 111, 126, 128, 135, 139ff
Brazil, 171
Brest-Litovsk, Treaty of, 125
Brezhnev, Leonid, 67

Brezhnev Doctrine, 69, 82, 95–96, 98
Bridge-building (see East-West relations)
Britain (see Great Britain)
British Bomber Command, 31
Brussels Treaty, 234n, 239
Brussels Treaty Organization (BTO), 30, 31, 234
Brzezinski, Zbigniew, 93
Buchan, Alastair, 182n
Bulganin, Nikolai, 57, 61
Bulgaria, 50, 55, 57, 157ff
Byrnes, James, 25, 29n

Camps, Miriam, 246n
Canada, 30, 39, 43
Carr, E. H., 28
Ceausescu, Nicolas, 80
Central Intelligence Agency (CIA), 93
China, Communist, 1, 20–21, 58, 65–66, 78, 82, 86ff, 161
Christ, Jesus, 131
Christian Democratic Union (CDU), 112, 122, 136ff
Churchill, Winston S., 7, 7n
Cleveland, Harold van B., 167
Cold war, 8, 16, 29, 51, 94–95, 98, 136, 231–232
COMECON, 20, 56, 66, 86, 89, 97, 188
Cominform, 56
Common Market (see EEC)
Common Nordic Market, 220
Commonwealth, British (see Great Britain)
Communist Party of the Soviet Union (CPSU), 57
Conference of Experts on the Prevention of Surprise Attack, 61
Congo (Brazzaville), 243
Conservative party (Britain), 176ff
Constantine I, King, 162
Cooper, Duff, 171n
Council for Mutual Economic Assistance (see COMECON)

Council of Europe, 221, 234
Crimean War, 157, 208
Cripps, Sir Stafford, 171
Croatia, 154ff
Cuban crisis of 1962, 61, 65, 67, 89
Cyprus, 43
Czechoslovakia, 20, 29, 32, 48–49, 50–51, 54, 55, 69, 74, 90ff, 116–17, 151, 183, 185, 188, 216

Dalmatia, 155
Debré, Michel, 122
Declaration of Interdependence of 1962, 36
de Gaulle, Charles, 36, 38–39, 39n, 69–70, 94, 99, 102, 109–10, 115, 119–20, 171, 177, 190, 225, 246, 249–51
Demirel, Suleyman, 164
Denmark, 4, 30, 35, 43, 168–69, 193ff
de Rougemont, Denis, 131
De-satellization, 75ff
d'Estaing, Valery Giscard, 126
De-Stalinization, 58, 75ff
Détente, 24, 55, 56, 67ff, 86ff, 94, 96–97, 102, 117, 138, 186–88
Deutsch, Karl, 195
Dillon, Douglas, 63
Dimitrov, Georgi, 159
Douglas-Home, Sir Alex, 178
Dubcek, Alexander, 69, 80
Dulles, John Foster, 56, 86, 93, 106

East Germany, 3, 54, 55, 63, 75ff, 143
East-West relations:
bridge-building, 3, 94, 153, 165
drawing-apart, 84–86
planes of interaction, 19ff, 24, 112, 124, 128–30
rivalry of superpowers, 13, 29, 57ff, 185
trade, 67, 90, 113
Eastern Europe, 75ff
definition of, 75, 81–82, 99

relations with West Germany, 143ff
relation to Western Europe, 82, 90, 101ff
Eastern Mediterranean subregion (*see* Balkans)
Eisenhower, Dwight D., 32, 33n, 61ff
Erhardt, Ludwig, 111
Erlander, Tag, 224
Ethiopia, 209
Europe:
definition of, 5ff, 13–14, 17–18, 76, 107–9, 112, 122, 126, 152, 166, 171
division of, 72–73, 76–77, 84–85, 168
European Atomic Energy Community (EURATOM), 44, 172, 240, 242ff
European Coal and Steel Community (ECSC), 31, 136, 172, 221, 234ff
European communities, 44, 103, 123
European Defense Community (EDC), 31, 137, 237ff, 250
European Economic Community (EEC):
and Baltic subregion, 219–20, 222
and Britain, 38–39, 170ff
and Common Agricultural Policy, 172
creation of, 34, 231ff
and Eastern Europe, 86, 103
and expansion of, 169
and France, 41
and integration, 103–4, 105ff, 116–18, 120, 122, 142–43, 181–82, 186–87, 248–51
and Treaty of Rome, 172ff, 220, 240–41, 251
and West Germany, 141, 251
European Free Trade Association (EFTA), 35, 169, 173ff, 198, 221ff
European integration (*see*

European Economic
    Community)
European Parliament, 184,
    244–45, 251
European Parliamentary Assembly,
    245
European Payments Union (EPU),
    234
European Political Community
    (EPC), 238
European Security Conference,
    20, 90
European Social Fund, 247

Faroe Islands, 195
Finland, 4, 35, 52, 78, 95, 169,
    193ff
Fischev-Calati, S., 87
Foster, William C., 62
Fouchet, Christian (see also
    European Political
    Community), 44–45
France (see also de Gaulle):
    and balance of power, 6, 138
    and Britain, 36, 44–45, 110,
    170–71, 190, 223, 225, 249–50
    and Eastern Europe, 102, 110,
    114, 138
    and European Coal and Steel
    Community, 31, 231ff
    and European Economic
    Community, 34, 36, 44–45,
    231ff
    and NATO, 37–38, 41, 43
    and nuclear weapons, 36
    and the United States, 36, 118
    and West Germany, 27, 31, 42,
    118
Franco-German Treaty of
    Friendship of 1963, 42

Gaitskell, Hugh, 178, 180
Garthoff, Raymond, 47n
General Agreement on Tariffs and
    Trade (see GATT), 174, 190,
    250
General and complete

disarmament, proposals for,
    63
Geneva spirit (see Superpowers)
Georgia (USSR), 166
German Democratic Republic (see
    East Germany)
German Federal Republic (see
    West Germany)
Germany:
    division of, 2, 3, 9, 15, 52, 72,
    95, 103–4, 106, 143ff
    pre-World War I, 6, 47
    Prussia, 6, 47, 134, 208
Gheorghiu-Dej, 86
Gibbs, Hubert, 231n
Goldwyn, Robert A., 59n
Gomulka, Wladyslaw, 58, 69, 90
Grand Coalition (see West
    Germany)
Great Britain:
    and Baltic subregion, 221
    and balance of power, 6
    and the Commonwealth, 35, 38,
    168, 172, 175
    and the European Economic
    Community, 38, 44–45, 110,
    170ff, 249–50
    and European Free Trade
    Association, 35, 231ff
    and France, 36, 44, 110, 120,
    190, 223, 225, 249–50
    and NATO, 30, 43
    and the United States, 35, 36,
    38, 44, 83, 168, 179
    and West Germany, 120
Greece, 30, 43, 84, 150, 160,
    161ff, 249
Greenberg, Stuart, 10
Griffith, William, 93
Gustavus Adolphus, 208
Gyorgy, Andrew, 9, 231n

Haas, Ernst B., 251n
Hallstein, Walter, 187, 244
Hallstein Doctrine, 90
Hapsburg monarchy (see Austro-
    Hungarian Empire)

Harkort, Gunther, 41
Harriman, Averell, 171
Harsch, Joseph C., 1n
Hassner, Pierre, 11, 73
Healey, Denis, 178
Heath, Edward, 122, 126, 170ff, 180
Herter, Christian, 63
Hitler, Adolph, 60, 205–6
Hoerlich, Arnold M., 55n
Holborn, Hajo, 23, 28n
Hungary, 50, 55, 57, 58, 74ff
Hunt, Kenneth, 38n
Hunter, Robert, 10

Iceland, 30
Inonu, Ismet, 163
Institute for Strategic Studies (London), 187
International politics:
  aspects of, 17ff
  levels of, 14ff
Iran, 166
Israel, 88, 166
Istanbul, Straits of, 149
Italy, 30, 34, 43, 209, 245ff

Japan, 27, 48, 204
Johnson, Lyndon, 93, 96
Jordan, Robert S., 33n, 231n
Just war, doctrine of, 95

Kadar, Janos, 58
Kalmar Union, 194–95
Kennan, George F., 51n, 61
Kennedy, John F., 19, 39, 64, 66, 93, 108, 147, 185
Kennedy Round, 116, 190, 250
Kenya, 243
Khrushchev, Nikita, 19, 48, 54, 55n, 57ff, 83ff, 109, 129, 151, 160
Kiessinger, Kurt-Georg, 111, 135
Korean War, 30, 51, 53, 237–38

Labor party (Britain), 176ff

Lange, Halvard, 208, 211
League of Nations, 28, 205–9
Lie, Trygve, 208
Lindsay, Kenneth, 251n
Little Entente, the, 151
Lloyd, Selwyn (Lord Holyoke), 63
Luxembourg (see also BENELUX), 234ff

Mackintosh, J. M., 49n
Macmillan, Harold, 36, 178ff
McNamara, Robert S., 36, 39
Malenkov, Georgi, 54, 55
Malenkov-Beria leadership, 85
Marshall Plan (see United States)
Marx, Karl, 107
Mendaras, Adnon, 163
Mendes-France, Pierre, 238
Micro-imperialism, 151
Mihailo of Serbia, Prince, 150
Moldavia, 157
Møller, Christmas, 206
Monnet, Jean, 105, 107–9, 117, 126, 136, 173, 239
Morgenthau, Hans, 8, 8n, 9n
Mussolini, Benito, 160

Nagy, Imre, 58
Nenni, Pietro, 127
Netherlands (see also BENELUX and NATO), 111, 234ff
New Zealand, 172, 191
Nixon, Richard, 43, 82, 97, 140, 152
NORDEK, 203, 226
Nordic Agreement on Cooperation of 1962 (Helsinki Treaty), 199ff
Nordic Committee for Economic Cooperation, 219
Nordic Council, 193, 197ff
Norstad, Lauris, 37
North Atlantic Alliance (see NATO)
North Atlantic Council (see NATO)

North Atlantic Free Trade Area (NAFTA), 190
North Atlantic Treaty (see NATO)
North Atlantic Treaty Organization (NATO):
and ANF, 37
and Anglo-French nuclear force, 183
and Baltic subregion, 169, 204, 215–16
Council, 42
creation of, 30–31
and deterrence, 37, 39–40, 70, 106
and Eastern Mediterranean, 133, 164
and "Europeanization," 116–17, 124, 181
Harmel Report, 42–43
and MLF, 20, 37, 67
Nuclear Planning Group, 42
Report of Committee of Three on Non-Military Co-operation, 33
strains in, 33, 37, 38–39, 110, 129, 215–16
and Treaty, 30, 39, 41, 43
troop withdrawals, 40
and Warsaw Pact, 39, 90–91
and West Germany, 4, 140ff
Norway, 4, 30, 35, 43, 169, 193ff
Novotny, Anton, 69
Nuclear Non-Proliferation Treaty (NPT), 37, 91, 96, 116, 138–39
Nuclear weapons:
de-nuclearized zone proposals, 87
inspection of, 61–62
limitation of, 116
and NATO, 30, 39–40, 42, 183
and Nuclear Non-Proliferation Treaty, 37, 67, 92, 94, 96, 116
prohibition of, 53
Soviet deterrent, 35–36, 61, 65, 70
strategic balance, 116

Obrenovic, Milos, 154
Oder-Niesse Line, 62, 113, 143–44, 146
Organization of Economic Cooperation and Development (OECD), 35, 250
Organization for European Economic Cooperation (OEEC) (see United States)
Östpolitik, 68, 87
Ottoman Empire, 6, 149, 159–61
Owen, Henry, 46n

Papandreou, George, 162
Papagos, Alexander, 162
Partial Nuclear Test-Ban Treaty of 1963, 67
Pasic, Nikola, 155
Peaceful coexistence (see Superpowers)
Peterson, Kathleen, 10
Pleven, René, 237
Poland, 29, 49, 50, 55, 57, 58, 75ff
Polycentrism, 9, 48, 60, 121
Pompidou, Georges, 42, 119, 121, 142, 172, 183
Portugal, 30, 35, 249
Potsdam Conference, 49
Posnan riots, 57

Randal, Jonathan, 41n
Ranger, Robert, 69n
Rankovic, Alexander, 156
Rapacki, Adam, 61
Rapallo, Treaty of 1922, 68
Renouvin, Pierre, 71
Roosevelt, Franklin D., 50
Roosevelt, Theodore, 27
Rumania, 20–21, 43, 50, 55, 70, 75ff, 97, 121, 129, 150, 156ff
Rush, Myron, 55n
Russia (see Soviet Union)

Saar, 235
San Stefano, Treaty of, 158
Sapilo, Frano, 155

Scandinavian Airlines System (SAS), 198
Scandinavian subregion (see Baltic subregion)
Schmidt, Helmut, 112
Schulman, Marshall, 47n
Schuman Plan (see European Coal and Steel Community)
Schumann, Maurice, 122
Scott, Andrew, 9
Serbia, 150, 154ff
Servan-Schreiber, J.-J., 1, 180
Shröder, Gerhard, 111
Sino-Soviet crisis, 87–88, 96–97
Six-day war (Arab-Israeli), 90
Skybolt, 36, 44
Social Democrats (SPD), 3, 87, 97, 104, 106, 111, 122, 136ff
Socialist Commonwealth (see Brezhnev Doctrine)
Somalia, 243
Southeastern Europe (see Balkans)
Soviet Union:
  and balance of power, 6, 47, 48
  and Baltic subregion, 206ff
  and Eastern Europe, 75ff, 161
  and Eastern Mediterranean, 43
  intervention in Europe, 14, 16, 24, 49–50, 70, 84–85, 95
  United States-Soviet relations (see Superpowers)
  and Warsaw Pact, 55
  and Western Europe, 186–87
Spaak, Paul-Henri, 240
Spanish Civil War, 49
Sputnik, 35, 38, 138
Stalin, Joseph, 7, 19, 48, 50, 52, 54–59, 69, 75, 83, 116, 127, 151, 159, 164, 238, 247
Stalinism, 55, 56, 58
Stockholm Convention, 175
Stockholm Peace Appeal, 53
Stoph, Willi, 146
Strategic Air Command, 31, 61
Strategic Arms Limitation Talks (SALT), 25, 96, 127, 169
Strauss, Franz-Joseph, 120, 122, 126–28, 135
Suez crisis of 1956, 25, 32–34, 36, 86, 240
Superpowers:
  and Baltic subregion, 204, 227–28
  deterrence of, 37–38, 59–60, 70
  Geneva Spirit, 56
  hot-line agreement of 1963, 67
  notion of, 2
  peaceful coexistence, 53, 98, 138, 188
  rivalry of, 8, 29, 30, 50, 91ff, 98, 111, 127, 132–33, 152, 227–28
  Summit Conference of 1955, 56–57
  Summit Conference of 1960, 62–63, 178
  Summit Conference of 1961, 64, 66
Sweden, 4, 35, 169, 177, 193ff, 248–49
Switzerland, 35, 248–49

Tanzania, 243
Taylor, A. J. P., 6, 6n
Tito, Josip, 51–52, 57, 84, 151, 155, 159
Titulescu, Nicolas, 157
Toynbee, Arnold, 161
Transylvania, 156, 157
Truman Doctrine, 8–9, 29–30, 50, 84
Turkey, 30, 43, 47, 84, 149ff, 163ff
Turkish Empire (see Ottoman Empire)
Twentieth Party Congress of the CPSU, 57, 59, 59n, 85

Uganda, 243
Ulbricht, Walter, 54, 60, 64, 85, 145
Ulbricht Doctrine, 90
Ullam, Adam, 50n
United Nations (UN), 32, 63, 95,

198, 206, 211, 226, 232–33, 247
United Nations Disarmament Committee, 63
United States:
  intervention in Europe, 1–2, 14, 16, 24, 33–34, 39–40, 50–51, 93, 115
  Marshall Plan and OEEC, 35, 50, 84, 103, 105, 110, 174, 211–12, 221, 234, 249–50
  mechanistic outlook, 11
  and NATO, 38–39, 40
  and the Soviet Union (see Superpowers)
  Truman Doctrine, 8–9, 29–30, 50, 84

Venizelos, Eleftherios, 161–62
Versailles, Treaty of, 28
Vietnam war, 90, 94, 96, 116, 217
von Kaenel, Margo, 10

Wallachia, 157, 161
Warsaw Pact, 20, 39, 43, 55, 58, 65, 68, 68n, 80, 86ff, 95, 144, 181, 215
Werth, Alexander, 170n
West Berlin (see Berlin)
West Germany:
  and the Baltic subregion, 217
  and Eastern Europe, 20, 86, 90, 103, 111, 138, 143–44, 185
  and the European Economic Community, 34, 136–37, 138ff, 173
  Franco-German relations, 27, 34, 42, 118
  and the Grand Coalition, 20, 90, 94, 111, 136, 139ff
  and NATO, 30, 43, 140ff, 183
  Peace Treaty with the Soviet Union, 62, 64, 137
  rearmament, 30–31, 54, 60, 104, 183, 239
  and the United States, 137, 148
Western Europe:
  relation to Eastern Europe, 14–16, 101ff, 104, 165
  relations with the United States, 33–34, 104, 116
  subregionalism, 124–28, 141, 169, 220
Western European integration (see European Economic Community)
Western European Union (WEU), 31, 171, 239, 245
Western Union Defence Organization (WUDO) (see Brussels Treaty Organization)
Wilson, Harold, 114, 122, 176ff, 224
Wilson, Woodrow, 27, 28
Windsor, Philip, 10, 50n
World War I, 6, 8, 132, 154–55, 162, 164, 207, 218
World War II, 2, 7, 24, 27–29, 65, 72–73, 110, 119–20, 132, 139, 145–46, 151, 155, 168, 186, 190, 205–6, 209–10, 213, 219, 231–32

Yalta Conference, 49, 93
Yugoslavia, 49, 51, 52, 57, 70, 75ff, 151, 153ff

Zhdanov, A. A., 84
Zveno, M., 158